Stefan Valentin

Cooperative Relaying and its Application

Stefan Valentin

Cooperative Relaying and its Application

From Analysis to Prototypes

Südwestdeutscher Verlag für Hochschulschriften

Impressum/Imprint (nur für Deutschland/ only for Germany)
Bibliografische Information der Deutschen Nationalbibliothek: Die Deutsche Nationalbibliothek verzeichnet diese Publikation in der Deutschen Nationalbibliografie; detaillierte bibliografische Daten sind im Internet über http://dnb.d-nb.de abrufbar.
Alle in diesem Buch genannten Marken und Produktnamen unterliegen warenzeichen-, marken- oder patentrechtlichem Schutz bzw. sind Warenzeichen oder eingetragene Warenzeichen der jeweiligen Inhaber. Die Wiedergabe von Marken, Produktnamen, Gebrauchsnamen, Handelsnamen, Warenbezeichnungen u.s.w. in diesem Werk berechtigt auch ohne besondere Kennzeichnung nicht zu der Annahme, dass solche Namen im Sinne der Warenzeichen- und Markenschutzgesetzgebung als frei zu betrachten wären und daher von jedermann benutzt werden dürften.

Verlag: Südwestdeutscher Verlag für Hochschulschriften GmbH & Co. KG
Dudweiler Landstr. 99, 66123 Saarbrücken, Deutschland
Telefon +49 681 37 20 271-1, Telefax +49 681 37 20 271-0
Email: info@svh-verlag.de
Zugl.: University of Paderborn, Germany, Dissertation, 2009

Herstellung in Deutschland:
Schaltungsdienst Lange o.H.G., Berlin
Books on Demand GmbH, Norderstedt
Reha GmbH, Saarbrücken
Amazon Distribution GmbH, Leipzig
ISBN: 978-3-8381-1858-1

Imprint (only for USA, GB)
Bibliographic information published by the Deutsche Nationalbibliothek: The Deutsche Nationalbibliothek lists this publication in the Deutsche Nationalbibliografie; detailed bibliographic data are available in the Internet at http://dnb.d-nb.de.
Any brand names and product names mentioned in this book are subject to trademark, brand or patent protection and are trademarks or registered trademarks of their respective holders. The use of brand names, product names, common names, trade names, product descriptions etc. even without a particular marking in this works is in no way to be construed to mean that such names may be regarded as unrestricted in respect of trademark and brand protection legislation and could thus be used by anyone.

Publisher: Südwestdeutscher Verlag für Hochschulschriften GmbH & Co. KG
Dudweiler Landstr. 99, 66123 Saarbrücken, Germany
Phone +49 681 37 20 271-1, Fax +49 681 37 20 271-0
Email: info@svh-verlag.de

Printed in the U.S.A.
Printed in the U.K. by (see last page)
ISBN: 978-3-8381-1858-1

Copyright © 2010 by the author and Südwestdeutscher Verlag für Hochschulschriften GmbH & Co. KG and licensors
All rights reserved. Saarbrücken 2010

Abstract

Mobile users often experience communication outage and low data rate. To efficiently and economically cope with this problem, *cooperative relaying* is promising. It exploits wireless broadcasts, providing tremendous *spatial diversity* gains in theory. Although these gains are consistently shown in theoretical work, their experimental proof and a theoretical justification of the underlying modeling assumptions are missing so far. In fact, it is not clear whether cooperative relaying can reach the performance promised by theory even under realistic assumptions. This leaves a large gap between theoretical and practical research on cooperative relaying protocols – bridging this gap is the objective of this thesis.

We do so in three steps. First, we study systematically how realistic scenario and system assumptions decrease the performance of ideal cooperative relaying protocols. Focusing on *selection relaying*, we find that the performance of ideal protocols substantially degrades when usual simplifications like perfect *channel knowledge*, error-free *control and feedback transmission*, perfect *network connectivity*, unlimited *system complexity*, or idealistic *fading* statistics are dropped. We analyze the performance of selection relaying without these simplifications and provide guidelines and theoretical tools to choose the most beneficial protocol.

Second, we develop new, practical techniques to maintain cooperative gains even under realistic assumptions and in new scenarios. More general fading channels, erroneous control transmissions, and beneficially applying cooperative relaying for *resource allocation* require significant extensions of a cooperative system. Our lightweight techniques can be readily integrated into many systems and closely approach the high performance promised by theory.

Third, we implement a transceiver prototype for *cooperative* Wireless Local Area Networks (WLANs). Extensive field measurements (e.g., using an actual train to move the cooperating nodes) not only show the feasibility and high performance of our solutions. Moreover, our lightweight integration into an *IEEE 802.11g* transceiver and our measurement results are the missing experimental proof that selection relaying protocols closely achieve the performance promised by theory. Even with today's wireless technology and in real mobile scenarios, letting nodes cooperate is feasible, efficient, and ready for standardization.

Acknowledgments

> *"Indes sie forschten, röntgten, filmten, funkten,*
> *entstand von selbst die köstlichste Erfindung:*
> *Der Umweg als die kürzeste Verbindung zwischen zwei Punkten."*
> —Erich Kästner

Studying cooperative relaying would have been less fruitful and less fun without the following people. First to thank, my Professor Holger Karl. At the Computer Networks Group, Holger provided me with an excellent environment where I neither missed the guidance, the tools, nor the freedom to finish this research project. Second, I thank Professor Halim Yanikomeroglu and his students at Carleton U. Our exciting discussions and Halim's ability to make me think out of the box significantly helped to improve Chapter 4. Third, I would like to thank Professor Gerhard Fettweis. Not only for acting as referee for this thesis but also for encouraging me during the final phase. Fourth to name, my colleague Hermann S. Lichte whom I thank for many productive hours, careful and quick proofreading, and for sustaining me as an office-mate. Fifthly, Tobias Volkhausen, Furuzan Atay Onat, Dereje H. Woldegebreal, Akram Bin Sediq, Sébastien Simoens, Guillaume Vivier, Josep Vidal, Adrian Agustin, Imad Aad, and Jörg Widmer – thank you for great collaboration and for many insightful discussions. Sixthly, I have to thank those students who contributed their high motivation and great ideas to implementation and experiments: Holger von Malm, Thorsten Pawlak, Thomas Freitag, Falk Eitzen, Daniel Warneke, Rafael Funke, and Thorsten Biermann – just to name a few of them. My seventh thanks go to Hajo Kraus for providing great mechanical solutions for the experiments and to Christian Henke for patiently driving the RailCab during our long measurements. Next to last, I would like to thank Sebastian S. Szyszkowicz and Abdulkareem Adinoyi for fascinating but not too serious discussions and, finally, a big hug goes to Helene and to the Valentins for believing in me and for being there.

Contents

1	**Introduction**	**1**
2	**Fading and diversity**	**7**
2.1	Fading channels	7
	2.1.1 Basic channel model and terminology	7
	2.1.2 Fading models	9
	2.1.3 Coherence time: Slow versus fast fading	12
	2.1.4 Performance metrics	14
2.2	Diversity systems	15
	2.2.1 Diversity order and gain	16
	2.2.2 Used diversity modes	17
	2.2.3 Combining	17
2.3	Basic constraints	18
2.4	Summary of basic assumptions	19
3	**Cooperative relaying – Protocols and theoretical performance**	**21**
3.1	Background on cooperative relaying protocols	21
	3.1.1 From relaying to cooperation diversity	22
	3.1.2 Fundamental cooperative relaying protocols	24
3.2	Selection relaying protocols	25
	3.2.1 Generalization and protocol classification	25
	3.2.2 Combining-based protocols	28
	3.2.3 Network path allocation-based protocols	30
3.3	Performance analysis of selection relaying	32
	3.3.1 Method and assumptions	33
	3.3.2 Outage probability for arbitrary flow networks	34
	3.3.3 Outage probability for one and two relays	36
	3.3.4 Outage capacity for arbitrary flow networks	42
	3.3.5 Outage capacity for one and two relays	45
3.4	Performance analysis under practical constraints	48
	3.4.1 Effect of limited CSI feedback	48

	3.4.2	Effect of limited network connectivity	54
	3.4.3	Occurrence-conditioned outage capacity	59
3.5	Summary of contributions and future work		59

4 Selection relaying with partial forwarding   63

4.1	Partial forwarding		63
4.2	Forwarding decision frequency		66
	4.2.1	Block lengths and decision frequency	66
	4.2.2	Analysis for block fading channels	67
	4.2.3	Discussion	70
4.3	Forwarding decision metric		72
	4.3.1	Related work and terminology	73
	4.3.2	Calculating Minimum Path Difference	74
	4.3.3	Decoder complexity and implementation remarks	77
	4.3.4	Accuracy study	79
4.4	Protocols for partial forwarding		85
	4.4.1	Single forwarding decision	85
	4.4.2	Two decision stages	88
	4.4.3	Transmitting control information	89
4.5	End-to-end performance study		91
	4.5.1	System model and parameters	91
	4.5.2	Effect of the decision metric	91
	4.5.3	Effect of the protocol and signaling functions	92
4.6	Summary of contributions and future work		97

5 Applying selection relaying to resource allocation   99

5.1	Asymmetric cooperation for media streaming		99
	5.1.1	Approach and scenario	100
	5.1.2	Related work	102
	5.1.3	Asymmetric diversity branch allocation (ACD)	103
	5.1.4	Outage probability and diversity order	103
	5.1.5	Traffic-aware cooperation diversity	108
	5.1.6	Video quality study	110
5.2	Cooperative feedback for multiuser diversity systems		115
	5.2.1	Multiuser diversity in OFDM systems	116
	5.2.2	Related work	118
	5.2.3	Cooperative feedback protocol	119
	5.2.4	Effects of feedback errors and overhead	120
	5.2.5	Performance study	123

		5.3	Summary of contributions and future work	130
6	**Cooperative WLANs – A prototype**			**133**
	6.1		Scope and related work	133
	6.2		Combining versus packet selection	136
		6.2.1	Packet selection	136
		6.2.2	Outage analysis	137
		6.2.3	Simulation results	138
	6.3		Cooperative medium access	139
		6.3.1	Signaling for cooperative WLANs	139
		6.3.2	CSIG control frames and overhead	143
		6.3.3	CSIG protocol operation	144
	6.4		A prototype for cooperative WLANs	146
		6.4.1	Transceiver design	146
		6.4.2	Implementing the prototype	147
	6.5		Measurement results	148
		6.5.1	Experimental setup and scenarios	148
		6.5.2	Indoor scenario results	150
		6.5.3	Vehicular scenario results	154
	6.6		Summary of contributions and future work	155
7	**Conclusions and future research**			**159**
A	**BER of partial forwarding**			**163**
B	**Details on the measurement platform and scenarios**			**165**
Bibliography				**179**

List of Figures

1.1	Main objective of this thesis	2
2.1	Direct transmission	8
2.2	Block fading channel	10
2.3	Effect of the Doppler frequency	12
2.4	Autocorrelation and coherence time	13
2.5	Diversity versus coding gain	16
3.1	Relaying with unicast and broadcast transmissions	22
3.2	A general selection relaying protocol	25
3.3	Selection relaying protocols	26
3.4	Flow of data packets in SDF	28
3.5	Flow of data packets in Coded Cooperation (CC)	29
3.6	Coding and protocol procedure of Coded Cooperation	30
3.7	Flow of control and data packets in OR	31
3.8	Flow of control and data packets in CoopMAC	32
3.9	Example flow network and cut sets	34
3.10	Flow networks for a single relay	36
3.11	*Diamond* flow networks in a four-node scenario	38
3.12	Outage probability, full CSI	41
3.13	Outage capacity: Comparing two approximations	44
3.14	Outage capacity as a fraction of AWGN capacity, full CSI	47
3.15	Outage capacity as a fraction of AWGN capacity, limited CSI	52
3.16	Region of operation for CSR and PSR with limited CSI	54
3.17	Studied propagation scenarios	55
3.18	Base configuration	56
3.19	Occurrence probability P^o of studied flow networks	58
3.20	Occurrence-conditioned outage capacity $C^{out,o}$	60
4.1	Autocorrelated vs. block fading	64
4.2	Partial Forwarding approach	64

4.3	Coherence time of an autocorrelated fading channel	65
4.4	Example of the block lengths for Case 1	68
4.5	Two examples of the block lengths for Case 2	69
4.6	Effect of forwarding decision frequency	71
4.7	Example: Extracting MPD from a trellis	75
4.8	MPD-extended Viterbi algorithm	75
4.9	BPSK constellation example	77
4.10	Realistic and ideal SNR measurement	82
4.11	BER vs. MPD measured over all symbols	83
4.12	Pairwise correlation coefficient of metric and true BER	84
4.13	Effect of block length on MPD accuracy	85
4.14	MPD-extended SDF relay, single-stage decision	86
4.15	Effect of MPD threshold on end-to-end Bit Error Rate (BER_{e2e})	87
4.16	Effect of MPD threshold on BER_{e2e}: Contour plot	88
4.17	MPD-extended SDF relay, two-stage decision	89
4.18	Source encoding for PF signaling	89
4.19	Signaling overhead for Partial Forwarding (PF)	90
4.20	Effect of decision metric on BER_{e2e}	93
4.21	Effect of relaying protocol on BER_{e2e}	95
4.22	Effect of relaying protocol on data rate	96
5.1	Structure of the proposed traffic-aware diversity allocation system	101
5.2	Basic scenario and MAC cycle of Coded Cooperation (CC)	101
5.3	Flow networks and cut sets of user a with ACD	104
5.4	Outage probability for $R = 1/4$	107
5.5	TACD's decision stages	108
5.6	Frame 1 of the MAF video sequence	112
5.7	Frame 139 of the MAF video sequence	112
5.8	Mean PER and DIV for the MAF video sequence	113
5.9	Occurrence of video frame types per MAC cycle	114
5.10	Example PSNR for a single MAF video sequence	115
5.11	Example of waterfilling power allocation	117
5.12	Simple example for cooperative feedback	119
5.13	MAC cycle for direct and cooperative feedback	119
5.14	Percentage of total overhead on ergodic sum capacity (downlink)	122
5.15	BER of the feedback channels vs. uplink SNR	124
5.16	MSE comparing the estimated CSI to the true value	125
5.17	Ergodic sum capacity (downlink) vs. uplink SNR	126
5.18	Outage probability (downlink) vs. uplink SNR	127

5.19	Uplink SNR regions required to reach full ergodic sum capacity	128
5.20	Ergodic sum capacity (downlink) vs. number of users	129
6.1	Comparing PS and MRC: Outage probability vs. mean SNR	138
6.2	Comparing PS and MRC: PER vs. mean SNR	139
6.3	MAC cycle for direct IEEE 802.11 transmission	140
6.4	MAC cycle for cooperative IEEE 802.11, direct signaling	141
6.5	Measured RTS control frame error rate for IEEE 802.11g	142
6.6	MAC cycle for cooperative IEEE 802.11 with CSIG	142
6.7	Layout of the extended control frames	143
6.8	Cooperative IEEE 802.11 MAC protocol automata	145
6.9	Cooperative IEEE 802.11g transceiver design	147
6.10	Indoor NLOS scenario	149
6.11	Vehicular scenario	151
6.12	Indoor: End-to-end PER, MRC vs. Packet Selection (PS)	152
6.13	Indoor: End-to-end UDP data rate	153
6.14	Indoor: End-to-end PER	153
6.15	Vehicular: End-to-end UDP data rate	154
6.16	Vehicular: End-to-end UDP PER	155
B.1	SORBAS 101 device	166
B.2	SORBAS 101 platform overview	167
B.3	Languages and tools for SORBAS programming	168
B.4	Setup to measure transmit power mismatch	169
B.5	Transmit power mismatch	170
B.6	Path loss of the indoor scenario	172

List of Tables

2.1	SNR gains of MRC for i.i.d. Rayleigh fading	18
3.1	Results of the outage analysis for CSR	39
3.2	Results of the outage analysis for PSR with full CSI	40
3.3	Results of the outage analysis for PSR, SSD with limited CSI	50
3.4	Connectivity conditions for occurrence counting	57
4.1	Computational complexity of several soft output decoders	78
4.2	Error events $\mathcal{E}$ for threshold-based forwarding decisions	86
5.1	Diversity order for two users	106
5.2	Parameters of the video quality study	110
6.1	Lengths of MAC frames used in IEEE 802.11 and CSIG	144
6.2	Example of DLC and PHY signaling overhead	144
B.1	Link budget: Constant power losses and gains	171
B.2	Hardware and software used in the indoor and vehicular scenario	175
B.3	Parameters and factors for the indoor scenario	175
B.4	Parameters and factors for the vehicular scenario	176

List of Acronyms

ACD	Asymmetric Cooperation Diversity
ACF	Autocorrelation Function
ACK	Acknowledgment
AF	Amplify-and-Forward
ARQ	Automatic Repeat Request
APP	A Posteriori Probability
AWGN	Additive White Gaussian Noise
AVC	Advanced Video Coding
BER	Bit Error Rate
BER_{e2e}	end-to-end Bit Error Rate
BPSK	Binary Phase Shift Keying
BS	Base Station
CC	Coded Cooperation
CCA	Clear Channel Assessment
CDF	Cumulative Distribution Function
CDMA	Code Division Multiple Access
CF	Compress-and-Forward
CFB	Cooperative Feedback
CIF	Common Intermediate Format
CSIG	Cooperative Signaling

CSR	Combining-based Selection Relaying
CRC	Cyclic Redundancy Check
CTR	Cooperative Triangle
CTS	Clear-To-Send
CSI	Channel State Information
DF	Decode-and-Forward
DIV	Distortion In interVal
DLC	Data Link Control layer
DMA	Direct Memory Access
DoF	Degree Of Freedom
DSP	Digital Signal Processor
DSSS	Direct Sequence Spread Spectrum
EA	Equivalent Addition
e2e	end-to-end
FDD	Frequency Division Duplexing
FEC	Forward Error Correction
FFT	Fast Fourier Transform
FPGA	Field Programmable Gate Array
FCS	Frame Check Sequences
GoP	Group Of Pictures
HARQ	Hybrid Automatic Repeat Request
HSDPA	High Speed Downlink Packet Access
HTS	Helper ready To Send
i.i.d.	independently identically distributed
IP	Internet Protocol

List of Acronyms

JTAG	Joint Test Action Group
LOS	Line Of Sight
LTE	Long Term Evolution
MAC	Medium Access Control
MAP	Maximum A Posteriori
MIMO	Multiple-Input Multiple-Output
MPD VA	MPD-extended Viterbi Algorithm
MAF	Mobile/Akiyo/Football
MPD	Minimum Path Difference
MRC	Maximum Ratio Combining
SC	Selection Combining
MSE	Mean Squared Error
MTU	Maximum Transmission Unit
MUD	Multiuser Diversity
NACK	Negative Acknowledgment
NAV	Network Allocation Vector
NCR	Non-Cooperative Relaying
NLOS	Non-Line Of Sight
OFDM	Orthogonal Frequency Division Multiplexing
OFDMA	OFDM Multiple Access
OR	Opportunistic Relaying
PDF	Probability Density Function
PER	Packet Error Rate
PF	Partial Forwarding
PHY	Physical layer

PLCP	Physical Layer Convergence Procedure	
PSD	Power Spectral Density	
PS	Packet Selection	
PSR	Path allocation-based Selection Relaying	
PSNR	Peak Signal-to-Noise Ratio	
OR	Opportunistic Relaying	
QAM	Quadrature Amplitude Modulation	
QPSK	Quadrature Phase Shift Keying	
RCPC	Rate-Compatible Punctured Convolutional	
RF	Radio Frequency	
RS	Relay Stations	
RTS	Request-To-Send	
RTP	Real-Time Transport Protocol	
RSSI	Received Signal Strength Indication	
SDF	Selection Decode-and-Forward	
2SDF	Two-stage SDF	
SDR	Software Defined Radio	
SER	Symbol Error Rate	
SDL	Specification and Description Language	
SFD	Strong Full Diamond	
SIFS	Short Inter-Frame Space	
SNR	Signal-to-Noise Ratio	
SINR	Signal-to-Interference plus Noise Ratio	
SOVA	Soft Output Viterbi Algorithm	
STC	Space-Time Coding	

SSD	Strong Sparse Diamond
TACD	Traffic-Aware Cooperation Diversity
TDD	Time Division Duplexing
TDMA	Time Division Multiple Access
UDP	User Datagram Protocol
VBR	Variable Bit Rate
VA	Viterbi Algorithm
WFD	Weak Full Diamond
WLAN	Wireless Local Area Network
WMAN	Wireless Metropolitan Area Network
WSD	Weak Sparse Diamond

List of Symbols

(i,j)	Unidirectional link from node i to node j
s	A node operating in *source* mode
r	A node operating in *relay* mode
d	A node operating in *destination* mode
CSI_{rx}	Channel State Information (CSI) at the receiver
CSI_{tx}	CSI at the transmitter
R	Spectral efficiency in bits/s/Hz specified at transmitter
L	Diversity order
C_A	AWGN capacity of system A, i.e., maximum mutual information between input and output of the band-limited AWGN channel.
$\bar{C}_A$	Ergodic capacity of system A
$\bar{C}_A^{\text{sum}}$	Ergodic sum capacity of system A
P_A^{out}	Outage probability of system A
C_A^{out}	Outage capacity of system A
ε	Outage probability constraint to calculate C^{out}
P	System-wide average transmission power
N_0	Noise Power Spectral Density
W	Signal bandwidth
α	Path loss exponent
$D_{i,j}$	Separation distance between node i and j

f_c	Carrier frequency
f_d	Doppler frequency; equivalent to maximum Doppler shift
v	Relative velocity between transmitter and receiver
$h_{i,j}$	Channel coefficient of link (i,j); the channel gain is $|h_{i,j}|^2$
Γ	System-wide reference Signal-to-Noise Ratio (SNR)
$\Gamma_{i,j}$	Mean of the channel gain $|h_{i,j}|^2$; also the variance of the circularly symmetric complex Gaussian random variable $h_{i,j} \sim \mathcal{CN}(0, \Gamma_{i,j})$.
$\gamma_{i,j}$	Instantaneous SNR of link (i,j)
$\bar{\gamma}_{i,j}$	Mean SNR of link (i,j)
$\hat{\gamma}$	A specified SNR threshold
T_b	Fading block time
T_c	Coherence time
T_p	Packet time
T_{cycle}	Total duration of a single Medium Access Control (MAC) cycle
$\wedge$	Logical *and* operator
$\vee$	Logical *or* operator
x^+	Operator $x^+ := \max(x, 0)$
$\Re\{x\}$	The real part of a complex variable x
$\Im\{x\}$	The imaginary part of complex variable x
$\mathbb{E}\{X\}$	Mean of the random variable X
$\mathbb{P}\{\mathcal{A}\}$	Probability of event $\mathcal{A}$
$p_X(x)$	Probability Density Function (PDF) of the random variable X
$R_0(\cdot)$	Autocorrelation Function (ACF) as a function of lag time
$J_0(\cdot)$	Zeroth-order Bessel function of the first kind
$\text{erfc}(\cdot)$	Complementary error function

Chapter 1

Introduction

Users of wireless networks demand a high data rate and seamless connectivity even in mobile scenarios. Fulfilling this need at reasonable costs is a challenge for research and development. In particular, technologies are required that maintain connectivity at high data rate but without requiring more bandwidth or substantial investments in infrastructure – *cooperative relaying* is one such technology.

Cooperative relaying achieves these benefits by joining two fundamental concepts of wireless communication: *multi-antenna communication* and *relaying*. Relaying uses intermediate nodes (briefly called *relays*) to retransmit the source's information towards the destination and, thereby, splits the overall distance into multiple *hops*. Compared to a directly transmitting source, each transmitter has to invest less power to reach the next hop. This saves transmit energy and allows to precisely focus the signal power to places where it is needed. For instance, in densely-connected *ad hoc* networks, relays focus the radio signal along a multi-hop path which limits the interference to neighboring paths. Consequently, more parallel paths in the network can be established which increases the overall network capacity [GK00].

In infrastructure-based *cellular networks* or in *Wireless Metropolitan Area Networks (WMANs)*, relays can help a base station to cover "blind spots" without significantly increasing the interference to neighboring cells [SPG+03, VLK+09]. The fact that conventional user nodes can act as relays (ad hoc networks) or that dedicated relay nodes are significantly simpler than full base stations (infrastructure-based networks) makes relaying also cost-efficient [THN08]. All these benefits have lead to the standardization of various relaying techniques in ad hoc networks [IEE99] and in infrastructure-based networks [IEE09a].

Cooperative relaying can be seen as an extension of conventional relaying that is inspired by multi-antenna communication. By overhearing the original broadcast of the source, the destination can combine the original and the relayed signal. Due to the spatial separation of the transmit antennas it is likely that both received signals were affected by statistically independent channels. In this case, *combining* these signals provides high so-called *spatial diversity* gains that protect the overall transmission from rapid channel fluctuations (so-called *fading*).

Spatial diversity reached by cooperative relaying is often called *cooperation diversity* and was first described in [SEA98]. Based on this fundamental concept, developing and studying cooperative relaying protocols has become a lively field of research. During the recent years many authors applied analytical

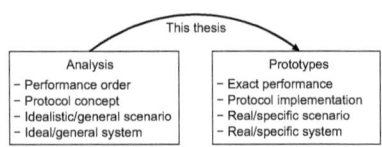

Figure 1.1: Main objective of this thesis: Bridging the gap between analysis and prototyping cooperative relaying protocols.

methods (usually classic information theory or Bit Error Rate (BER) analysis) but also early prototypes and measurement results were presented.

Naturally, prototyping and analysis have their individual strengths and limitations. Figure 1.1 summarizes these differences. Analysis allows to assess the performance order (and sometimes even to derive the performance bounds) of a cooperation protocol. Thereby, analysis is a strong fundament and valuable guidance for designing fundamental concepts for cooperative relaying but it is limited by its idealistic assumptions. In particular, many analytical papers on cooperative relaying assume ideal coding, unlimited system complexity, ideal system accuracy, ideal channel knowledge, and ideal channel statistics. Due to these idealistic assumptions, protocol engineers have to take a large step from (1) designing and analyzing a theoretical protocol concept to (2) transforming this design into a practical protocol that approaches the theoretical performance at reasonable complexity and overhead.

This large gap between theoretical and practical research on cooperative relaying protocols is highlighted by the fact that, so far, none of the previous prototyping attempts could reproduce the cooperation diversity gains (or at least the order of magnitude) promised by theory [BL06b, KNBP06, LTN$^+$07, ZJZ09, KKEP09]. Thus, we have to expect that the current theoretical performance results for cooperative relaying protocols are not robust to *practical constraints* that are imposed by real systems and real scenarios. So far, the performance degradation due to such practical constraints was not consistently studied in previous work.

Objectives and scope   It is the objective of this thesis to bridge the gap between the theoretical analysis and practical implementation of cooperative relaying protocols. In particular, we aim to:

1. Show how cooperative relaying protocols perform under realistic scenario and system assumptions.
2. Develop new, practical techniques to maintain cooperative gains in realistic scenarios and to obtain benefits in new scenarios.
3. Demonstrate the feasibility and high performance of cooperative relaying in reality by implementing a prototype and by field measurements.

We start with the general models and idealistic assumptions commonly used in analytical papers on cooperative relaying. Then, to achieve each of our three objectives, we gradually increase the "level of reality" by adding more and more practical constraints. This is done until our prototype is implemented and measured in real scenarios.

Adding more and more practical constraints, naturally, limits the scope of our studies. While the results of our theoretical studies and most of the proposed techniques can be applied to a variety of systems, implementing a prototype requires to focus on a particular technology. We integrate cooperative relaying into a *Wireless Local Area Network (WLAN)* transceiver that follows the IEEE 802.11g standard [IEE03]. This technology is widely employed, a foundation of upcoming wireless systems (e.g., IEEE 802.11n, IEEE 802.16e [Per08, IEE05]), and well-understood for direct transmission. In terms of cooperation protocols, we focus on the general approach of *selection relaying* where the relay avoids error propagation by deciding not to forward incorrect packets [LWT01]. Selection relaying is the basis of many practical cooperation protocols such as Selection Decode-and-Forward (SDF), Coded Cooperation (CC), and Opportunistic Relaying (OR) [LWT04, HN02, BSW07]. Therefore, studying selection relaying and, in particular, the forwarding decision of the relay is highly relevant for applying cooperative relaying protocols.

Contributions to state of the art The first contribution in this thesis is the joint analysis of *Path allocation-based Selection Relaying (PSR)* and *Combining-based Selection Relaying (CSR)* protocols. While previous work has studied these selection relaying protocols separately [LWT04, BSW07], we unify their analysis assuming ideal channel knowledge. Based on these idealistic assumptions we derive two new approximations for the *outage capacity* (i.e., the maximum transmission rate at a required error rate) which are valid for any network topology, match simulation results closely, and clearly show how the required error rate and the employed links degrade the capacity of an ideal multi-antenna system.

These outage capacity approximations enable us to study our first practical constraints: *limited channel knowledge* and *limited network connectivity*. Both constraints were not studied by previous work. Limited channel knowledge significantly degrades the outage capacity for PSR protocols but not for CSR; for limited network connectivity the situation reverses. Thereby each of these selection relaying protocols performs best in different settings. We provide lookup tables to choose between these protocols according to the SNR region and error rate. Further selection relaying protocols or scenarios can be analyzed with the presented methods; they are easy to use and general.

The third practical constraint that we focus on is the statistical model of the time-selective fading channel. So far, the research community focused on so-called *block fading* channels to analyze cooperative relaying protocols. By assuming the channel states to be uncorrelated but static per packet time, this model represents the ideal case for selection relaying. By taking the *second order statistics* (i.e., the autocorrelation) of the fading process into account, we study selection relaying protocols in a more general fading scenario. Our analysis points out that selection relaying protocols perform poorly when fades occur during the packet time. By not deciding frequently "enough", the relay ignores a significant amount of correctly received symbols and performance drops. Our so-called *Partial Forwarding (PF)* approach generalizes selection relaying from an optimization in the value domain (find SNR threshold to decide if a packet is correct) to an optimization in the value *and* time domain (find SNR threshold *and* block length to decide if a block is correct). We describe a practical system that employs *soft output decoding* [BCJR74] for a frequent forwarding decision, imposes only low calculation complexity, and reaches a performance close to the theoretical ideal case even with autocorrelated fading.

Our fourth contribution demonstrates two beneficial applications of selection relaying in systems with resource allocation. First, we propose *Traffic-Aware Cooperation Diversity (TACD)* – an extension of selection relaying to provide higher diversity gains to more relevant parts of a video stream. This extension substantially improves the video quality of a cooperative transmission and can be implemented without communication overhead. Our second scheme is called *Cooperative Feedback (CFB)* and strengthens the feedback channels of *Multiuser Diversity (MUD)* systems by cooperation. Thereby, CFB avoids scheduling errors and improves the error rate and sum capacity of MUD systems. TACD and CFB are simple, can be applied in various systems, and provide tremendous gains if combined with resource allocation.

To demonstrate a further beneficial application of selection relaying we implement a transceiver prototype for *cooperative* WLANs. This requires several contributions. Since previous *Medium Access Control (MAC)* protocols for cooperative relaying [LTN+07, TWT08, SZW09] perform poorly with *erroneous control frames*, we develop the *Cooperative Signaling (CSIG)* protocol that efficiently copes with this practical constraint. Further, we study a combining scheme that reaches a performance close to the ideal scheme but substantially simplifies the transceiver design. Our design of a cooperative IEEE 802.11g transceiver is lightweight, transparent, and includes standard IEEE 802.11g operation as legacy mode. Implementing this design results in a WLAN transceiver that performs selection relaying at the high transmission rates of IEEE 802.11g. Until now, such high rates are not reached by any other prototype for cooperative networks [BL06b, KNBP06, LTN+07, ZJZ09, KKEP09]. Based on several prototypes we establish a cooperative WLAN in an indoor and vehicular scenario (using a train to move the cooperating nodes) and perform extensive field measurements. Our measurement results not only demonstrate the feasibility and high performance of our cooperative IEEE 802.11g extensions but also that selection relaying is a promising approach for future WLAN generations.

Thesis organization This work is divided into seven chapters. Chapter 2 introduces the basic terminology, quantities, channel models, and assumptions that are used throughout this thesis. Note that in the remaining chapters related work is discussed when needed.

In Chapter 3, we start with the basic principles of cooperation diversity. We classify the cooperative relaying protocols from literature into Path allocation-based Selection Relaying (PSR) and Combining-based Selection Relaying (CSR) and jointly analyze both protocol classes under idealistic assumptions. Accounting for the practical constraints, we study how the performance of these protocols degrades with limited channel knowledge and limited network connectivity.

In Chapter 4 we validate the performance of selection relaying for autocorrelated fading channels. We propose Partial Forwarding (PF) and analyze this approach under idealistic assumptions. The closed-form results are summarized in Appendix A. Then, we integrate PF into IEEE 802.11 and study the resulting practical system by simulation.

Chapter 5 applies selection relaying to resource allocation. As efficient examples, TACD and CFB are proposed. We describe both cooperation schemes in detail, study TACD in terms of outage probability and video quality, and analyze the outage probability and sum capacity of CFB in a multiuser system.

Chapter 6 details our development of the cooperative WLAN prototype. In particular, a simplified combing scheme is studied, the cooperative CSIG protocol and a cooperative IEEE 802.11g transceiver are specified, and the results of our field measurements are presented. Details on the experimental setup, studies of the scenarios, and an overview of the testbed are provided in Appendix B. In Chapter 7 this thesis is concluded and promising future research is summarized.

Bibliographical notes Parts of this thesis have been published in collaboration with other researchers. The related publications are listed here.

The survey and classification of relaying protocols in Chapter 3 is an extension of [VLK$^+$06, VLK$^+$07]. The outage analysis from Section 3.3 and the degradation due to feedback and limited connectivity from Section 3.4 was published in [VLK$^+$08]. This paper also includes the outage capacity approximations from Section 3.3 which are applied in [LVvM$^+$09] on the problem of cooperative rate adaptation. Our analytic results from Section 3.3 are also employed in [LVK$^+$09b] to study coverage/capacity tradeoffs; a study that led to the new interference model in [HSLK10].

The problem of selection relaying with autocorrelated fading in Chapter 4 was found in early studies [VK07b, VK07a]. The Partial Forwarding (PF) approach was first described in [VVA$^+$08b]. The decoding-based metric for partial channel estimation was formalized and studied in [VVA$^+$08a] and the system design was detailed in patent applications [VVK08, VVK$^+$09]. The analysis of ideal PF for a generalized block fading model and the metric complexity studies are original to this thesis.

Both cooperative resource allocation approaches from Chapter 5 are published. The Traffic-Aware Cooperation Diversity (TACD) scheme was first described and studied in [VvK07]. Further outage probability and video quality results are given in Section 5.1. An extensive description of the system is given in a patent [VKA07]. The idea and a first analysis of cooperative feedback was published in [VK09]. The analysis in Section 5.2 is a significant extension of this paper.

The closer look at the combining schemes in Section 6.2 and their simplification was published in [VWVK09]. The Cooperative Signaling (CSIG) protocol from Section 6.3 is based on the early cooperative MAC protocols [VLK$^+$09, LVK$^+$08, LAW$^+$08] and was first published in [VLW$^+$08]. In [LV08] some properties of CSIG are formalized to a specification language for cooperative MAC protocols which enables their compiler-based generation [LVK09a] and easy integration into simulators [KSW$^+$08]. Nonetheless, the formal description of the complete CSIG protocol is original to this thesis.

The paper [VLW$^+$08] also contains the first description of the cooperative WLAN prototype in Section 6.4 and the measurement results for the vehicular scenario in Section 6.5. The measurements for the indoor scenario are not published elsewhere so far. The detailed description of the testbed and experimental framework in Appendix B is partially published in [LVE$^+$07, VFK08].

Chapter 2

Fading and diversity

This chapter introduces the basic terminology, models, and assumptions in this work. First, fundamental models and performance metrics for fading channels are described. Then, we focus on diversity as an approach to cope with fading and describe conventional diversity modes on which cooperative relaying is based. Finally, we summarize the main system assumptions and resource constraints.

2.1 Fading channels

With multipath propagation, multiple reflected signals interfere at the receiver antenna. This superposition causes rapid fluctuations of the received signal at a small time scale – an effect called *small scale fading* or, briefly, *fading*.

In this thesis we focus on multipath propagation environments with mobility where fading is frequency-flat but time-selective. *Frequency-flat fading* corresponds to scenarios where (1) the delay spread – measuring the difference between the path echos – is much smaller than the symbol time or (2) when techniques are used to flatten the spectrum of the received signal, e.g., Orthogonal Frequency Division Multiplexing (OFDM) and/or power allocation (Section 5.2). *Time-selective fading* results from mobility in a multipath propagation environment, which (1) changes the position of the receiver antenna and, thus, the superposition of the path signals and (2) induces a frequency shift of the received signal due to the Doppler effect.

2.1.1 Basic channel model and terminology

To describe the employed channel model, let us focus on *direct transmission*. Figure 2.1 illustrates this basic scenario. Here, node i transmits signal x_i via a wireless channel in order to establish the unidirectional link (i,j) to node j.

Baseband model and noise The signal vector $y_{i,j}$ received at node j is given by the classic discrete baseband channel model as

$$y_{i,j} = h_{i,j} x_i + n_{i,j} \qquad (2.1)$$

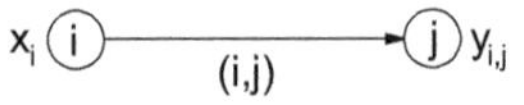

$$x_i \bigcirc \xrightarrow{\quad (i,j) \quad} \bigcirc y_{i,j}$$

Figure 2.1: Direct transmission from node i to node j via a wireless channel to establish the unidirectional link (i,j).

where all variables are time-discrete complex amplitudes and specific to an arbitrary link (i,j). The signal vector x_i is transmitted at an *average transmission power* of P Watts using a *signal bandwidth* of W Hz. At the receiver j, the noise vector $n_{i,j}$ adds to x_i. With the standard Additive White Gaussian Noise (AWGN) model, $n_{i,j}$ is a zero-mean, circularly symmetric, complex random sequence where the real and imaginary components are independently identically distributed (i.i.d.) Gaussians with variance $N_0/2$. N_0 is the Power Spectral Density (PSD) of the received, band-passed noise and $N_0/2$ is the PSD of the white Gaussian noise [Pro00, (4.1-56)].

Channel gain and path loss The *channel coefficient* $h_{i,j}$ models the multiplicative effect of both path loss and fading. Fading causes a random variation of the channel coefficient, which is detailed below. In power, the magnitude of this random variable is given by the *channel gain* $|h_{i,j}|^2$ with mean $\Gamma_{i,j}$.[1] We assume that the *mean channel gain* $\Gamma_{i,j}$ is only given by the distance-dependent path loss. Hence, we define

$$\Gamma_{i,j} = \mathbb{E}\{|h_{i,j}|^2\} := \left(\frac{D_{i,j}}{D_0}\right)^{-\alpha} \quad (2.2)$$

using the common power law model for path loss [Rap02, (4.67)] where the distance $D_{i,j}$ between the nodes i and j is normalized by a reference distance D_0. The *path loss exponent* α depends on the propagation scenario and is typically between 2 and 5.

SNRs Throughout this thesis several expressions for the *Signal-to-Noise Ratio (SNR)* are used. As common in theoretical studies [LWT04, Her05, AT07], we account for noise and average transmission power by a *reference SNR*

$$\Gamma := \frac{P}{N_0 W} \quad (2.3)$$

and express channel-related effects as scaling factors to this reference. While this example is given for a single system-wide transmission power P, we will similarly define other reference SNRs for different transmission powers. With definition (2.3), the *mean SNR* received at j is

$$\bar{\gamma}_{i,j} = \Gamma_{i,j} \Gamma \quad (2.4)$$

where $\Gamma_{i,j}$ is used as a scaling factor to incorporate path loss. The *instantaneous SNR* at j is then

$$\gamma_{i,j} = |h_{i,j}|^2 \Gamma \quad (2.5)$$

---

[1] In the literature, $\Gamma_{i,j}$ is also referred to as $\sigma_{i,j}^2$.

where path loss is captured by the the mean of $|h_{i,j}|^2$ and its random variation captures fading that node j experiences per discrete time interval. Let us take a closer look on the fading assumptions and models.

2.1.2 Fading models

Two basic models for time-selective fading are common in the literature and also used in this thesis. The first, so-called *i.i.d. Rayleigh fading model* accounts for *uncorrelated fading* where all channel coefficients h are i.i.d. random variables. The second, so-called *Clarke's model* captures *autocorrelated fading* and is a more-complex generalization of the first model. We will now discuss both models in detail.

Modeling uncorrelated fading

The i.i.d. Rayleigh fading model is widely employed, e.g., [LWT04, Her05, AT07] and extensively described in the literature, e.g., [TV05, Section 2.4.2], [SA04, Section 2.2.1]. Let us focus on the basic properties and implications of this model.

Probability Density Function (PDF) This model uses an uncorrelated complex Gaussian process to capture the effect of fading on the amplitude and phase of $y_{i,j}$. In particular, the channel coefficient $h_{i,j}$ is a random sequence with i.i.d. Gaussian real and imaginary components, zero mean, and a variance $\Gamma_{i,j}$. Such a complex random variable is called *circularly symmetric complex Gaussian* and denoted by $h_{i,j} \sim \mathcal{CN}(0, \Gamma_{i,j})$. The magnitudes $|h_{i,j}|$ are i.i.d. Rayleigh distributed and the channel gains $|h_{i,j}|^2$ follow an exponential distribution where mean $\Gamma_{i,j}$ accounts for path loss as described above. With (2.5), this leads to i.i.d. instantaneous SNRs with the PDF

$$p_{\gamma_{i,j}}(\gamma_{i,j}) = \frac{1}{\bar{\gamma}_{i,j}} \exp\left(-\frac{\gamma_{i,j}}{\bar{\gamma}_{i,j}}\right) \qquad (2.6)$$

around the mean SNR $\bar{\gamma}_{i,j}$.

Block fading channels This channel type is a common implementation of the above i.i.d. fading model. An exemplary channel gain is illustrated in Figure 2.2. For each discrete time interval, a single fading coefficient is independently generated and is assumed to hold until the next interval begins. Each interval is called a *fading block* and we denote its duration by the *fading block time* T_b.

This discrete model is based on the assumption that T_b is equal to the *coherence time* T_c, i.e., the time over which the channel gain stays approximately constant. Beside assuming $T_b = T_c$, each fading block is seen as an independent coherence period. We will see in Section 2.1.3 how both assumptions depend on the channel's autocorrelation and when block fading can be reasonably applied.

Model premises Modeling fading as a Gaussian process relies on a large number of independently reflected signals. This requires a scenario with many small reflectors and no dominating signal paths.

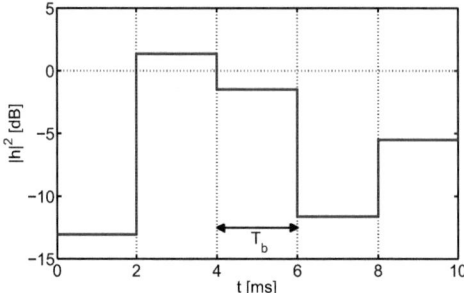

Figure 2.2: Channel gain $|h|^2$ vs. time with the block fading model and block time $T_b = 2$ ms.

Consequently, the i.i.d. Rayleigh fading model is usually employed for Non-Line Of Sight (NLOS) situations in urban and indoor scenarios [TV05, Section 2.4.2].

The i.i.d. property implies that the modeled fading channels are (1) non-reciprocal, i.e., $h_{i,j} \neq h_{j,i}$, (2) independent in space, and (3) independent in time. Each of these properties is highly relevant for the following chapters.

First, without reciprocal channels, the transmitter cannot observe the channel state of link (i, j) from the received signal $y_{j,i}$ (e.g., from a packet readily received with bidirectional communication). If the transmitter wants to adapt to link (i, j), some form of explicit *Channel State Information (CSI) feedback* from receiver j to i is required. As feedback imposes signaling overhead, errors, and delay, it is an important criterion to classify and analyze cooperation protocols (Chapter 3) and allows significant performance gains with improved feedback strategies (Section 5.2).

Second, throughout this thesis we will assume spatially independent fading channels. This is justified by the fact that the separation distance between cooperating nodes is typically much larger than the coherence distance [PNG03, Section 2.2.2]. This significant benefit of cooperative relaying above multiple antenna systems (where multiple antennas have to be packed on a single device) is further discussed in Section 3.1.1.

Third, by neglecting autocorrelation, the i.i.d. Rayleigh fading model does not describe how the channel gain varies in time. This neglects the Doppler effect and, as we will discuss in Section 2.1.3, limits the application of this model to specific mobility cases. Let us now describe a more general model for autocorrelated fading which accounts for the Doppler effect as well.

Modeling autocorrelated fading

So far, we modeled fading only by first-order statistics, i.e., the PDF, of the Gaussian process. We can generalize this model by using the fact that a Gaussian process can be completely characterized by its second-order statistics, namely, its Autocorrelation Function (ACF) [Ros96, Chapter 8]. The resulting model keeps the above PDFs of Rayleigh fading but additionally expresses autocorrelation due to the

2.1. Fading channels

Doppler shift. In the literature, this basic model for *autocorrelated fading* is known as *Clarke's model* [TV05, Section 2.4.3], *Jakes-like model* [Cav00, Section 5], or *land mobile model* [SA04, Section 2.1.2]. We describe its basic properties only briefly and focus on the underlying assumptions that are relevant for this work.

Doppler frequency/shift/spread A general autocorrelated fading model accounts for each individual reflected path. In this case the channel coefficient h depends on the Doppler shift $\Delta f = f_d \cos \tau$ of each reflected path where τ is the angle of arrival of a path with respect to the direction of motion. The *Doppler frequency* is calculated by $f_d = f_c v/c$ with carrier frequency f_c, speed of light c, and the relative velocity v between transmitter and receiver. The quantity f_d also denotes the *maximum Doppler shift* when the reflected path comes directly from the direction of motion (or $-f_d$ if directly from behind). Hence, the Doppler effect shifts the carrier frequency in $\Delta f \in [-f_d, f_d]$ and the *Doppler spread* $2f_d$ denotes the maximum range of this shift.

Autocorrelation Function (ACF) Clarke's model now simplifies the general autocorrelated fading model by placing many reflectors on a ring around the omnidirectional receive antenna. This isotropic scenario results in equal amplitudes and uniformly distributed phase shifts across all angles τ (cp. [Cav00, Section 5.1] for a detailed derivation). In this case, the Central Limit Theorem allows to model the contribution of all individual paths as Gaussian process. The lag-time dependent ACF is then given by

$$R_0 = \Gamma_{i,j} \cdot J_0(2\pi f_d \tau) \tag{2.7}$$

using the mean channel gain $\Gamma_{i,j}$ as a scaling factor to the zeroth-order Bessel function of the first kind

$$J_0(x) := \frac{1}{\pi} \int_0^\pi \exp(\iota x \cos \tau) d\tau \tag{2.8}$$

with the imaginary unit ι. Transforming (2.7) to the frequency domain provides the *Doppler spectrum* as the well-known U-shaped PSD ("bathtub curve") as introduced by Jakes in [Jak62, Chapter 1].

In (2.7), $\Gamma_{i,j}$ accounts for the magnitude of the channel gain (i.e., path loss) while the temporal stability of the fading process is defined by the Doppler frequency f_d. The effect of this parameter on the channel gain and on R_0 is illustrated in Figure 2.3. For increasing f_d the channel gain decorrelates in time and the ACF narrows until the characteristic form of J_0 is clearly shown. Thus, a large f_d accounts for scenarios with high speed where the channel gain changes frequently.

Model premises As stated above, Clarke's model is based on an isotropic antenna gain pattern with a circular placement of many scatterers. This leads to a Gaussian process which, again, provides Rayleigh distributed magnitudes $|h_{i,j}|$ and exponentially distributed channel gains $|h_{i,j}|^2$ with mean $\Gamma_{i,j}$ for an NLOS situation. However, unlike in the above i.i.d. Rayleigh fading model, the channel gains are now correlated in time. Clarke's model is very popular for mobile urban and indoor scenarios [TV05, Sec-

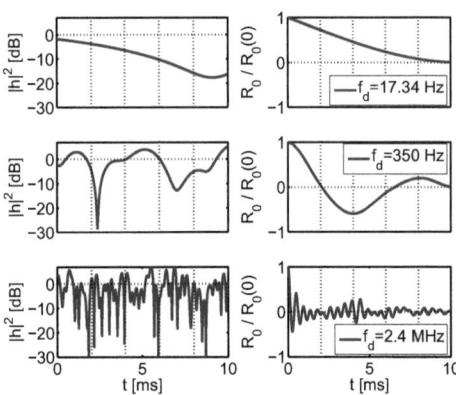

Figure 2.3: Effect of the Doppler frequency f_d (rows) on the channel gain $|h|^2$ vs. time (left column) and on the ACF (2.7) vs. lag time (right column). Shown for a vertical grid of 2 ms.

tion 2.4.3] and is often used as a reference even if more accurate channel models for specific vehicular scenarios and frequencies ranges are employed [AMI07, HKK+07].

Unlike block fading, the autocorrelated fading model accounts for the fact that a fading channel can change at any time. Even after a long stable period, an instant deep fade can occur (e.g., Figure 2.3, $f_d = 350\,\text{Hz}$). To this end, autocorrelated fading has to be studied at significantly smaller time scales than block fading channels.

2.1.3 Coherence time: Slow versus fast fading

Definition and approximation As stated above, the *coherence time* T_c is the time over which the channel gain stays approximately constant. More formally, the coherence time is often defined as the *minimal lag time* T_c' until the ACF R_0 decays below a given threshold [TV05, Section 2.4.3]. We illustrate this relationship between the coherence time and R_0 in Figure 2.4 using 5 % of the ACF's initial value as a threshold. With this common threshold, we find T_c' as the smallest lag time such that $R_0(T_c') = 0.05 R_0(0)$. However, significant correlation is still found for lag times larger than T_c' due to the slowly decreasing envelope of the Bessel function. Hence, the time over which the channel gain decorrelates is typically much larger than T_c' making the coherence time only a very rough estimate for decorrelation [Cav00, Section 5.1].

Moreover, it depends on the scenario (and is to some extent subjective) below which level one can ignore autocorrelation. Although the above 5 % threshold is often used [TV05, (2.61)], various other approximations of the coherence time are given in literature. All of them are reciprocal to the Doppler frequency which scales R_0 on the time axis (cp. Figure 2.3) but differ in an empirical factor. In this work,

2.1. Fading channels

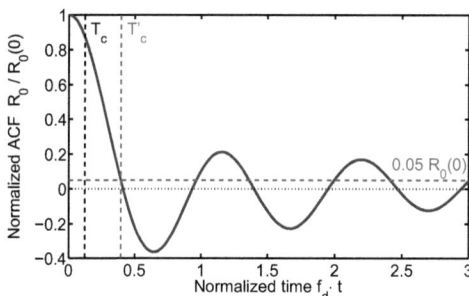

Figure 2.4: ACF (2.7) shown vs. normalized lag time $f_d \cdot t$ for $f_d = 120\,\text{Hz}$; Coherence time T_c' found at threshold $0.05 R_0(0)$ and T_c approximated by (2.9).

we use

$$T_c \approx \frac{1}{8 f_d} \qquad (2.9)$$

[TV05, (2.44)]. Depending on f_d, this approximation is three to four times smaller than the above T_c' (cp. Figure 2.4) and, thus, serves well as a pessimistic estimate of the coherence time. Other approximations of T_c in standard literature are either between (2.9) and T_c' [Rap02, (5.40.b)] or even larger than T_c' [Cav00, (5.1.17)].

Slow versus fast fading The coherence time is often used to distinguish between *slow fading* and *fast fading* channels but there is little consensus on these terms. In this thesis we will use a terminology similar to [TV05, Section 2.3.1]. We call a fading channel *fast* when T_c is much shorter than the packet time T_p and *slow* when T_c is longer than T_p.

Choosing the fading model In principle, the ACF (2.7) sufficiently characterizes Rayleigh fading for any value of T_c and T_p. However, slow and fast fading represent asymptotic cases for which autocorrelation is often neglected.

For a fast fading channel, i.e., $T_c \ll T_p$, each packet (usually a single codeword) spans a very large number of coherence times. Such a decorrelated situation occurs when the mobility is high (i.e., high f_d, low T_c) with respect to the packet time and allows to assume i.i.d. channel gains among the blocks [TV05, Section 5.4.5]. Figure 2.3 ($f_d = 2.4\,\text{MHz}$) illustrates such rapid fluctuations with respect to a typical packet time of $T_p = 2\,\text{ms}$ (marked by the vertical grid lines in the figure).

If fading is slow, i.e., $T_c \gg T_p$, the channel can be considered static over the packet time and deep fades occur only occasionally. This quasi-static situation is found when the mobility is low (i.e., very low f_d, high T_c) with respect to T_p. An example is illustrated in Figure 2.3 ($f_d = 17.34\,\text{Hz}$). Although for this continuous observation the channel gain is strongly correlated in time, many studies assume that the channel coefficients of consecutive blocks are uncorrelated [LWT04, AT07, BSW07, OAF+08]. This assumption can be justified when a long time is spent between channel uses or when the channel gain is decorrelated by other methods (e.g., interleaving or coding over many packet times).

To sum up: By focusing on the extreme cases of slow and fast fading, many studies ignore the second order statistics (i.e., ACF) of the fading process and model only its PDF. In this case the simple block fading model is used.

We will frequently use block fading in the following chapters but also justify our results for autocorrelated fading when needed. We do so in Chapter 4 and Section 6.2 where we focus on the $T_c \approx T_p$ case. In such intermediate situation neither the fast nor the slow fading assumption clearly holds. Figure 2.3 ($f_d = 350$ Hz) shows an example.

2.1.4 Performance metrics

In this thesis we use the following performance metrics.

Outage probability   The outage probability provides an information-theoretic measure of error rate for fading channels. A transmission is in *outage*, if the instantaneous SNR at the receiver γ falls below a specified *SNR threshold* $\hat{\gamma}$. We can compute the probability of this *outage event* – the so-called *outage probability* P^{out} – as the Cumulative Distribution Function (CDF) of γ evaluated at $\gamma = \hat{\gamma}$. With the PDF of γ, we can write this general definition as

$$P^{\text{out}} := \int_0^{\hat{\gamma}} p_\gamma(\gamma) \mathrm{d}\gamma \qquad (2.10)$$

giving the outage probability for arbitrary links and fading channels.

This metric can be easily illustrated for direct transmission and block fading by treating each block as an AWGN channel [TV05, Section 5.4.1]. The capacity of this channel – formally the maximum mutual information between input and output of the band-limited AWGN channel – is well known as *Shannon* or *AWGN capacity* [Sha49]. For an arbitrary fading block of the direct link (i,j), the AWGN capacity is $C(\gamma_{i,j}) = \log_2(1 + \gamma_{i,j})$ bits/s/Hz and only depends on the instantaneous SNR $\gamma_{i,j}$.

Assuming that the transmitter selects a data rate of R_{tx} bits/s (given by the *spectral efficiency* $R := R_{\text{tx}}/W$ in bits/s/Hz), at least an SNR of

$$\log_2(1 + \hat{\gamma}) = R \Leftrightarrow \hat{\gamma} = 2^R - 1$$

is required to communicate reliably over such block. Otherwise an outage occurs and – as a direct consequence of the Shannon-Hartley theorem – no code can lead to an arbitrary small error rate. Consequently, the outage probability of direct transmission with block fading is

$$P^{\text{out}}_{\text{DIR}} = \mathbb{P}\{\gamma_{i,j} < \hat{\gamma}\} = \mathbb{P}\{C(\gamma_{i,j}) < R\}$$

and depends on $\gamma_{i,j}$ and on the specified R. By inserting threshold $\hat{\gamma}$ and the exponential PDF (2.6) into

2.2. Diversity systems

(2.10) we obtain

$$P_{\text{DIR}}^{\text{out}} = \frac{1}{\bar{\gamma}_{i,j}} \int_0^{2^R-1} \exp\left(-\frac{\gamma_{i,j}}{\bar{\gamma}_{i,j}}\right) d\gamma_{i,j} = 1 - \exp\left(-\frac{2^R-1}{\bar{\gamma}_{i,j}}\right) \qquad (2.11)$$

as explicit outage probability of direct transmission via an i.i.d. Rayleigh fading channel. Writing the mean SNR as $\bar{\gamma}_{i,j} = \Gamma_{i,j}\Gamma$ we approximate

$$P_{\text{DIR}}^{\text{out}} \approx \frac{1}{\Gamma_{i,j}} \frac{2^R-1}{\Gamma} \qquad (2.12)$$

for asymptotically high SNR, i.e., $\Gamma \to \infty$. Note that in this approximation the link-dependent factor $\Gamma_{i,j}$ can be well separated from the system-wide parameters R and Γ. We will extensively use this property in Chapter 3 when we approximate P^{out} for large cooperative networks.

Outage capacity The outage capacity C^{out} is defined as the highest data rate such that a given *outage probability constraint* ε is not exceeded [TV05, 5.4.1]. We can obtain

$$C^{\text{out}} := \max(R) \quad \text{s.t.} \quad P^{\text{out}}(R) \leq \varepsilon \qquad (2.13)$$

by solving $P^{\text{out}}(R) = \varepsilon$ for R.

Practically speaking, C^{out} measures the maximum data rate guaranteed for at least $(1-\varepsilon) \cdot 100\%$ of the time. Such target error rates are an important design parameter of many wireless systems, e.g., the IEEE 802.11 standard specifies a maximum Packet Error Rate (PER) of 10% [IEE99]. Especially in multi-hop systems and under strict delay constraints (e.g., with voice transmission) high error rates can significantly decrease the performance. For such scenarios, C^{out} is often seen as a more functional performance metric than the ergodic capacity $\bar{C} := \mathbb{E}\{C\}$ which, in fact, implies an error rate close to zero [ASH+08].

Other performance metrics In addition to these fading-specific metrics we will study performance in terms of data rate, ergodic capacity $\bar{C}$, Bit Error Rate (BER), and Packet Error Rate (PER). We will detail these metrics when they are used.

2.2 Diversity systems

Unlike for an AWGN channel, the error rate of a fading channel decays only linearly if the SNR increases. An effective approach to cope with this poor performance is called *diversity*. By transmitting redundancy via independently faded channel representations, the slope of the error rate can be significantly improved. After discussing the basics and terminology in the field of diversity, we will focus on *combining* as a fundamental scheme to realize this approach.

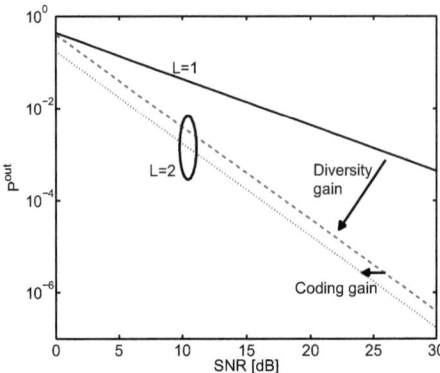

Figure 2.5: Outage probability vs. SNR comparing diversity and coding gain. Numerical results for two diversity orders L and $R = 1/4$ bits/s/Hz. Illustration similar to [PNG03, Figure 5.2].

2.2.1 Diversity order and gain

In Section 2.1.4 we used the error event $\{\gamma_{i,j} < \hat{\gamma}\}$ to derive the outage probability for direct transmission with block fading. In this example a single deep fade suffices for the overall transmission to be in outage. The result is an outage probability (2.12) that decays only linearly if the SNR increases. This poor performance of fading channels is well known, can be shown for an arbitrary error rate metric P^e, and is not found for AWGN channels where the decay is exponential [TV05, Section 3.1].

A *diversity scheme* can dramatically improve P^e for fading channels by distributing a single codeword over L independently faded channel representations (so-called *diversity branches*). In our above example, the diversity branches are given by L i.i.d. fading blocks over which a single packet can be distributed simply by repeating it once per block (so-called *repetition coding*). In this case, all L diversity branches have to be *simultaneously* affected by a deep fade such that the overall transmission is in outage. Since with increasing L this event becomes less and less likely, the error rate substantially decreases for higher L. In fact, P^e decays exponentially in L when L i.i.d., Rayleigh-faded diversity branches are employed [TV05, (3.41)]. The number of employed independent fading branches L is called the *diversity order* of the communication system and a scheme is said to reach *full diversity* if it exploits all available diversity branches of the channel.

Increasing L substantially improves the slope of P^e. This improvement is called *diversity gain* and illustrated in Figure 2.5. Full diversity and, therefore, the maximum diversity gain can be already reached by simple repetition coding but more sophisticated coding shifts the error rate curve to the left [TV05, (3.158)]. This offset is called *coding gain* and remains constant for increasing SNR while the diversity gain improves with the SNR (Figure 2.5). Mathematically, we can state this behavior by

$$P_e \approx \left(\frac{1}{G_c \bar{\gamma}}\right)^L \qquad (2.14)$$

for asymptotically high SNR and i.i.d. Rayleigh fading block fading. Here, $G_c \geq 1$ denotes the coding gain as a factor to the mean SNR while the large improvement due to diversity is represented by the exponent L. This standard form for the error rate will be found frequently when we analyze the coding and diversity gain of cooperative relaying systems in the following chapters.

2.2.2 Used diversity modes

With fading channels diversity gains can be reached in multiple dimensions. The diversity schemes studied in this thesis – cooperation diversity and Multiuser Diversity (MUD) – combine the following basic diversity modes.

Temporal diversity distributes a codeword over multiple coherence times. A simple temporal diversity scheme was described in Section 2.2.1. By repeating a packet in each of L fading blocks, L coherence times are used and a diversity order of L is reached. More sophisticated temporal diversity schemes interleave code symbols over the coherence times and are, thus, often combined with Forward Error Correction (FEC) coding. We will focus on the interaction of temporal and cooperation diversity in Chapter 4 and Section 5.

Spatial diversity schemes employ multiple antennas which have to be placed such that the *coherence distance* (i.e., the antenna separation distance above which the channel coefficients are assumed to be spatially uncorrelated) is exceeded. In this case, independent diversity branches can be reached by repeating the same symbol (or some form of redundancy) over multiple transmit antennas using only a single antenna for reception. This multipoint-to-point approach is called *spatial transmit diversity* and is the fundament of all cooperation diversity protocols discussed in the remaining chapters. On the other hand, if only a single transmit antenna is used but multiple antennas receive independently faded signal paths, *spatial receive diversity* is exploited. This point-to-multipoint approach is employed by the MUD schemes in Section 5.2.

2.2.3 Combining

In many cases, the receiver reaches a diversity gain by combining multiple signals. The following standard combining schemes perform this task at signal level prior to FEC decoding, are used in our system models in Chapter 3, 4, and 5, and are the basis for the practical combining schemes described in Chapter 6.

Assuming coherent reception, the signals $y_{1,d}, \ldots, y_{L,d}$ that a destination d receives from L transmitters are in phase and can be combined linearly by their summation. In this case, the signal at d *after* combining is given by

$$y_d = \sum_{l=1}^{L} a_l y_{l,d}$$

where each received signal is weighted by its combining coefficient $a_{1,d}, \ldots, a_{L,d}$.

With Selection Combining (SC), the receiver selects only the "best" of the L signals. Thus, SC defines $a_k = 1$ for channel k with the highest instantaneous SNR γ_k, while all other weights are 0. In practice, this

Table 2.1: SNR gains of MRC for i.i.d. Rayleigh fading [Bre03, Table 1].

L	SNR gain of MRC [dB] compared to SC	Direct
2	1.25	3.01
3	2.14	4.77
4	2.83	6.02
...	...	...
∞	∞	∞

technique is usually simplified by selecting the signals with the highest power instead of SNR [Bre03]. In this case, no further CSI is required.

Maximum Ratio Combining (MRC) is a more sophisticated technique where each weight is time-variant and proportional to the signal's root mean square and inversely proportional to the mean square noise. Hence, a weight value is given by $a_l = \sqrt{y_{l,d}^2 / n_{l,d}^2}$. If these coefficients are used to calculate y_d as above, its instantaneous SNR γ is equal to the sum of the instantaneous SNR of all combined signals. Consequently, MRC obtains the highest SNR from all linear combining schemes and, thus, reaches the best BER performance [Bre03]. The SNR gain of MRC compared to SC and direct transmission ($L = 1$) is listed in Table 2.1 for several values of L i.i.d. Rayleigh fading diversity branches. Nonetheless, to reach these gains, MRC adds several restrictions to the system. First, accurate knowledge of the noise and signal power is required which is not easily available in many receivers. Second, the combined signals have to be transmitted at equal modulation and code. This restricts the choices and, thus, performance of rate adaptation. We will get back to these aspects when we describe a practical combining scheme in Chapter 6.

2.3 Basic constraints

Throughout this thesis, we apply the following fundamental resource and system constraints to assure a fair comparison of the transmission schemes.

Single antennas and bandwidth Each node employs only a single antenna. All nodes operate in the same frequency band of signal bandwidth W and each node uses W Hz per transmission.

Orthogonality constraint In this thesis, one node has to employ at least a single orthogonal subchannel per transmission. This *orthogonality constraint* reflects two restrictions of typical wireless systems. First, many single-antenna devices are restricted to *half duplex* operation and, thus, cannot transmit and receive at the same time on the same frequency band. Overcoming this limitation would require expensive transceiver hardware to decouple the transmit and receive process, e.g., by strict time/frequency synchronization [Rap02, Section 1.4]. Therefore, half duplex is the typical operation mode for mobile handhelds, WLAN devices, and wireless sensor nodes so far.

Second, the orthogonality constraint reflects that the performance of many wireless networks is *interference limited* [GK00]. This significant limitation results from the fact that most single-antenna receivers have to treat interfering signals as additive noise [Rap02, Section 3.5] and that approaches to eliminate interference from the received signal [GK08] are not practical so far. Instead, most wireless networks avoid interference by multiplexing multiple transmissions onto orthogonal subchannels and by using a MAC protocol to coordinate the use of these subchannels.

Medium Access Control (MAC) and multiplexing loss For the sake of explanation, we assume that duplexing and MAC realize orthogonal subchannels by separate time slots. Assuming this, Time Division Duplexing (TDD) and Time Division Multiple Access (TDMA) operation come at no loss of generality for the results of our theoretical studies (Chapter 3 to 5). In these chapters, we assume perfect MAC operation but account for MAC errors and overhead in Chapter 6.

As a result, K transmissions within a single propagation domain are multiplexed onto K orthogonal subchannels. This completely avoids interference between these transmissions but significantly reduces the capacity by the so-called *multiplexing loss*. Since per propagation domain each transmitter can use only $1/K$ of the channel resources, the overall capacity is divided by K. Note that this ignores quasi-orthogonal subchannels and spatial reuse and is, thus, a very strict interpretation of the orthogonality constraint.

Energy and power constraints The theoretical studies in Chapter 3 to 5 are made under the following *total energy constraint*. Independent of the number of transmitters, always the same number of Joules is injected into the channel to transmit an information bit from the source to the destination. This is a very conservative constraint which assures a fair comparison between relaying (where multiple transmitters may inject energy) and direct transmission (with a single transmitter) in terms of radiated energy.

The total energy constraint is relaxed to the *per-node power constraint* in our practical studies in Section 4.5 and Chapter 6. Here, each transmitter spends P Watts of average transmission power. As additional transmitters increase the duration of a single MAC cycle T_{cycle}, the overall radiated energy increases with the number of transmitters K. Although this constraint is less strict than the total energy constraint, it reflects the practical operation in WLANs and other wireless networks.

2.4 Summary of basic assumptions

In this thesis, we use the following general models and assumptions. More specific assumptions are described when they are used.

Fading Based on the classic discrete baseband model with Additive White Gaussian Noise (AWGN), we focus on time-selective, frequency-flat fading. The magnitudes of the channel coefficients are assumed to be Rayleigh distributed which leads to an exponentially distributed instantaneous SNR. Correlation in time is modeled using Clarke's model with an J_0 Autocorrelation Function (ACF) but also temporally uncorrelated fading blocks are used when appropriate. In space, received signals are assumed to be not correlated due to the typically large separation distance of cooperating nodes.

Performance metrics In our theoretical studies the outage probability P^{out} is used to measure the error rate. This metric accounts for decoding errors due to deep fades which are the typical error event at high SNR in fading channels. From P^{out}, the outage capacity C^{out} is derived as the highest data rate which can be guaranteed at a specified outage probability level ε. Unlike ergodic capacity, C^{out} explicitly accounts for non-zero error rates which are the usual case with practical transceivers, multi-hop communication, and delay constraints. Beside these fading-specific metrics, we observe data rate, ergodic capacity, BER, and PER.

Diversity Diversity is a powerful approach to improve the error rate of fading channels. Even simple repetition coding reaches full diversity order L and, thus, improves the error rate exponentially in L. More sophisticated coding can further improve the error rate by a coding gain. Cooperation diversity and Multiuser Diversity (MUD) are based on the basic diversity modes temporal and spatial diversity. One fundamental scheme to reach a diversity gain at the receiver is combing. Coherent Maximum Ratio Combining (MRC) maximizes the SNR gain and is assumed in the theoretical parts of this thesis; Selection Combining (SC) is the basis of the practical combining scheme in Chapter 6.

Constraints Several fundamental resource and system constraints assure a fair comparison of the studied transmission schemes. In particular, each node uses only a single antenna and requires at least an orthogonal subchannel for its transmission. For simplicity, the transmissions are separated in time and each node uses the full signal bandwidth W per transmission. While the theoretical studies in Chapter 3 to 5 are performed under the total energy constraint, the per-node power constraint reflects practical WLAN operation in Chapter 6.

Confidence level and units To account for statistical significance, simulation and measurement results are presented with 95 % confidence intervals.

Unless noted by dB, all constants and variables are defined in the linear domain.

Chapter 3

Cooperative relaying – Protocols and theoretical performance

We described in Chapter 2 that a source node exploits temporal diversity simply by repeating its own information. Now we focus on wireless networks where the source's information is repeated by a relay node. Relaying is very appealing in wireless networks where

1. the broadcast medium allows a relay to overhear other nodes' signals without requiring additional channel resources;
2. it is likely that source and relay antennas are differently affected by fading which can provide spatial diversity gains.

These properties of wireless channels have motivated the design of a variety of relaying protocols that exploit spatial diversity. The basics of these so-called *cooperative relaying protocols* are described in Section 3.1. Then, we focus on *selection relaying* as a class of many practical cooperation protocols such as Selection Decode-and-Forward (SDF), Coded Cooperation (CC), and Opportunistic Relaying (OR) [LWT04, HN02, BSW07]. We discuss these protocols in Section 3.2 and classify them into two fundamental types: *Combining-based Selection Relaying (CSR)* and *Path allocation-based Selection Relaying (PSR)*.

For a first insight, we jointly derive the outage probability and outage capacity of both protocol types under idealistic assumptions in Section 3.3. Based on this unified analysis, we systematically study the effect of limited Channel State Information (CSI) and network connectivity on the outage capacity and outage probability of CSR and PSR (Section 3.4). This allows a fair comparison of CSR and PSR protocols according to their individual CSI and connectivity demands and, finally, highlights in which cases either combining-based or path allocation-based selection relaying should be used.

3.1 Background on cooperative relaying protocols

Many cooperative relaying protocols were developed to improve error rate, coverage, or data rate. While each of these schemes has its specific benefits and constraints, all these protocols are based on common

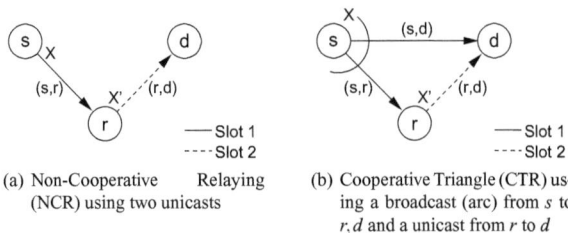

Figure 3.1: Simple example of cooperative and non-cooperate relaying. Each figure shows the packet flow from a source s via relay r to destination d. The transmission employs two orthogonal channels, e.g., time slots.

principles of the channel, coding, and medium access. These fundamentals are only briefly discussed in this section. Extensive surveys on cooperative relaying protocols are provided in [LSSK09, Part II] and [KMY06, VLK+07, VLK+09].

3.1.1 From relaying to cooperation diversity

In conventional wireless networks, a Medium Access Control (MAC) scheme reinforces a point-to-point link for a transmission from source s to destination d. The simplest relaying scenario for such unicast transmission is called *Non-Cooperative Relaying (NCR)* and illustrated in Figure 3.1(a). Here, a single relay r receives and forwards a packet X from s to d via the links (s,r) and (r,d). Even this simplest scenario already includes two basic elements of more complex cooperative relaying systems.

Multiple access and node processing

The first element is the *multiple access channel*. Unlike direct transmission, the end-to-end transmission of X from s to d via relay r requires two nodes to transmit. Each of the transmitters s and r demands an orthogonal subchannel (Section 2.3). These subchannels are realized by a Medium Access Control (MAC) scheme, e.g., by non-overlapping time slots. In the first slot, node r has to receive the packet from the source (solid line in Figure 3.1(a)). Then, in the second slot, r forwards the source's packet to the destination (dashed line).

We call the second basic element of relaying *node processing*. After reception, a relay may *regenerate* the bits of the source's packet X by demodulation and decoding. The relay may further store and process the regenerated bits, e.g., combine these bits with different information and re-encode the result using a different code than the source. Figure 3.1(a) illustrates this operation by letting r forward a possibly modified version of X that is denoted by X'. While node processing is ignored in traditional *store-and-forward* network models [CLRS01, Chapter 26] it is extensively used by cooperative relaying protocols. We will discuss specific protocols below.

The relay channel

Despite these basic elements, the simple point-to-point scenario in Figure 3.1(a) ignores one inherent attribute of the radio channel – its broadcast nature. Including this aspect extends point-to-point relaying to the point-to-multipoint scenario in Figure 3.1(b). We call this most basic three-terminal cooperative network the *Cooperative Triangle (CTR)*. It was defined by van der Meulen in [vdM71] and was later called the *relay channel* [CG79].

One important characteristic of the relay channel is that it combines the multiple access channel with the broadcast channel. While the multiple access channel is already implied by two channel uses of conventional point-to-point relaying, the broadcast arises naturally if s sends its packet X via a wireless channel. Here, X reaches r and d via a broadcast (Figure 3.1(b)) before the relay conventionally forwards X' to d. As opposed to NCR, the broadcast introduces a redundant transmission of X via the so-far unutilized (s,d) link but requires no additional channel use to convey the packet to both nodes r and d. Finally, two versions of the source packet are received at d which can improve the end-to-end performance by redundancy and diversity. This is not achieved with point-to-point relaying where d ignores the broadcast and receives only a single packet during the first slot.

Since van der Meulen's early work [vdM71], the capacity of the relay channel is a classic problem in information theory. Cover and El Gamal [CG79] showed that random binning [SW73] and block Markov superposition coding [CT91, Chapter 8] achieve the capacity of the so-called *degraded relay channel*, i.e., point-to-point relaying where link (s,d) is not considered. By generalizing Block-Markov coding, Kramer, Gastpar, and Gupta provided fundamental coding strategies which reach the capacity of specific relay channels with a broadcast and with multiple sources in N terminal networks [KGG05]. Similar results were obtained by Høst-Madsen and Zhang from the scope of power allocation [HMZ05].

However, despite this seminal work, the capacity of the general relay channel with three terminals and without degradation is still not known [Kra06]. So far, only an upper capacity bound can be given by the cut set theorem [CG79].

Cooperation diversity

Instead of studying ergodic capacity for asymptotically long codewords, one can study the performance of the relay channel from the perspective of outage probability and error rate. This perspective is important in wireless networks with fading channels when the transmission delay is limited such that errors do not average-out over long codewords.

One of the first studies in this field was performed by Sendonaris, Erkip, and Aazhang [SEA98]. The authors observed that the links (s,d) and (r,d) in Figure 3.1(b) may experience a different channel state only due to the different position of the source's and relay's transmit antennas. Consequently, cooperative relaying introduces spatial transmit diversity which can significantly decrease the error rate at the destination (Section 2.2). The authors called this concept *cooperation diversity* and left open how cooperative nodes share their transmit antennas.

Even without a specific method for cooperation, cooperation diversity already points out important similarities and differences between cooperative and multi-antenna systems. Similar to Space-Time Coding (STC) systems, a cooperation diversity system employs multiple transmit antennas to profit from spatial diversity. Therefore, cooperative networks are sometimes called "virtual Multiple-Input Multiple-Output (MIMO)" or "distributed antenna arrays" [PWS+04]. Unlike MIMO, cooperation does not rely on multiple antennas per node. Cooperative relaying is possible even with single antenna devices but can also be combined with MIMO techniques if multiple antennas per node are available. Furthermore, in a cooperative network inter-antenna distances larger than the coherence distance are easily achieved. Cooperating nodes are further apart than several to tens of wavelengths which assures spatially uncorrelated channels in many propagation environments [TV05, Section 3.3]. Achieving such distances is not straightforward with MIMO where the inter-antenna distance is constrained by the device size. This makes the design of small MIMO devices difficult and can dramatically decrease the performance of MIMO systems due to spatially correlated shadowing [PNG03, Chapter 5].

Beside these benefits, a cooperative system connects the distributed transmit antennas via a wireless link, e.g., (s,r) in Figure 3.1(b), which can introduce unpredictable transmission errors and delay. This is a significant drawback compared to MIMO where the inter-antenna link can be seen as an ideal out-of-band channel. Therefore, classic capacity results and coding techniques for MIMO systems, e.g., STC [Ala98], cannot be directly applied to cooperative diversity systems. Instead, a method is required to invoke, maintain, and synchronize a cooperative transmission via error-prone wireless links. This is achieved by cooperative relaying protocols whose fundamentals are described next.

3.1.2 Fundamental cooperative relaying protocols

A cooperative relaying protocol defines how the cooperating nodes exchange and process information. A first approach for an asynchronous Code Division Multiple Access (CDMA) system is provided in [SEA03a]. Results for non-ideal spreading codes and receivers are given in [SEA03b] and significant gains in outage probability are shown.

Without restricting their assumptions to a specific medium access technique, Laneman, Wornell, and Tse provide an early systematic comparison of cooperative relaying protocols in [LWT01]. The authors extended this paper to their seminal work [LWT04]. Focusing on the scenario in Figure 3.1(b), Laneman et al. compare the fundamental relaying strategies *Amplify-and-Forward (AF)* and *Decode-and-Forward (DF)* from the perspective of diversity. Both strategies represent extreme cases of the general *Compress-and-Forward (CF)* strategy [CG79] where the relay forwards an arbitrarily coded signal to the destination. With AF (also called non-regenerative relaying) the relay simply amplifies and retransmits both the source signal and noise in the analog domain. With DF (also called regenerative relaying), the relay decodes and re-encodes the source signal in the digital baseband before forwarding.

With either of these forwarding strategies, the destination combines the signals received from s and r using MRC and obtains diversity gains if the channel coefficients of (s,d) and (r,d) differ (cp. Section 2.2). The authors show that AF achieves full diversity, i.e., a diversity order L equal to the number of transmitters in the cooperative network. Outage probability results for asymptotic high SNR are provided

3.2. Selection relaying protocols

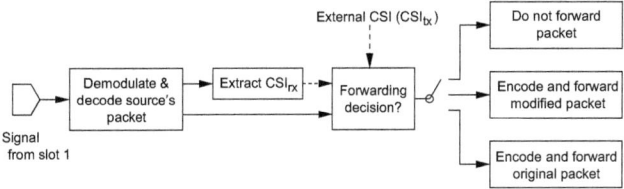

Figure 3.2: Operation of a general selection relaying protocol: After receiving and regenerating the source packet, the relay decides whether to forward the packet based on CSI.

showing that the outage probability decreases exponentially in the number of transmitters.

A further important result is that regenerative relaying only achieves full diversity if the relay perfectly avoids error propagation. To this end, Laneman et al. introduce the concept of *selection relaying* where the relay only forwards a packet if it has decoded it reliably. The authors introduced the *SDF* protocol where the relay always forwards correct packets and the *incremental relaying* protocol where the destination requests a packet from the relay only if the direct transmission fails.

Based on these fundamental approaches a variety of relaying protocols was proposed to exploit cooperation diversity in the relay channel. Focusing on the class of selection relaying protocols, we now describe and classify those protocols which are relevant for this work.

3.2 Selection relaying protocols

In the basic Selection Decode-and-Forward (SDF) approach [LWT04], a relay filters out erroneous packets to reach full diversity. Therefore, a relay regenerates and detects erroneously received packets, e.g., by performing a Cyclic Redundancy Check (CRC). From this example, we can identify two basic properties of a *selection relaying protocol*. First, the relay performs a *forwarding decision*. With SDF it decides either to drop or to forward the received packet. Second, this forwarding decision is based on some form of CSI, e.g., on a CRC checksum extracted from the received packet. These two characteristics are the basis of all previously developed cooperative relaying protocols that are compared in this section. Note that under this definition even NCR performs selection relaying if the relay does not forward erroneous packets.

3.2.1 Generalization and protocol classification

Based on Laneman's previous work [LWT04] we can generalize the basic operation of a selection relaying protocol as in Figure 3.2. The relay performs the illustrated functions after receiving the source packet and prior to forwarding, e.g., between slot 1 and slot 2 in Figure 3.1(b). As illustrated, the relay regenerates the source packet and performs its forwarding decision. Unlike in the basic Selection Decode-and-Forward (SDF) approach [LWT04], in general the relay has more than two alternatives. For instance, the relay may decide to either forward the received packet, a modified variant of the received packet, or not to forward

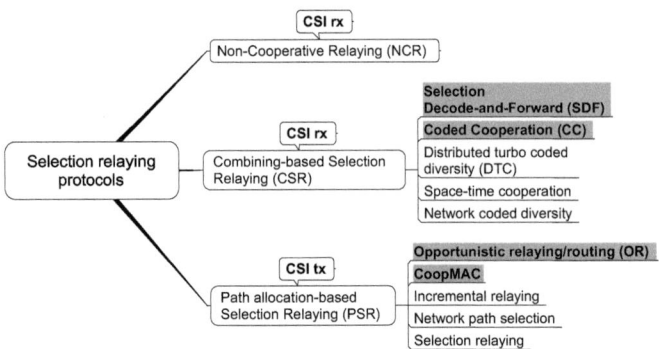

Figure 3.3: Selection relaying protocols and their employed CSI: The protocols either follow the CSR or the PSR approach. The shaded protocols are relevant for this thesis. NCR is included for comparison.

the received packet.

This forwarding decision can be based on two types of CSI: Either on so-called *receiver CSI* (CSI_{rx}) or on so-called *transmitter CSI* (CSI_{tx}). While the relay locally extracts CSI_{rx} from the received packet, CSI_{tx} refers to channel knowledge from external sources. If the relay bases its forwarding decision on such external CSI, this channel knowledge has to be available prior to transmission. The term *full CSI* denotes that CSI_{rx} as well as CSI_{tx} is available.

Combining-based Selection Relaying (CSR)

The employed CSI defines the further operation and performance of a selection relaying protocol. If only CSI_{rx} is used, a relay forwards irrespective of the state of other parallel links in the cooperative network. For instance, in Figure 3.1(b) the relay even forwards if the destination has already correctly received the packet via the (s,d) link. Without CSI_{tx}, this correct reception cannot be signaled to r and the multiplexing loss due forwarding cannot be avoided. Especially with multiple relays, such parallel transmissions decrease the effective rate by a high multiplexing loss. Without intermediate adaptation due to CSI_{tx}, this form of relaying can exploit spatial diversity only by combining the received signals at the destination. Therefore, we call this protocol type *Combining-based Selection Relaying (CSR)*.

Various protocols in literature follow the CSR approach. A representative selection is listed in Figure 3.3. All these protocols employ only CSI_{rx}. They primarily differ in their coding scheme. While the SDF protocol uses repetition coding [LWT04], i.e., the forwarded codeword equals the received codeword, *Coded Cooperation (CC)* [HN02] and *Distributed Turbo Coded Diversity (DTC)* [ZV03, LVWD06] employ Rate-Compatible Punctured Convolutional (RCPC) codes [Hag88] or turbo codes [HWR07], respectively. In addition to one of such FEC coding schemes, a CSR protocol may use network coding [CKL06, BL06a, WVK07, WVK08] or even space-time coding [SE03, JHHN04] during the relaying process.

In this thesis we will not study such combinations of various coding schemes. Instead, our focus

3.2. Selection relaying protocols

is on protocol aspects and on the effect of limited CSI and other practical constraints on the protocol's performance. To this end, we limit our scope to the fundamental SDF protocol and to CC as a practical example with more-sophisticated FEC coding. Since we focus only on the protocol operation, our results apply to protocols that use different FEC codes or employ space-time or network coding on top of a cooperation protocol. We will detail the CSR protocols that are relevant for this thesis in Section 3.2.2.

Path allocation-based Selection Relaying (PSR)

One method to overcome the high multiplexing loss of Combining-based Selection Relaying (CSR) protocols is to avoid unnecessary retransmissions. If a relay knows the state of other links (i.e., CSI_{tx} is available) it can choose not to retransmit if direct transmission succeeds or if a different relay has a better channel state towards d. More general, if CSI_{tx} is available, only the nodes on the "best" end-to-end network path from s to d need to transmit. Naturally, these nodes have to be chosen *before* they transmit, i.e., they have to be selected *a priori*. We call protocols that utilize CSI_{tx} to select the transmitters on the "best" network path a priori *Path allocation-based Selection Relaying (PSR)* protocols.

Choosing the transmitters a priori is an important difference between PSR and CSR. As discussed above, without CSI_{tx} a cooperation protocol can only reach diversity gains by combining. This operation can be interpreted as choosing the symbols from the "best" network path *a posteriori*, i.e., after the transmission of all signals related to packet X has ended. With this operation, each node requires only local channel knowledge, i.e., CSI_{rx}. On the other hand, PSR protocols choose the "best" path before the transmission to d has ended. This *a priori* selection requires CSI_{tx} at the relays to inform them either about a centralized choice or about the state of other links for a distributed choice of the network path. With ideal CSI_{tx}, PSR protocols can choose the SNR-maximizing path and achieve the same diversity order as CSR [BSW07].

In previous work, many PSR protocols were described. Figure 3.3 lists the most relevant. The protocols differ in the form of CSI_{tx} and how this CSI_{tx} is fed back from the destination to the transmitters. While *incremental relaying* [LWT04] and *CoopMAC* [LTP05] use explicit feedback from d to s and r, *opportunistic relaying/routing* rely on implicit negotiation among the nodes at MAC [BKRL06] or at routing level [BM05]. PSR protocols are also known under the names *network path selection* [BKRL06] and *selection relaying* [BA07].[1]

To study representative PSR protocols with explicit and implicit CSI_{tx} feedback, we focus on Coop-MAC and Opportunistic Relaying (OR) in this thesis. Both protocols are the basis of many derivative variants and, as prototyping attempts have shown, are also practical. We describe related work and detail their operation in Section 3.2.3.

---

[1] As in [LWT04], we use the term *selection relaying* to denote the selection of the forwarded packet during the relay's local forwarding decision and not the selection of the relay or the network path. Hence, the terminology of [BA07] does not coincide with the one adopted here.

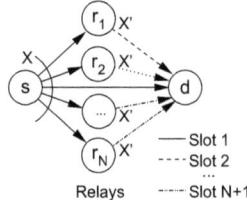

Figure 3.4: Flow of data packets in a generalized SDF scenario.

3.2.2 Combining-based protocols

In a CSR protocol, all N relays forward a correct packet and the destination achieves spatial transmit diversity gains by combining the received signals. Only local CSI_{rx} is employed to perform an error test at the relay and for coherent detection and weighted combining at the destination.

Selection Decode-and-Forward (SDF)

As described above, a basic CSR protocol is SDF [LWT04]. It exploits spatial transmit diversity in the relay channel (Figure 3.1(b)) but may employ more than a single relay. A general network with the relays $r_1, \ldots, r_N$ is illustrated in Figure 3.4. After the source broadcasts packet X in slot 1, each of the N relays decodes and the received packet and performs an error test. Correctly received packets are re-encoded using the same code as the source – a procedure known as *repetition coding*. Consequently, each of the N relays forwards either packet $X' = X$ or does not forward in the subsequent slots. If each relay forwards, $K = N+1$ slots are required and $N+1$ signals are combined at the destination. With ideal error detection and combining, finally, a diversity order of $L = N+1$ is reached [LWT04].

While this approach assumes that a relay employs a CRC or similar error detecting code, in principle, any form of CSI_{rx} can serve as an error detection metric. Using SNR was proposed by Herhold, Zimmermann, and Fettweis [HZF04]. This provides a more general forwarding decision model than the CRC-based SDF protocol but introduces the problem of SNR-threshold selection. For uncoded systems, the threshold minimizing the BER can be found analytically [OAF+07]. For coded systems, also the FEC decoder output can serve as an error detection metric [VVA+08b]. We will discuss details of this approach in Chapter 4.

Coded Cooperation (CC)

This CSR protocol was proposed by Hunter and Nosratinia [HN02]. The authors proofed full diversity $L = N+1$ and approximated outage probability at high SNR [HSN06]. Unlike SDF, CC supports multiple sources and the retransmission of incremental redundancy. We employ this flexibility for our adaptive CC protocol in Section 5.1.

CC differs from SDF in its coding process and protocol operation. With CC, the nodes cooperate *mutually*, i.e., each transmitter may alternatively act as source s and relay r. Figure 3.5 reflects this by the

3.2. Selection relaying protocols

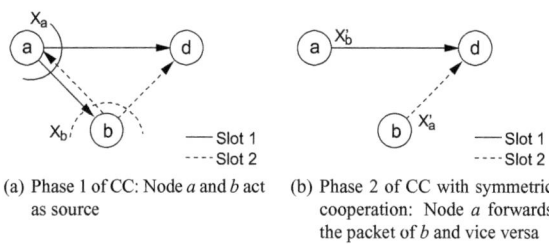

(a) Phase 1 of CC: Node a and b act as source

(b) Phase 2 of CC with symmetric cooperation: Node a forwards the packet of b and vice versa

Figure 3.5: Flow of data packets in the Coded Cooperation (CC) protocol with $N+1=2$ cooperating nodes a and b.

cooperating nodes a and b. As shown, mutual cooperation splits the MAC cycle in two phases. In phase 1, all $N+1$ transmitter act as sources. This initial data exchange requires $N+1$ slots. Afterwards, the nodes switch to relay mode and forward correct packets in the second phase using $N+1$ slots. If each node forwards, the nodes cooperate *symmetrically* (Figure 3.5(b)). *Asymmetric cooperation* occurs if a packet was not correctly received. In this case a node employs its slot in phase 2 to retransmit its own information. For instance, if node b does not correctly receive packet X_a, it retransmits its own packet X'_b even if node a has already forwarded X'_b. Consequently, three versions of X_b can be combined at the destination but only one version of X_a reaches d. In any case, $K = 2(N+1)$ slots are used in total and transferring a single packet flow requires $N+1$ slots.

Unlike SDF, the CC protocol integrates the cooperation and combining process into FEC coding. Instead of repetition coding, CC is based on RCPC [Hag88] which allows to retransmit incremental redundancy of a packet X in phase 2, i.e., $X \neq X'$. Although each cooperating node transmits k information bits coded at rate $R_c = k/n$ to $n = n_1 + n_2$ bits, the number of bits n_2 that are transmitted in phase 2 may differ from the number of bits n_1 transmitted in phase 1. The values n_1 and n_2 are defined by the free parameter *cooperation level* $\beta = n_1/n$ and are known at each node.

Figure 3.6 extends Figure 3.5 by the coding process at the nodes. At the beginning of the transmission cycle, each node operates in *source mode*. As illustrated, a node removes n_2 bits from n by puncturing and stores these bits. During phase 1, the nodes broadcast the remaining n_1 bits to d and to a potential relay.

After phase 1, each node switches to *relay mode* and decodes and error tests the k bits received from the partner. If the error test succeeds, the partner's bits are re-encoded to n bits and puncturing extracts n_2 bits according to β. These regenerated n_2 bits are relayed to d. If a node in relay mode cannot correctly decode its partner's k bits, it transmits its own n_2 bits which were stored initially.

After both phases, n_1 and n_2 bits may be available per node. In this case d combines these bits by de-puncturing [Pro00, Section 8.2.6] which can introduce a spatial transmit diversity gain. De-puncturing requires matching coded bits between the phase 1 and phase 2 packets which is provided with RCPC codes.

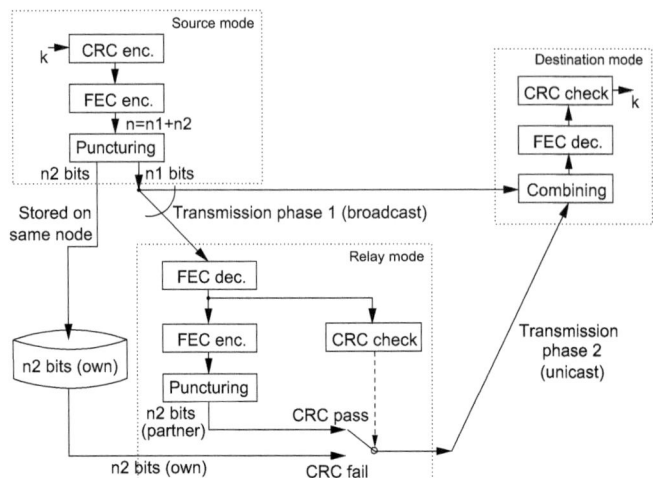

Figure 3.6: Coding and protocol procedure of Coded Cooperation. Flow chart based on [NHH04, Figure 5] and [LSSK09, Figure 4.8].

3.2.3 Network path allocation-based protocols

In PSR protocols either only a single relay forwards correct packets or the direct link is chosen. Instead of choosing the "best" symbols a posteriori by combining, PSC employs CSI_{tx} to allocate the "best" links prior to the transmission of the relays. With N alternatively transmitting relays this provides full diversity order of $N+1$ [BSW07], costs only a single retransmission per MAC cycle but requires CSI_{tx} at the relays. With non-reciprocal fading channels this channel knowledge has to be obtained by CSI feedback via wireless channels which can reduce the end-to-end performance by overhead and errors.

Opportunistic Relaying (OR)

This basic PSR protocol was introduced at the routing layer by Biswas and Morris [BM05]. At high SNR, Bletsas, Khisti, Reed, and Lippmann provided outage probability approximations, showed full diversity [BSW07], and showed that OR significantly improves the diversity-multiplexing tradeoff of CSR protocols by reducing the number of retransmissions [BKRL06]. At low SNR, Beres and Adve approximated outage probability [BA07] and Adinoyi, Fan, Yanikomeroglu, and Poor provided closed-form solutions for the approximate BER [AFYP08]. All this work shows that OR significantly improves the error rate of direct transmission under idealistic system and CSI assumptions.

Figure 3.7 illustrates an example scenario for OR with N relays. In this two-hop scenario, allocating the "best" end-to-end network path is equivalent with choosing the best relay. Many OR protocols aim for minimal end-to-end error rate and, thus, choose the path which maximizes the SNR at d. If an OR protocol aims to maximize throughput, even the direct link may be included.

3.2. Selection relaying protocols

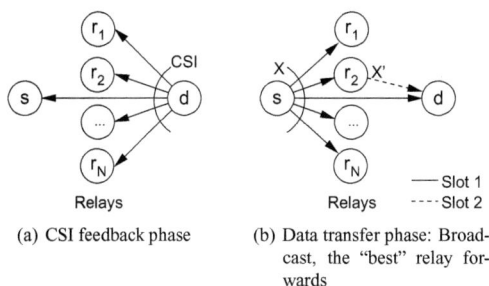

(a) CSI feedback phase

(b) Data transfer phase: Broadcast, the "best" relay forwards

Figure 3.7: Flow of control and data packets in the OR protocol. Figure based on [BSW07].

To allocate this "best" path, CSI_{tx} has to be provided to either the source or the relays. With non-reciprocal fading channels, d has to extract this channel knowledge from a received packet and has to transfer it back to the transmitters. As illustrated in Figure 3.7(a) this so-called *CSI feedback* can be efficiently realized by a broadcast.

Where the feedback phase in Figure 3.7(a) is placed in the protocol cycle depends on when OR performs its path allocation. In *proactive* OR protocols [LTL+06, BSW07], the source chooses the path before its data transmission (Figure 3.7(a)). Therefore, the feedback phase is typically performed directly before the broadcast in slot 1. With *reactive* protocols the relays choose the path between slot 1 and slot 2, e.g., by reacting to outstanding Acknowledgment (ACK) packets or to explicit Negative Acknowledgment (NACK) packets. To this end, many reactive protocols [BM05, BSW07] transmit CSI feedback (e.g., as an ACK or NACK) between slot 1 and slot 2 of the data transfer phase in Figure 3.7(b). Once the "best" path is allocated, only the chosen relay forwards the packet using the second slot of the data transfer phase. To this end, typically repetition coding is assumed, i.e., $X' = X$.

As a matter of fact, current papers on OR protocols ignore the feedback phase in Figure 3.7(a). Either full CSI is assumed to be available at no cost [BKRL06, BA08, AFYP08] or feedback procedures are given but assumed to operate at no cost and without error [BM05, BSW07]. Neither of these assumptions is realistic with non-reciprocal fading channels which are common in cooperative relaying scenarios. In this case, the overhead and errors due to CSI feedback can highly degrade throughput and error rate of OR protocols. Therefore, the constraints of the feedback channel have to be included in the analysis of OR's performance. We do so in Section 3.4.

CoopMAC

CoopMAC aims to increase the throughput in IEEE 802.11 WLANs by the help of a relay. Liu, Tao, and Panwar introduced this protocol [LTP05] and described an extended version and a first implementation [LTN+07]. An extended prototype is discussed in [KKEP09]. This practical PSR protocol is a relevant benchmark for our prototype in Chapter 6.

CoopMAC integrates PSR into the IEEE 802.11 MAC sublayer [IEE99]. To this end, it extends the IEEE 802.11 Request-To-Send (RTS)/Clear-To-Send (CTS) cycle by a so-called *Helper ready To*

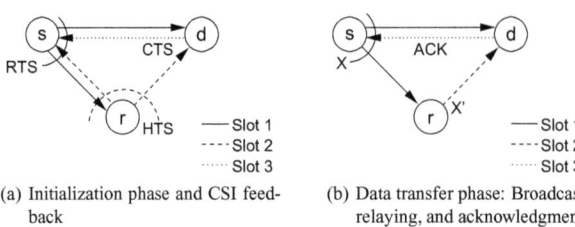

(a) Initialization phase and CSI feedback

(b) Data transfer phase: Broadcast, relaying, and acknowledgment

Figure 3.8: Flow of control and data packets in the CoopMAC protocol. Extended figure based on [LTN+07].

Send (HTS) packet as illustrated in Figure 3.8. In CoopMAC the source overhears CSI_{tx} from ACK and CTS packets, estimates the end-to-end throughput, and maintains a list of these estimates for all possible relays. Based on this list, s proactively chooses the relay which provides the highest estimated throughput. To initialize the CoopMAC cycle, s broadcasts an extended RTS packet to the chosen relay and d (Figure 3.8(a)). This RTS packet includes the requested data rate and the relay only replies with an HTS packet if its own estimation of the data rate matches. The source then broadcasts its data packet X to the relay and d. If received correctly, the relay re-encodes and modulates the packet at a potentially higher rate, i.e., $X' \neq X$, and retransmits this packet to d. The destination performs no combining but selects the first correctly received packet from both paths and, finally, answers with an ACK.

With the help of a relay the source can select a transmission rate larger than the direct link supports. Nevertheless, this comes at the cost of a significant amount of control transmissions and CSI feedback. The literature on CoopMAC [LTP05, LTL+06, LTN+07, KKEP09] and its derivatives [TWT08, SZW09] shows two important aspects. First, none of these studies compares the effective rate of CoopMAC vs. the direct case at equal injected energy. Such a global energy constraint is, however, crucial for a fair comparison (Section 2.3). Second, CoopMAC implies that the control packets are received at negligible error rate, e.g., by using a robust modulation and code. This assumption may not hold with fading channels where diversity gains are required to overcome deep fades and, thus, lost control packets may significantly degrade throughput. We study both aspects theoretically in terms of outage capacity in Section 3.4 and practically by measuring throughput and error rate in Chapter 6.

3.3 Performance analysis of selection relaying

We compare the performance of PSR and CSR in two steps. First, we derive the diversity order, outage probability, and outage capacity. We provide approximations for general cooperative networks at high SNR and illustrate these methods for networks with one relay and with two relays. Idealistic assumptions allows us to jointly analyze PSR and CSR.

This unified analysis is a starting point for the individual discussion of PSR and CSR in the second step of our study. In Section 3.4, the general performance results of selection relaying are degraded according to the individual constraints of PSR and CSR. Although under ideal assumptions the results of both protocols match, PSR and CSR have different requirements on CSI and network connectivity. Accounting for each of these constraints separately leads to individual performance results and provides a systematic comparison of both selection relaying approaches.

3.3.1 Method and assumptions

Our study is based on *cut set analysis* known as a useful method to derive the outer capacity bound of a network from its graph [CT91, Section 14.10]. Before we apply this graph-theoretical approach to approximate diversity order, outage probability, and outage capacity for cooperative networks, let us define the basic terminology and assumptions.

Channel and system assumptions

Our channel and system assumptions are widely used in theoretic studies of cooperative relaying protocols [LWT04, BFY04, SSL07, BSW07, OFYT08]. Assuming the constraints from Section 2.3, we compare direct transmission and cooperative networks with multiple transmitters at equal energy, transmission time, and bandwidth.

Fading channels are modeled using the block fading model from Section 2.1.2 choosing a block time equal to the duration of a MAC cycle, i.e., $T_b := T_{\text{cycle}}$. According to this model, the instantaneous SNR $\gamma_{i,j}$ of an arbitrary link (i, j) is an i.i.d. exponential random variable with the mean $\bar{\gamma}_{i,j} = \Gamma_{i,j}\Gamma$. As described in Section 2.1.1, Γ is the system-wide reference SNR (2.3) while $\Gamma_{i,j}$ accounts for the path loss of the individual link. We employ (2.2) as path loss model. For all shown numerical results we assume a reference distance of $D_0 = 1$ and a path loss exponent of $\alpha = 2.4$ with no loss of generality.

At system level, we assume that an ideal MAC scheme provides an orthogonal subchannel for each transmitter, perfectly avoiding interference among the studied nodes (Section 2.3). We denote the number of orthogonal subchannels by K. We further assume *common codebooks*, i.e., all nodes employ the same channel code. This implies repetition coding at the relays. As common in outage analysis we assume deep fades to be the only error event. Other causes of decoding errors are ignored by assuming ideal error correcting and error detecting codes. Assuming ideal coherent signal detection and ideal Maximum Ratio Combining (MRC) ignores power losses in imperfect receivers (Section 2.2). This implies that d extracts ideal CSI_{rx} from the received packets and is a common assumption for analyzing coherent receivers [SA04, Section 3.1].

Besides these standard assumptions, we explicitly study the effect of limited channel knowledge on the performance of selection relaying protocols. To this end, we assume full CSI in this section but limit CSI_{tx} in Section 3.4 to account for limited feedback. We study scenarios with multiple relays. In addition to the general case with N relays, we study networks with $N = 1$ and $N = 2$ representing the minimal scenarios for CSR and PSR, respectively.

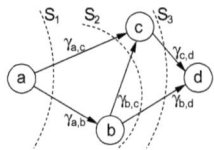

Figure 3.9: Example flow network using instantaneous SNR $\gamma_{i,j}$ as capacity weight for any link (i,j) and the unidirectional cut sets $S_1, \ldots, S_3$.

Flow networks and cut sets

Our analysis is based on common graph-theoretical network models and definitions [CLRS01, Section 26.1]. A cooperative or non-cooperative network is modeled as a *flow network*, i.e., a finite directed graph where each link (i,j) is weighted by its AWGN capacity. Only links with a positive capacity are included.

Each flow network includes a dedicated source node a and destination node d. We assume that any potential relay node between a and d lies on some *path*, i.e., for any node r there is a path $s \to r \to d$. Unlike most graph-theoretical approaches [CLRS01, Section 26.1], we do not require *flow conservation*. Instead, the rate of the information flow leaving a relay may be different from the rate of the incoming flow. This accounts for node processing, where a relay may drop packets or may encode these packet at a different rate prior to forwarding.

Figure 3.9 shows an example of a flow network. Here the potential relays b and c are located on the paths $a \to b \to d$, $a \to c \to d$, and $a \to b \to c \to d$ between source a and destination d. We call any path between the source and the destination an *end-to-end path*. As discussed in Section 2.1.4, the AWGN capacity $C(\gamma_{i,j}) = \log_2(1+\gamma_{i,j})$ of a link (i,j) only depends on the instantaneous SNR $\gamma_{i,j}$. Hence, it suffices to weight each link only by the corresponding instantaneous SNR (cp. Figure 3.9).

The figure further includes three *cuts* illustrated as dashed lines. A cut separates the network into disjoint subsets and a *cut set* S_n includes all links crossing this cut, e.g., $S_1 = \{(a,c),(a,b)\}$ in Figure 3.9. The number of links within a cut set S_n is given by the *cardinality* $|S_n|$ of this cut set. For example, S_1 in Figure 3.9 includes two links and is, thus, of cardinality $|S_1| = 2$. We denote all N cut sets of a flow network by the superset $\mathbb{S}$ with $\mathbb{S} := \{S_1, \ldots, S_n, \ldots, S_N\}$. Note that only *unidirectional cut sets* are defined in Figure 3.9. That is, all links within a cut set cross this set only in a single direction. This results from the fact that the capacity $C(S_n)$ of an arbitrary cut set S_n is composed only of nonnegative flows [CLRS01, Section 26.2]. Therefore, no cut set $\{(a,b),(b,c),(c,d)\}$ is defined in Figure 3.9, as (b,c) would cause this set to be bidirectional.

3.3.2 Outage probability for arbitrary flow networks

In classic literature [HM02, LWT04] and many follow-up papers the outage probability and diversity order of cooperative relaying protocols is directly derived from the outage events. This allows to analyze specific networks but cannot provide general results. To analyze arbitrary flow networks with any number of relays we employ *cut set analysis* [CT91, Section 14.10]. Boyer, Falconer, and Yanikomeroglu extended

3.3. Performance analysis of selection relaying

this method to derive diversity order and outage probability for cooperative networks [BFY07]. We will now describe this method and apply it to several network examples.

Diversity order

With cooperative relaying, multiple links are employed in parallel and these links are included in N cut sets. Given all cut sets $\mathbb{S}$, we can find the diversity order L by searching the cut sets

$$\mathbb{S}_M := \{S \in \mathbb{S} \mid |S| = L\} \tag{3.1}$$

that include the *minimum* number of links

$$L = \min_{S \in \mathbb{S}}(|S|). \tag{3.2}$$

Hence, the diversity order L of the flow network is the smallest cardinality over all its cut sets.

The rationale behind this definition is that L represents the number of independent links which at least have to fail to cause the end-to-end transmission to be in outage. Over all cut sets that a cooperative end-to-end transmission traverses, this "bottleneck" is given by the cut set of smallest cardinality.

Outage probability

Deriving the end-to-end outage probability at the destination d for arbitrary flow networks with selection relaying is given in [BFY07]. The resulting end-to-end outage probability of selection relaying for common codebooks at high SNR is

$$P^{\text{out}} \approx \frac{1}{L!} \Theta \left(\frac{2^{KR} - 1}{\Gamma} \right)^L \tag{3.3}$$

and depends on the number of orthogonal channels K, the spectral efficiency R, and the diversity order L. Equation 3.3 further includes the link-dependent term

$$\Theta = \sum_{\forall S_m \in \mathbb{S}_M} \left(\prod_{\forall (i,j) \in S_m} \frac{1}{\Gamma_{i,j}} \right) \tag{3.4}$$

where we define the M cut sets $\mathbb{S}_M \subseteq \mathbb{S}$ of minimal cardinality L as in (3.1).

The derivation in [BFY07] makes use of the fact that, given common codebooks, the end-to-end outage probability is upper bounded by the outage probability of the cut sets $\mathbb{S}_M$. Put less formally, no cut set with more than L links can decrease the overall P^{out} below the outage probability given by this "bottleneck". Therefore, (3.4) accounts only for the links of those cut sets $\mathbb{S}_M$ that define the diversity order L.

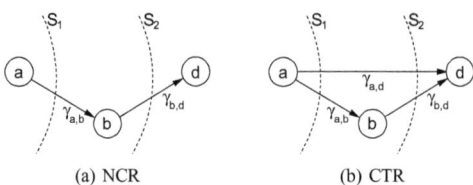

Figure 3.10: Flow networks for a single relay either performing Non-Cooperative Relaying (NCR) or CSR in the Cooperative Triangle (CTR). Each graph includes all distinct directed cut sets S_1, S_2 and the instantaneous SNR $\gamma_{i,j}$ for each employed link (i,j).

3.3.3 Outage probability for one and two relays

We will now apply the methods from Section 3.3.2 to derive diversity order and outage probability of selection relaying for specific networks. Introducing the methods for a single relay, we extend this basic scenario to $N = 2$ relays on two alternative paths which represents the minimal scenario for many PSR protocols [BM05, BSW07, BA07]. For this scenario, we classify the possible flow networks and compare PSR and Combining-based Selection Relaying (CSR) at full CSI. We further assume *ideal connectivity* which means that a given flow network can always be established. Networks without these idealistic assumptions are studied in Section 3.4.

Single relay

We start our analysis with the single relay case. As discussed in Section 3.1, this can lead to the two networks in Figure 3.10. With Non-Cooperative Relaying (NCR) the nodes establish the point-to-point network in Figure 3.10(a). With cooperative relaying the point-to-multipoint flow network in Figure 3.10(b) is established. We call the latter network graph Cooperative Triangle (CTR) and assume that a Combining-based Selection Relaying (CSR) protocol is employed. This case is equivalent to the basic SDF protocol [LWT04] and allows a consistent comparison of the results. Both flow networks in Figure 3.10 only differ in the direct link (a,d) which is only included in the CTR as only the CSR protocol d makes use of this link by combining.

In both protocols $K = 2$ orthogonal subchannels are required per end-to-end transmission from a to d. This splits the MAC cycle into two phases. In the first phase, relay b overhears the signal from a. In the second phase, b may forward this signal to d. Note that even with CTR, only $K = 2$ is required as node d overhears the signal from a as a broadcast and, thus, requires no additional phase to receive the first packet.

In the CTR network, we obtain the diversity order as in (3.2). Both cut sets include two links, already at minimum cardinality $|S_1| = |S_2| = 2$. Hence, the diversity order of the CTR is $L = 2$. The end-to-end outage probability of the CTR is derived according to Section 3.3.2. Applying (3.4) to both cut sets in

3.3. Performance analysis of selection relaying

Figure 3.10(b) provides the link-dependent term $\Theta_{\text{CTR}} = \Theta_T / \Gamma_{a,d}$ where

$$\Theta_T = \frac{\Gamma_{a,b} + \Gamma_{b,d}}{\Gamma_{a,b}\Gamma_{b,d}} \tag{3.5}$$

includes all links other than (a,d). Inserting Θ_{CTR} and the above-derived values for K and L in (3.3) yields

$$P_{\text{CTR}}^{\text{out}} = \frac{1}{2\Gamma_{a,d}}\Theta_T \left(\frac{2^{2R}-1}{\Gamma}\right)^2 \tag{3.6}$$

for the end-to-end outage probability of a CSR protocol operating in the CTR network. Note that this result consistently matches the outage probability given in [LWT04, (22)] that was approximated using a different method.

For NCR, the derivation is similar to the cooperative case. As d cannot exploit channel (a,d), both cut sets in Figure 3.10(a) include only a single link. This means that even if only a single link in Figure 3.10(a) is in outage, an outage at d occurs. Consequently, the diversity order is $L = 1$ which is equal to direct transmission. Applying (3.4) and (3.3) results in

$$P_{\text{NCR}}^{\text{out}} = \Theta_T \left(\frac{2^{2R}-1}{\Gamma}\right) \tag{3.7}$$

for the end-to-end outage probability of NCR. This result is similar to the P^{out} approximation for direct transmission in (2.12). Compared to direct transmission, NCR still only achieves $L = 1$ but adds $K = 2$ as a factor to R since now two slots are required.

We will further discuss these analytic results and provide numerical examples below. Let us first derive diversity order and outage probability for the two-relay case.

Two relays

The diversity order and outage probability can be further improved by adding more relays to the CTR. Besides employing CSR protocols like SDF or CC, multiple relays allow to use PSR protocols such as OR or CoopMAC (Section 3.2). While with CSR, d combines the signals received from all relays and from the direct link, a PSR protocol aims to choose the relay which provides the best path towards d. Naturally, such relay selection is only possible with at least $N = 2$ relays.

To systematically study the two-relay case, we account for all possible flow networks. Therefore, we add node c to the CTR which, like node b, performs regenerative selection relaying to d. This leads to the four flow networks in Figure 3.11. As in [LVK+08], we call these networks *diamonds*. Flow networks where the direct link (a,d) is included are called *strong*; networks making use of the inter-relay link (b,c) are called *full*. Networks without these links are called *weak* or *sparse*, respectively. In each of the resulting four diamonds, any of the nodes a, b, c may transmit. If these nodes transmit, $K = 3$ orthogonal subchannels are required.

For both sparse diamonds, we define the cut sets $\mathbb{S} := \{S_1, \ldots, S_4\}$ as illustrated in Figure 3.11(a) and

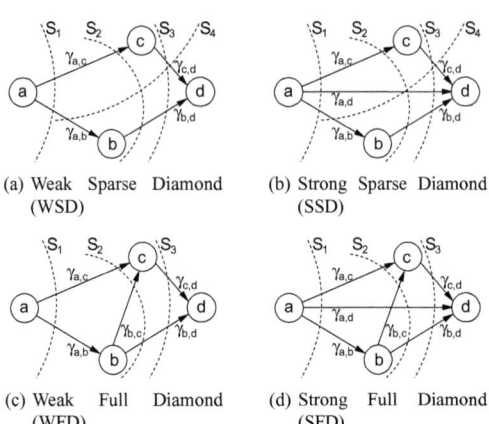

Figure 3.11: *Diamond* flow networks in a four-node scenario with unidirectional transmission from a to d: Instantaneous SNR $\gamma_{i,j}$ for any link (i,j) and all distinct, unidirectional cut sets $\mathbb{S} := \{S_1, \ldots, S_N\}$.

3.11(b). For the full diamonds, defining a cut set S_4 is not defined as the inter-relay link (b,c) would cause S_4 to be bidirectional. Hence, for both full diamonds, only the cut sets $\mathbb{S} := \{S_1, \ldots, S_3\}$ are defined in Figure 3.11(c) and 3.11(d).

Combining-based Selection Relaying (CSR) This protocol type can operate in each flow network in Figure 3.11. For each network, we obtain the diversity order after combining at d as above. Searching the M cut sets $\mathbb{S}_M \subseteq \mathbb{S}$ with minimum cardinality provides the diversity order L as the number of links in these sets. If CSR is employed in the sparse diamonds, we find the four sets $\mathbb{S}_M := \{S_1, \ldots, S_4\}$ while, for the full diamonds, only the two sets $\mathbb{S}_M := \{S_1, S_3\}$ include L_M channels. Counting the channels in these sets results in diversity order $L = 2$ for the weak and in $L = 3$ for the strong diamonds.

Note that with full diamonds even c can combine the two signals from (a,c) and (b,c). This causes a CTR $a - b - c$ to appear *inside* the diamond improving diversity order at node c. Naturally, the diversity order of this CTR at node c is $L_c = 2$. Formally, this is derived as above handling node c as a destination. Finding all $\mathbb{S}_M^c$ cut sets of minimum cardinality at node c and calculating the cardinality for any of these sets $S_m^c \in \mathbb{S}_M^c$ leads to $L_c = |S_m^c| = 2$.

Using (3.3) and (3.4) provides the outage probability approximations for high SNR as in Table 3.1. The link-dependent terms are

$$\Theta_S = \frac{\Gamma_{a,b}\Gamma_{a,c} + \Gamma_{a,b}\Gamma_{c,d} + \Gamma_{a,c}\Gamma_{b,d} + \Gamma_{b,d}\Gamma_{c,d}}{\Gamma_{a,b}\Gamma_{a,c}\Gamma_{b,d}\Gamma_{c,d}} \qquad (3.8)$$

for the sparse diamonds and

$$\Theta_F = \frac{\Gamma_{a,b}\Gamma_{a,c} + \Gamma_{b,d}\Gamma_{c,d}}{\Gamma_{a,b}\Gamma_{a,c}\Gamma_{b,d}\Gamma_{c,d}} \qquad (3.9)$$

3.3. Performance analysis of selection relaying

Table 3.1: Results of the outage analysis for CSR.

Flow network	Outage probability at high SNR, $P^{\text{out}} \approx$	Div. order, L	Div. order at c, L_c	# subchan. K
Direct	$\frac{1}{\Gamma_{a,d}} \frac{2^R-1}{\Gamma}$	1	–	1
NCR	$\Theta_T \left(\frac{2^{2R}-1}{\Gamma} \right)$	1	1	2
CTR	$\frac{1}{2\Gamma_{a,d}} \Theta_T \left(\frac{2^{2R}-1}{\Gamma} \right)^2$	2	1	2
WSD	$\frac{1}{2} \Theta_S \left(\frac{2^{3R}-1}{\Gamma} \right)^2$	2	1	3
WFD	$\frac{1}{2} \Theta_F \left(\frac{2^{3R}-1}{\Gamma} \right)^2$	2	2	3
SSD	$\frac{1}{6\Gamma_{a,d}} \Theta_S \left(\frac{2^{3R}-1}{\Gamma} \right)^3$	3	1	3
SFD	$\frac{1}{6\Gamma_{a,d}} \Theta_F \left(\frac{2^{3R}-1}{\Gamma} \right)^3$	3	2	3
Any	$\frac{1}{L!} \Theta \left(\frac{2^{KR}-1}{\Gamma} \right)^L$	$\lvert S_m \rvert$	$\lvert S_m^c \rvert$	$N+1$

for the full diamonds. For the weak diamonds, Θ_S and Θ_F directly result from (3.4). For the strong diamonds, Θ_S or Θ_F occur if $1/\Gamma_{a,d}$ is factored out from the result of (3.4).

We summarize the analytic results for CSR in the four diamond networks in Table 3.1. For comparison and to highlight the uniformity of the P^{out} formulas, we include direct transmission and the general approximation for selection relaying in any flow network.

Path allocation-based Selection Relaying (PSR) If path allocation is based on full CSI, PSR protocols can be treated similarly to combining-based protocols (Section 3.2). To minimize P^{out}, any of the above PSR protocols would choose one of the paths $a \to d$, $a \to b \to d$, or $a \to c \to d$. As no combining is performed, node c cannot profit from links (c,b) or (b,c). Without combining, both links can only increase the end-to-end outage probability at d and are, thus, not chosen by PSR.

Consequently, PSR only operates in the sparse diamonds WSD and SSD making (3.8) the relevant link-dependent term. Assuming ideal CSI$_{\text{tx}}$, PSR chooses the best out of two paths in the WSD and the best out of three paths in the SSD. Thereby, PSR reaches equal diversity order L as CSR at the destination – a result also shown by Bletsas et al. [BKRL06]. This leads to $L=2$ for the WSD. For the SSD and any denser configuration with four nodes $L=3$ is reached. For any number of relays, PSR reaches L at the cost of either $K=1$ if the direct path $a \to d$ is chosen or at $K=2$ if any relay is chosen.

These results for PSR with full CSI are summarized in Table 3.2. Although the outage probability is derived equally for PSR and CSR, the obtained P^{out} functions differ in their parameters K, L, and L_c. We will now discuss the differences between the two protocols in detail.

Table 3.2: Results of the outage analysis for PSR with full CSI.

Flow network	Outage probability at high SNR, p^{out}	Div. order, L	Div. order at c, L_c	# subchan. K
WSD	$\frac{1}{2}\Theta_S \left(\frac{2^{2R}-1}{\Gamma}\right)^2$	2	1	2
SSD	$\frac{1}{6\Gamma_{a,d}}\Theta_S \left(\frac{2^{2R}-1}{\Gamma}\right)^3$	3	1	2
Any	$\frac{1}{L!}\Theta \left(\frac{2^{KR}-1}{\Gamma}\right)^L$	$|S_m|$	1	$\{1,2\}$

Discussion

Analytic results Let us first discuss the above analytic results for CSR (Table 3.1). Comparing the link-dependent terms for the sparse (3.8) and full diamonds (3.9) shows that Θ_S has a larger numerator than Θ_F while the denominators are equal. As the SNR scaling factor $\Gamma_{i,j}$ can only take positive values, we obtain

$$\Theta_S > \Theta_F. \tag{3.10}$$

This means that the outage probability of a CSR protocol can be improved by connecting the relays by an intermediate link, i.e., link (b,c) in our full diamond configurations. This result holds for any network geometry (here expressed by the $\Gamma_{i,j}$ values). The inter-relay link (b,c) provides this gain by causing a CTR $a-b-c$ to appear inside the diamond, improving diversity order at node c to $L_c = 2$. Hence, even with the WFD where the direct link cannot be used, cooperation within the diamond can improve overall outage performance for CSR.

Comparing the outage probabilities of CSR for the weak and strong diamonds shows that using the direct link adds a factor $1/\Gamma_{a,d}$ and increases the diversity order by one. Both significantly improves the outage probability for a strong diamond if compared to the corresponding weak diamond.

The parameter K accounts for the number of orthogonal subchannels required for a an end-to-end transmission from a to d. As the multiplexing loss increases linearly in K, this parameter represents the cost for the additional transmissions due to relaying. With CSR protocols the multiplexing loss depends on the number of relays. As source and all N relays can transmit, $K = N + 1$ orthogonal subchannels are required. Comparing configurations of equal K shows that NCR and the weak diamonds make only inefficient use of the channel by spending K phases for reaching a diversity order $L = K - 1$. In contrast, direct transmission, CTR, and the strong diamonds reach $L = K$. While this difference has only a small effect on the outage probability, it highly affects the outage capacity reached in a configuration. We will further discuss this aspect in Section 3.3.4.

The outage probability of PSR protocols with full CSI (Table 3.2) is similar to that of CTR. The first difference result from the lack of combining. Without combining, PSR cannot profit from the inter-relay links to increase L_c and, thus, employs only the sparse diamonds. The second difference is that PSR can achieve full diversity at the cost of $K = 1$ or $K = 2$ orthogonal subchannels. This can be beneficial in terms of outage capacity and is further discussed below.

3.3. Performance analysis of selection relaying

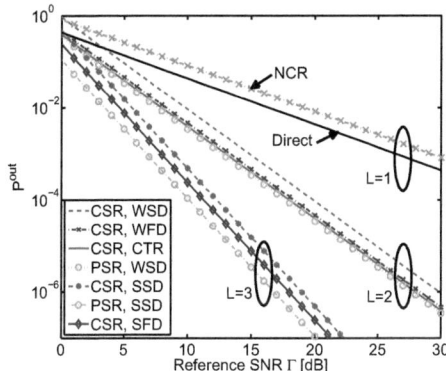

Figure 3.12: Outage probability vs. reference SNR for several flow networks: Numerical results for $R = 1/4$ bits/s/Hz.

Numerical results As an example for the above analytical results, Figure 3.12 shows numerical results for the parameters from Section 3.3.1 and a symmetric diamond geometry. Here, all node-to-node distances are 1 unit except for the direct link where the diamond geometry requires a distance of $D_{a,d} = \sqrt{2}$ units between node a and d. Figure 3.12 compares different flow networks as well as different protocols. CSR protocols operate in any diamond network from Figure 3.11 and in the CTR. PSR protocols operate only in the WSD and in the SSD.

Clearly, the diversity order L has the largest effect on the outage probability. Its exponential effect divides the results into three groups: The outage probability that CSR and PSR reach in the strong diamonds ($L = 3$) is clearly below the probability reached in the CTR and in the weak diamonds ($L = 2$). Naturally, the worst outage probability is obtained with direct transmission and NCR ($L = 1$).

Within these groups defined by L, the link-dependent factors Θ and $1/\Gamma_{a,d}$ as well as factor $1/L!$ lead to outage probability offsets. These offsets are called coding gains (Section 2.2.1) and have different origins. The coding gain of direct transmission over NCR results from the fact that for NCR the P^{out} of both independent links adds up. This causes the P^{out} for NCR to be significantly larger than for direct transmission. Consequently, NCR reaches the worst outage probability of all studied systems. Comparing the outage probability that CSR reaches with sparse and full diamonds shows a coding gain with the full diamonds. As discussed above (3.10), this results from the intermediate link which improves the outage probability with the full diamonds. Comparing PSR and CSR in the corresponding configuration shows a significant coding gain for PSR. This gain results from the fact that PSR utilizes, at worst, $K = 2$ orthogonal channels while CSR employs $K = 3$ at high SNR.

From these analytic and numerical results, we suggest that exploiting as many links as possible should be the major focus of a cooperation protocol if minimal outage probability is desired. This includes even combining at intermediate nodes.

3.3.4 Outage capacity for arbitrary flow networks

Before studying specific cases, we extend the theoretical framework from Section 3.3.2 to the *outage capacity* C^{out} for general flow networks at high SNR. As described in Section 2.1.2, C^{out} is the largest spectral efficiency R such that the outage probability $P^{\text{out}}(R)$ does not exceed the *outage probability constraint* ε.

Several studies approximated C^{out} for cooperative relaying and Rayleigh fading. Without further constraints, C^{out} at high SNR for DF [HM02] and at low SNR for DF and AF [AT07] were approximated. With practical constraints on synchronization and duplexing, the C^{out} of DF and CF was studied [HMZ05]. All these studies show significant gains for cooperative relaying at low and medium SNR in terms of C^{out} but all of them are limited to the CTR network. Although we will include this special case for comparison, our C^{out} results apply to general flow networks with N relays.

We can now obtain the outage capacity for high SNR by solving $P^{\text{out}}(R) = \varepsilon$ for R. This results in

$$C^{\text{out}} \approx R = \frac{1}{K}\log_2\left(1 + \Gamma \sqrt[L]{\frac{L!\varepsilon}{\Theta}}\right) \text{ [bits/s/Hz]} \tag{3.11}$$

as the end-to-end outage capacity at high SNR for any given flow network. It should be noted that for any feasible value of ε, L, and Θ, the term

$$\Psi := \frac{L!\varepsilon}{\Theta} \tag{3.12}$$

in (3.3) is non-negative and, hence, a real-valued solution of C^{out} can be obtained.

The outage capacity is linearly reduced by the multiplexing loss $1/K$. This clearly expresses the costs of relaying via orthogonal subchannels (Section 2.3). With relaying, $K > 1$ nodes may transmit per end-to-end transmission and the channel resources have to be split into K orthogonal subchannels. At equal bandwidth this, naturally, divides the end-to-end capacity by K.

Second approximation for high SNR and large L

The outage capacity can be further characterized by simplifying (3.11) for high SNR and large L. At high SNR, we can approximate $\log_2(1+\Gamma) \approx \log_2(\Gamma)$. Applying this approximation to (3.11) leads to

$$C^{\text{out}} \approx \tilde{C}^{\text{out}} = \frac{1}{K}(\log_2 \Gamma + \log_2 \sqrt[L]{\Psi}) \tag{3.13}$$

where we can write

$$\log_2 \sqrt[L]{\Psi} = \frac{1}{L}(\log_2(L!) + \log_2 \varepsilon - \log_2 \Theta). \tag{3.14}$$

Here, we can approximate for large L [BS04]

$$\log_2(L!) = \sum_{l=1}^{L} \log_2 l \approx \int_1^L \log_2 x \, dx = L\log_2 L - L. \tag{3.15}$$

3.3. Performance analysis of selection relaying

Inserting this approximation in (3.14) and the resulting term in (3.13) provides

$$\tilde{C}^{\text{out}} = \frac{1}{K}(\underbrace{\log_2(L\Gamma)}_{=C_L} + \underbrace{\frac{1}{L}\log_2 \varepsilon}_{\text{Fading}} - \underbrace{\frac{1}{L}\log_2 \Theta}_{\text{Relaying}} - 1) \text{ [bits/s/Hz]} \quad (3.16)$$

as a simple approximation of the outage capacity (3.11).

Apart from the multiplexing loss, this approximation is dominated by three terms: First, the *AWGN capacity at high SNR* $C_L = \log_2(L\Gamma)$ for an L-fold reception of the same signal. Second, the ε-dependent term which significantly reduces C_L since, typically, $\varepsilon \ll 1 \Leftrightarrow \log \varepsilon \ll 0$. Third, the Θ-dependent term which includes all link-dependent scaling factors according to the flow network of the employed relaying protocol.

Discussion

Analytic results Due to the C_L term in (3.16), the outage capacity increases logarithmically with the SNR Γ and the diversity order L. With the subtrahends in the logarithmic domain, the outage capacity is only a small fraction of the AWGN capacity C_L. This reduction is independent on the SNR and does only depend on the outage probability constraint ε, on the link-dependent term Θ, and on the diversity order L.

The degradation of C_L due to ε accounts for the overall effect of fading. This degradation increases for smaller ε and decreases for larger L. This result shows that a stricter error rate constraint decreases the outage capacity and that this effect can be mitigated by increasing the diversity order. Similar results where found for low SNR [AT07] that consistently matches to our approximation for high SNR.

In (3.16) the AWGN capacity is further degraded by the Θ-dependent term. Again, this degradation is reduced if L increases. Further, this degradation depends on Θ which accounts for the SNR scaling factors, for the available relays, and for which relays and links are employed by a relaying protocol. Hence, the third term in (3.16) clearly captures the effect of the network geometry and of the relaying protocol. Note that for general networks this effect is not characterized in previous approximations of the outage capacity [HM02, HMZ05, AT07]

Numerical results We compare both outage capacity approximations to simulation results in Figure 3.13. As a simple example, we focus on the CTR where CSR achieves a diversity order $L = 2$. Two levels of ε are studied; each accounting for different traffic requirements. For example, a low ε represents the strict error rate constraint of real-time voice or video traffic. Such a transmission is very vulnerable to fading and only a low ε is acceptable. On the other hand, ε can be usually larger with non-real time traffic, e.g., file downloads or web pages.

For these parameters, Figure 3.13(a) shows absolute outage capacity results. In Figure 3.13(b) outage capacity is plotted as a fraction of the corresponding AWGN capacity, i.e., $C_L = \log_2(L\Gamma)$ with $L = 2$, isolating the impact of fading and relaying. The figures show that, at high SNR, both approximations are tight. Even at $L = 2$, the simple approximation $\tilde{C}^{\text{out}}$ (3.16) matches well with the simulation results. As

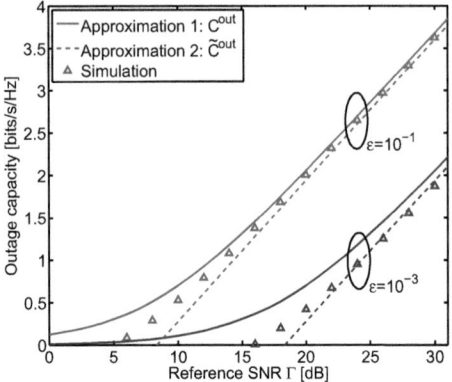

(a) Outage capacity vs. reference SNR

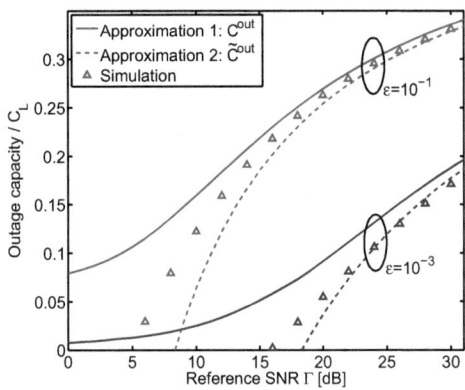

(b) Outage capacity as a fraction of AWGN capacity vs. reference SNR

Figure 3.13: Comparing the outage capacity approximations (3.11) and (3.16) to simulation results: CTR with symmetric geometry, $\varepsilon = 10^{-1}$ and $\varepsilon = 10^{-3}$. For simulation results, no confidence intervals are shown due to their small size.

the accuracy of the approximation (3.15) improves in L, also $\tilde{C}^{\text{out}}$ becomes more accurate if L increases in larger cooperative setups.

For decreasing SNR, both approximations disperse and do not match to the simulation results. This is expected as the underlying P^{out} approximation (3.3) is only valid at high SNR. At low SNR, the approximation C^{out} and the simulation results become convex (Figure 3.13(a)). This shape of the outage capacity for Rayleigh fading is known [AT07] and shifts to higher SNR if the impact of fading increases, i.e., ε or L decrease. Vice versa, in scenarios with high ε or high L (e.g., soft robustness constraints or many relays) both approximations are still accurate in the medium SNR regime.

All in all, we can conclude that at high SNR both approximations of C^{out} closely match the simulation results. At low C^{out} (e.g., due to low SNR or high ε) both approximations become less accurate but the new approximation (3.16) matches closer to the empirical results than (3.11).

3.3.5 Outage capacity for one and two relays

Let us now use the derived C^{out} approximation to rate the outage capacity of flow networks with $N = 1$ and $N = 2$ relays. With this relatively low (but practical) number of relays cooperation reaches at best a diversity order of $L = 3$. Hence, we employ the first approximation (3.11) which holds even for low L. Similar to our P^{out} analysis we focus on CSR and PSR protocols and ignore practical constraints on CSI and network connectivity.

CSR with one and two relays

For general flow networks, the high SNR outage capacity C^{out} is readily provided by (3.11). For a particular flow network, we obtain C^{out} by deriving $\Theta, L,$ and K as above (or by using the values from Table 3.1 if this network was already studied) and by inserting into (3.11).

For "weak" flow networks without the direct link (NCR, WSD, WFD), the respective Θ_T, Θ_S, Θ_F from Table 3.1 can be inserted directly. For the "strong" networks, we factored out $1/\Gamma_{a,d}$ from Θ, which now needs to be re-included before we can insert the values from Table 3.1 in (3.11). This is simply done by $\Theta = \Theta'/\Gamma_{a,d}$ where Θ' represents one of the channel-dependent Θ-terms from Table 3.1.

For example, the outage capacity for the "strong" CTR is obtained by choosing $K = 2$, $L = 2$, and $\Theta' = \Theta_T$ from Table 3.1. Therewith, $\Theta = \Theta_T/\Gamma_{a,d}$ and (3.11) yield

$$C_T^{\text{out}} = \frac{1}{2}\log_2\left(\sqrt{\frac{2\varepsilon\Gamma_{a,d}}{\Theta_T}} \cdot \Gamma + 1\right) \tag{3.17}$$

for this single-relay SDF case.

PSR with two relays and full CSI

With full CSI, PSR can employ perfect CSI_{tx} to choose the path that minimizes P^{out}. This ideal case corresponds to the Opportunistic Relaying (OR) protocol studied in [BSW07, BA07] and in Section 3.3.3.

Alternatively, a PSR protocol may choose a path which maximizes outage capacity. Such protocols aim for a beneficial tradeoff of diversity gains and multiplexing loss and would, thus, choose the direct link even if it increases P^{out} but (due to the lower K) improves C^{out}. A practical example of such a C^{out}-maximizing protocol was described as CoopMAC [LTN+07]. Let us now analyze the outage capacity of both PSR strategies.

Minimize outage probability For this min(P^{out}) strategy, the general outage capacity $C^{\text{out}}_{\text{ORF}}$ is directly given by (3.11). For the studied $N=2$ network we insert the values from Table 3.2 into (3.11) and obtain

$$C^{\text{out}}_{\text{PSR,WSD}} = \frac{1}{2}\log_2\left(\sqrt{\frac{2\varepsilon}{\Theta_S}} \cdot \Gamma + 1\right) \tag{3.18}$$

as approximate outage capacity for the WSD at high SNR and

$$C^{\text{out}}_{\text{PSR,SSD}} = \frac{1}{2}\log_2\left(\sqrt[3]{\frac{6\varepsilon\Gamma_{a,d}}{\Theta_S}} \cdot \Gamma + 1\right) \tag{3.19}$$

for the SSD.

Maximize outage capacity Based on full CSI, a max(C^{out}) protocol simply selects the "best" network path assuring max(C^{out}) from all network paths. Although direct transmission cannot achieve a P^{out} smaller than the outage probabilities in Table 3.2, its outage capacity $C^{\text{out}}_{\text{DIR}}$ can exceed (3.18) and (3.19) since it may meet ε at lower K.

Following this strategy, a max(C^{out}) PSR protocol achieves outage capacity

$$C^{\text{out}}_{\text{PSR,M}} = \max(C^{\text{out}}_{\text{PSR}}, C^{\text{out}}_{\text{DIR}}) \tag{3.20}$$

with full CSI where $C^{\text{out}}_{\text{PSR}}$ represents the outage capacity of the available configuration.

Discussion

Numerical results for the most interesting configurations of the P^{out} study are shown in Figure 3.14. We use the parameters from Section 3.3.1 but study two levels of ε. As in Figure 3.13, a low and a high error rate constraint is chosen. To highlight the effect of this constraint and of the capacity degradation due to relaying, we plot C^{out} as a fraction of the AWGN capacity C_L. To this end, we choose diversity order L of the studied relaying scheme (Table 3.1 or 3.2) and divide C^{out} by $C_L = \log_2(L\Gamma)$. Both figures show direct transmission, NCR, and CSR and PSR protocols. CSR is shown for the CTR and SFD configuration and PSR is shown for the SSD. For PSR both optimization objectives (min(P^{out}) and max(C^{out})) are shown.

Figure 3.14(a) illustrates the outage capacity of these cases for $\varepsilon = 10^{-3}$. With this strict error rate constraint, direct transmission performs poorly. Due to (3.20), this link is never chosen by PSR if it aims to maximize C^{out}. Thus, both PSR strategies perform equal. At high SNR, PSR outperforms CSR

3.3. Performance analysis of selection relaying

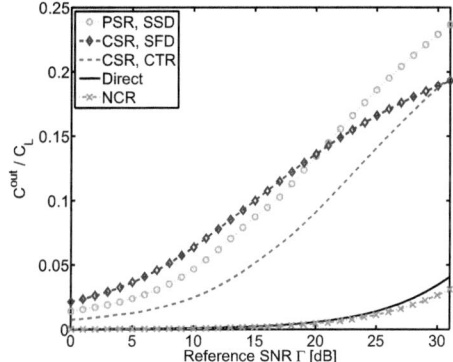

(a) Outage capacity as a fraction of AWGN capacity vs. reference SNR for $\varepsilon = 10^{-3}$. The results for *PSR* $\max(C^{\text{out}})$ and *PSR* $\min(P^{\text{out}})$ are equal.

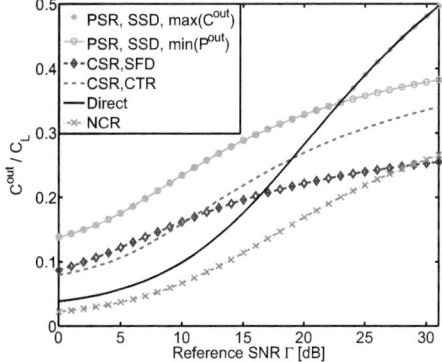

(b) Outage capacity as a fraction of AWGN capacity vs. reference SNR for $\varepsilon = 10^{-1}$.

Figure 3.14: Outage capacity as a fraction of AWGN capacity: Numerical results for various flow networks and two levels of ε.

for all studied flow networks until PSR reaches 24 % of the respective AWGN capacity. Consequently, at high SNR and low ε, PSR is a better choice than CSR. With decreasing SNR the situation reverses. Here, CSR performs best if it can employ as many links as possible (cp. Figure 3.12), i.e, if an SFD can be established. The CTR cannot achieve this high performance due to its lower diversity order L. Consequently, with strict error rate constraints and medium or low SNR, CSR protocols in full networks (e.g., the SFD) are preferable.

Figure 3.14(b) with $\varepsilon = 10^{-1}$ represents a typical error rate acceptable for non-real time traffic in WLAN systems [OP99]. At this high ε, even direct transmission shows its benefits. For high SNR it achieves up to 50 % of the AWGN capacity and, thus, outperforms any relaying scheme. To this end, at high SNR, direct transmission is chosen by C^{out}-maximizing PSR. This choice is represented by the sharp bend of the C^{out} function at 23 dB (Figure 3.14(b)) which results from (3.20). Compared to all other relaying cases and direct transmission, PSR max(C^{out}) achieves the highest outage capacity for all studied SNR levels. At high SNR, it outperforms the P^{out}-minimizing PSR and the CSR strategies which suffer from a high multiplexing loss due to relaying.

3.4 Performance analysis under practical constraints

In our above analysis we compared the performance of CSR and PSR protocols assuming full CSI and ideal network connectivity. With full CSI, perfect channel knowledge is available at all nodes at no cost. Assuming ideal network connectivity implies that a flow network employed by a relaying protocol can be always established. That is, relays always occur in the source's propagation domain and links are never shadowed by obstacles. These idealistic assumptions suit well for a unified performance analysis but can only provide a starting point for practically relevant studies.

Before studying realistic scenarios by simulation and field measurement (Chapter 4 and 6), we study outage probability and capacity under more practical assumptions. To this end, we limit CSI and network connectivity which degrades the above analytic results individually for CSR and PSR. The results highlight that – despite the unified results for the ideal case – the performance of CSR and PSR significantly differs under practical constraints. This leads to different scenarios where each of these protocols is beneficial.

3.4.1 Effect of limited CSI feedback

With full CSI, perfect channel knowledge is assumed to be available at all transmitters at no costs. Although this CSI assumption is along the line with most theoretic work on PSR [BSW07, BA07, AFYP08], it unfairly favors PSR above CSR.

Unlike CSR, PSR protocols require *transmitter CSI* (CSI_{tx}) for their network path allocation. This type of CSI is not required by CSR and is usually costly to obtain. With non-reciprocal channels, CSI_{tx} has to

3.4. Performance analysis under practical constraints

be obtained by feedback. The receiver measures CSI and transmits it back to the transmitter via an error-prone wireless channel. As this feedback channel is always limited, CSI feedback introduces overhead, delay, and transmission errors. So far, the effect of limited CSI feedback on PSR protocols is only rarely studied in literature. Lo, Heath, and Vishwanath [LHV07] study throughput and error rate for distributed path allocation under limited CSI feedback. However, the authors make very specific assumptions on the employed codes and path allocation method and ignore feedback errors imposed by fading channels. Both is not the case in the following outage probability and outage capacity analysis.

In addition to costly CSI_{tx}, PSR systems require *receiver CSI* (CSI_{rx}) for coherent detection. This type of CSI is also required by CSR for coherent detection and combining. In most systems the receiver observes CSI_{rx} from a short training sequence withing the received packets at low overhead.[2] Since both protocol types equally rely on CSI_{rx} and obtain this channel knowledge at equal (typically low) cost, we compare both protocols for perfect CSI_{rx}. On the other hand, we account for the specific CSI_{tx} demands of PSR by limiting this type of channel knowledge.

Outage probability

For PSR's diversity order and outage probability, the available CSI_{tx} (either at the source or at all relays) is crucial. With ideal CSI_{tx}, a PSR protocol can always choose the P^{out}-minimal path, thus reaching full diversity order and ideal outage probability. As we ignore CSI_{rx} constraints, ideal CSI_{tx} is equivalent to full CSI and, naturally, the same results as in Section 3.3 are obtained. If PSR operates in the SSD, it reaches full diversity order $L = 3$ and the P^{out} in Table 3.2. We include these results in Table 3.3 for comparison.

Assuming no CSI_{tx} allows a fair comparison of PSR to CSR protocols, which only require CSI_{rx}. Under this CSI assumption, PSR cannot choose the best path and reaches only $L = 1$ (Table 3.3) [BSW07]. We treat such PSR protocol as a special case of NCR and, thus, include (3.7) in Table 3.3. Note that in the symmetrical scenario the average gain provided by choosing relay c is equal to the gain of choosing relay b. Thus, Θ_T suffices as link-dependent term.

The results for these two extreme cases are summarized in Table 3.3. Without CSI_{tx}, PSR only reaches the poor outage probability of NCR. On the other hand, with CSI_{tx}, the minimal outage probability of the WSD with full diversity is reached. This simple comparison clearly points out that PSR protocols heavily rely on CSI_{tx} and that PSR without feedback is no option. Let us now study how obtaining CSI_{tx} via possibly erroneous feedback channels reduces outage capacity.

Outage capacity

While perfect CSI_{tx} requires feedback at every channel change, even limited CSI_{tx} occasionally employs feedback channels. At which transmitter this channel knowledge is required depends on the PSR protocol. Proactive OR protocols and CoopMAC require CSI_{tx} at the source while reactive OR protocols require

---
[2] For instance, in IEEE 802.11a/g systems the first $16\mu s$ of a Physical layer (PHY) frame are employed for training, i.e., only 1.6 % of a typical 1 ms frame.

Table 3.3: Results of the outage analysis for PSR, SSD with limited CSI.

CSI	Outage probability at high SNR, P^{out}	Div. order, L	Div. order at c, L_c	# subchan. K
Rx and Tx	$\frac{1}{6\Gamma_{a,d}}\Theta_S\left(\frac{2^{2R}-1}{\Gamma}\right)^3$	3	1	2
Rx only	$\Theta_T\left(\frac{2^{2R}-1}{\Gamma}\right)$	1	1	2

CSI$_{\text{tx}}$ at all relays (Section 3.2). In each of these cases, the most efficient CSI feedback in terms of K is a single broadcast from d. Focusing only on this broadcast and ignoring that reactive OR requires further coordination overhead, e.g., a contention phase among the relays, provides an upper bound of the overhead-degraded C^{out} for proactive and reactive protocols.

In our two-relay scenario, the CSI broadcast of d has to reach both relays if a reactive protocol is employed. During the broadcast, d utilizes the links $\{(d,b),(d,c)\}$ for $K=1$ phase. Applying (3.4), (3.3), and (3.11) as above yields the capacity of this feedback channel as

$$C_{\text{FB}}^{\text{out}} := \log_2(\varepsilon\Gamma_{d,b}\Gamma_{d,c}\Gamma+1). \tag{3.21}$$

In a proactive protocol, only unidirectional feedback to a is required. In this case, we employ $C_{\text{FB}}^{\text{out}} := \log_2(\varepsilon\Gamma_{d,a}\Gamma+1)$ instead of (3.21).

For proactive and reactive PSR protocols, we assume that b_{FB} bits of CSI are transferred once per *feedback period* of N_T protocol cycles. The *share of the feedback channel's outage capacity* that remains after this feedback is defined as

$$R_{\text{FB}}(b_{\text{FB}}, N_T) := \begin{cases} \frac{C_{\text{FB}}^{\text{out}} - b_{\text{FB}}/N_T}{C_{\text{FB}}^{\text{out}}} & ; \; b_{\text{FB}}/N_T \leq C_{\text{FB}}^{\text{out}} \\ 0 & ; \; \text{otherwise} \end{cases} \tag{3.22}$$

and captures the feedback overhead (b_{FB}), frequency (N_T) as well as channel capacity and error constraints ($C_{\text{FB}}^{\text{out}}$).

With R_{FB} and C^{out} from (3.11), the end-to-end outage capacity of a PSR protocol degraded by CSI feedback overhead and errors is

$$C_{\text{PSR,FB}}^{\text{out}} = C_{\text{PSR}}^{\text{out}} \cdot R_{\text{FB}}(b_{\text{FB}}, N_T). \tag{3.23}$$

The term $C_{\text{PSR}}^{\text{out}}$ depends on the PSR objective and configuration. If PSR aims for minimal P^{out}, (3.18) accounts for the WSD and (3.19) for the SSD configuration. With the max(C^{out}) strategy, we insert (3.20).

To simplify the above discussion, we assumed that a PSR protocol gives up if no transmission via the feedback channel is possible, i.e., if $b_{\text{FB}}/N_T > C_{\text{FB}}^{\text{out}}$. In this case, (3.22) and (3.23) are zero. Furthermore, we assumed that the outage probability constraint for data $\varepsilon_{\text{Data}}$ is equal to the outage probability constraint of CSI feedback ε_{FB}. Due to the high relevance of CSI feedback usually, $\varepsilon_{\text{FB}} \leq \varepsilon_{\text{Data}}$. Our assumption

3.4. Performance analysis under practical constraints

$\varepsilon := \varepsilon_{\text{FB}} = \varepsilon_{\text{Data}}$ is, therefore, optimistic. It leads to a higher $C_{\text{FB}}^{\text{out}}$ than usual and is, thus, feasible for an upper bound of $C_{\text{PSR,FB}}^{\text{out}}$.

Number of CSI feedback bits Choosing the number of CSI feedback bits b_{FB} depends on the required CSI_{tx} accuracy. If d reactively selects the "best" out of N relays and the direct link, $b_{\text{FB}} = \log_2(N+1)$ bits have to be transferred. In our two-relay example, this leads to $b_{\text{FB}} = \log_2 3$ bits. Naturally, b_{FB} increases with more sophisticated forms of channel adaptation, e.g., if d also assigns the transmission rate to the relays.

Feedback period The destination transmits b_{FB} once every N_T cycles. Choosing this feedback period depends on the coherence time of the fading channel. To synchronize CSI_{tx} to a block fading channel, CSI feedback is required once per fading block. As we assumed one block per MAC cycle, this case is expressed by $N_T = 1$, i.e., one feedback transmission per cycle.

The more practical case, however, is limited CSI_{tx} which requires only occasional feedback. In this case, $N_T > 1$ can be chosen if the channel's coherence time is larger than T_{cycle}. For instance, with typical IEEE 802.11a WLAN parameters (i.e., 5.2 GHz carrier frequency, 1 ms transmission time per packet) an approximate channel coherence time of 57 ms can be assumed at a slow walking speed of 1 m/s. CSI_{tx} can be synchronized to this channel by updating feedback once per coherence time, i.e., once every $N_T = 57$ protocol cycles with $T_{\text{cycle}} = 1$ ms. Naturally, more frequent feedback is required with faster nodes or if the coherence time cannot be accurately approximated for the used fading channels (Section 2.1.2). Let us now use $N_T = 57$ and $b_{\text{FB}} = \log_2 3$ bits to study our two-relay networks by numerical results.

Discussion

Feedback errors can substantially degrade the performance of a PSR protocol especially if it operates under strict error rate constraints. As such constraints are typical for cooperative relaying protocols, it is interesting to study how the performance of PSR degrades with erroneous CSI feedback.

Analytic results Unlike the outage capacity of CSR protocols, the capacity of PSR is reduced by CSI feedback. In (3.23), the feedback loss linearly reduces PSR's outage capacity and depends on the desired CSI_{tx} accuracy in time and value. This loss increases with the feedback frequency $1/N_T$ and is small if the destination assigns the transmission to the "best" relay. More sophisticated channel adaptation or a contention phase among the relays will decrease the feedback-degraded outage capacity of PSR.

Moreover, the capacity of the feedback channel depends on the error rate constraint ε. Decreasing ε leads to a lower outage capacity of the feedback channel (3.21). This logarithmically degrades the end-to-end outage capacity of PSR (3.23).

Numerical results In Figure 3.15 the outage capacity for PSR operating in the SSD configuration with several degrees of CSI is shown. We use the same parameters as above and include the results for direct transmission and for CSR in the CTR configuration from Figure 3.14 for comparison.

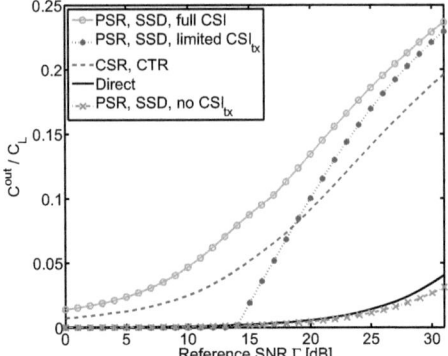

(a) Outage capacity as a fraction of AWGN capacity vs. reference SNR for $\varepsilon = 10^{-3}$

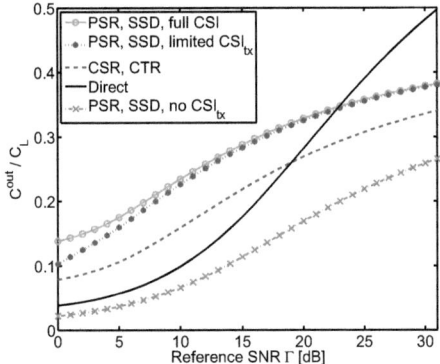

(b) Outage capacity as a fraction of AWGN capacity vs. reference SNR for $\varepsilon = 10^{-1}$

Figure 3.15: Outage capacity as a fraction of AWGN capacity: Numerical results for PSR with ideal, limited, and no CSI_{tx}. Shown for CTR and direct transmission and two levels of ε.

PSR without CSI_{tx} and PSR with full CSI_{tx} represent the lower and upper bound, respectively. As a realistic case, PSR with limited CSI_{tx} obtained by feedback is studied. Figure 3.14(a) illustrates the capacity for the different CSI degrees under strict error constraints. As in Figure 3.14(a), direct transmission performs poorly and PSR without CSI_{tx} is no option. Even with only a single relay, CSR reaches acceptable performance. It is only outperformed by PSR if full CSI is assumed.

The outage capacity of this idealistic case is significantly degraded if realistic feedback is assumed. While at high SNR even with limited feedback a C^{out} close to the upper bound is reached, at decreasing SNR C^{out} quickly drops to zero. This is a result of using only a single broadcast transmission for feedback. Such a feedback channel cannot achieve a diversity order larger than $L = 1$ and would require infeasible coding redundancy to meet a strict outage probability as $\varepsilon = 10^{-3}$ (Section 2.2.1). Consequently, at medium and low SNR, the capacity (3.21) of the broadcast channel is too low to transfer the full b_{FB} bits even if, as in this example, b_{FB} is very small.

The poor performance of PSR with limited CSI clearly shows that a single feedback phase is not sufficient if PSR operates under strict error constraints. Instead, additional protection, e.g., by cooperating even during the feedback phases, is required. We will discuss the implementation of this *cooperative feedback* technique in Chapter 5 and Chapter 6.

Figure 3.14(b) shows the above protocols and CSI degrees at a relaxed error rate constraint $\varepsilon = 10^{-1}$. At such high ε the full CSI case is only slightly degraded by feedback errors. Here, a single broadcast channel provides sufficient capacity to transfer the feedback information. Consequently, even if we account for overhead and feedback errors, CSR protocols are significantly outperformed by PSR when the acceptable error rate is high.

Region of operation

The above results show that choosing the "best" relaying protocol to maximize outage capacity C^{out} highly depends on available CSI, the outage probability constraint ε, and on the SNR regime. Depending on these parameters, the C^{out} functions intersect, making either PSR or a particular CSR a good choice. This preferred *region of operation* for a specific protocol is summarized in Figure 3.16. For various ε, the figure shows the reference SNR value Γ where the capacity functions C_A^{out} and C_B^{out} of the compared cases A and B intersect. If Γ increases above the plotted value, C_A^{out} exceeds C_B^{out}. Hence, for an SNR above a shown line, case A is preferable while, below the line, case B achieves higher capacity.

In Figure 3.16, PSR is studied in the SSD configuration for full and limited CSI. This protocol is compared to CSR which operates in the CTR and SFD. Direct transmission always requires largest SNR and is, thus, not included. At a low ε, PSR demands a lower SNR than CTR to outperform the SFD if full CSI is available. Taking limited CSI feedback into account, however, shows that OR is only efficient for an ε larger than 10^{-2}. As discussed above, this results from the direct feedback channel that represents a "bottleneck" if a small ε is chosen. Here, CTR and SFD reach significant SNR gains above PSR if limited CSI has to be obtained via feedback.

All in all, Figure 3.16 allows to choose the relaying protocol and network that maximizes the outage

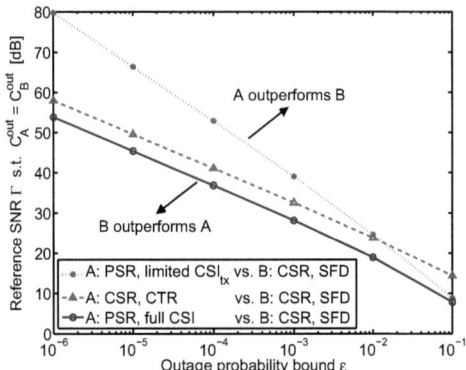

Figure 3.16: Region of operation: Reference SNR at intersection of the two capacity functions $C_A^{\text{out}} = C_B^{\text{out}}$. Numerical results shown vs. ε.

capacity at a given error rate constraint and an expected mean SNR. During operation, it also can be employed as a lookup table for an adaptation scheme selecting the "best" relaying protocol according to the measured SNR.

3.4.2 Effect of limited network connectivity

So far we assumed that all links of a given flow network can be established. In this model, deep fades cause short-time channel outages but on the average, all links and relays that a protocol can employ are available. This assumption is unrealistic in urban scenarios where only a limited number of relays may be available in the source's propagation domain or where obstacles shadow links for multiple MAC cycles. In this case only subsets of the above flow networks are available, limiting a cooperation protocol's performance. As PSR and CSR employ different flow networks, shadowed links degrade the performance of both protocol types differently.

To compare PSR and CSR on a fair basis, we count how often the above two-hop flow networks occur in large simulated networks. The resulting *occurrence probability* P^o is counted exclusively for each flow network in Figure 3.10 and 3.11 and it is assumed that a cooperation protocol can employ J different networks. Expressing these networks by their link-dependent terms $\Theta_1,\ldots,\Theta_J$ allows us to condition the outage capacity on the occurrence probabilities of those networks the cooperation protocol employs. Mathematically speaking, we define this *occurrence-conditioned outage capacity* as

$$C^{\text{out},o} := \sum_{j=1}^{J} P^o(\Theta_j) \cdot C^{\text{out}}(\Theta_j). \tag{3.24}$$

This connectivity-degraded capacity metric accounts for the fact that even a cooperation protocol with superior C^{out} reaches only poor performance if it relies on flow networks that almost never occur.

3.4. Performance analysis under practical constraints

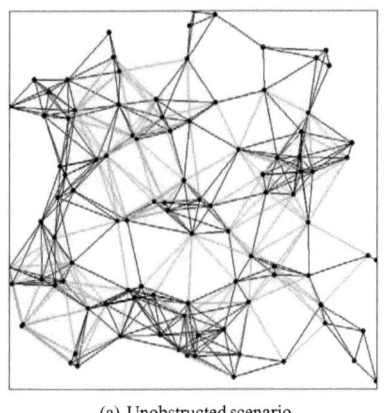
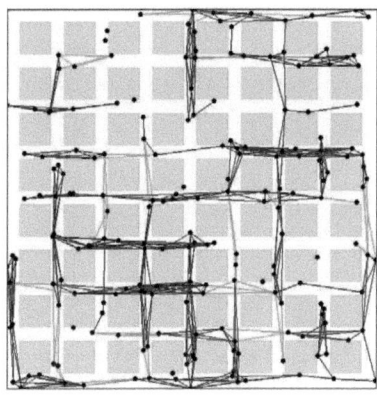

(a) Unobstructed scenario   (b) Manhattan grid scenario

Figure 3.17: Screen shot from the simulation software [VLK+08]: Example node placement for both studied propagation scenarios. The network graph is shown by black lines; counted diamonds are highlighted as subsets of this graph.

Counting triangles and diamonds

To obtain P^o, we count the occurrence of the Cooperative Triangle (CTR) and of the four diamond networks (Figure 3.10) by simulation. We use the following method, models, and parameters.

Propagation scenarios We study the unobstructed and the Manhattan grid scenario. An example for each of these basic propagation scenarios is shown in Figure 3.17. Without obstacles the signal propagates freely and is, at a large time-scale, only affected by path loss. The resulting network graph traverses the full playground as in Figure 3.17(a). Note that even in the unobstructed scenario deep fades still occur as a result of many small scatterers in the propagation environment. However, in this scenario no large obstacle shadows all signal paths of a link.

Placing such obstacles in a grid structure leads to the so-called *Manhattan grid* scenario. The result is the simple chess-board structure in Figure 3.17 where signals are assumed to propagate only in narrow streets. Thus, only on these corridors a network graph can be established. This classic model is often used to gain a first insight in urban environments with large buildings [CBD02]. The model captures mobility by randomly re-placing the nodes over many iterations.

Node placement and connectivity checks Figure 3.17 also shows an example for the node placement. Initially, all nodes are placed randomly on the playground. Without obstacles the node locations are uniformly distributed. In the Manhattan grid scenario the nodes are only placed on the streets. We ignore nodes on rooftops and assume that each node may operate as source, relay, or destination. Thus, this scenario represents a pure cooperative ad hoc network without a centralized infrastructure or dedicated node positions.

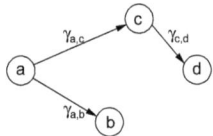

Figure 3.18: Base configuration and corresponding instantaneous SNR values.

Based on the initial node positions, the simulation establishes a network graph and then splits this graph into flow networks that we want to count. An example of these subgraphs is shown by the highlighted links in Figure 3.17. The simulation separates and counts the flow networks for all possible source/destination pairs. After all pairs are evaluated, the nodes are randomly re-placed. This process is repeated until the confidence intervals of P^o reach a specified size.

To count the flow networks for each source/destination pair the simulation has to perform a large number of connectivity checks. We limit the complexity of these checks by using two thresholds. If a signal's SNR falls below the so-called *decoding threshold* th_D it is assumed to be not correctly decoded anymore. If the SNR falls below the *sensing threshold* th_S it is assumed to be not coherently detected anymore. Using threshold th_S we model a building as an *ideal absorber*, i.e., $\gamma_{a,b} \ll \text{th}_S$ if a building lies on the shortest path between a transmitter a and a receiver b. Further propagation effects, e.g., scattering or reflection, are ignored. This model simplifies the connectivity check to only determining whether the line segment representing the shortest path intersects with any line segment corresponding to a building wall.

Normalization and connectivity conditions To make the occurrence probability independent on the playground size we obtain P^o as follows. First, we count all triangle and diamond networks along the two-hop path $a \to c \to d$. Second, the occurrence of a so-called *base configuration* is counted. This base configuration can constitute any of the counted flow networks and is shown in Figure 3.18. Nodes form this base configuration if (1) data can be transferred via path $a \to c \to d$, i.e., $(\gamma_{a,c} \geq \text{th}_D) \wedge \gamma_{c,d} \geq \text{th}_D$ and if (2) the potential relay node b successfully decodes a's data, i.e., $\gamma_{a,b} \geq \text{th}_D$.

Based on the occurrence of this base configuration, finally, P^o of an arbitrary flow network Θ_j is calculated by

$$P^o(\Theta_j) := \frac{\text{Number of found } \Theta_j}{\text{Number of found base configurations}}.$$

Since the base configuration is included in the CTR and every diamond but cannot *always* be extended to a triangle or diamond graph, this normalization assures $P^o \leq 1$ and that P^o does not increase with the playground size.

The additional conditions that complement a base configuration to a diamond are summarized in Table 3.4. In place of $(<;\geq)$ either the operator $<$ or $\geq$ is used as defined in the table. Let us illustrate these conditions for the CTR which simplifies a diamond due to $b := c$. To extend Figure 3.18 to the CTR, we require $\gamma_{a,d} \geq \text{th}_S$, i.e., the destination must be able to detect the source signal. Further, the condition

Table 3.4: Connectivity conditions for counting the occurrence of flow networks.

Comparison	CTR	WSD	WFD	SSD	SFD
$\gamma_{a,c}$ $(<;\geq)$ th_D		$\geq$		$\geq$	
$\gamma_{a,d}$ $(<;\geq)$ th_S	$\geq$	$<$	$<$	$\geq$	$\geq$
$\gamma_{b,c}$ $(<;\geq)$ th_S		$<$	$\geq$	$<$	$\geq$
$\gamma_{a,d} + \gamma_{c,d}$ $(<;\geq)$ th_D	$\geq$				
$\gamma_{a,c} + \gamma_{b,c}$ $(<;\geq)$ th_D			$\geq$		$\geq$
$\gamma_{b,d} + \gamma_{c,d}$ $(<;\geq)$ th_D		$\geq$	$\geq$	$<$	$<$
$\gamma_{a,d} + \gamma_{b,d} + \gamma_{c,d}$ $(<;\geq)$ th_D				$\geq$	$\geq$

$\gamma_{a,d} + \gamma_{c,d} \geq th_D$ must hold for a correct end-to-end transmission to d (Table 3.4) where the SNR sum accounts for MRC (Section 2.2.3). If both conditions and the conditions for the base configurations hold, a CTR is counted. Note that a CTR may be included in a diamond but the four diamonds are mutually exclusive (Figure 3.10).

Parameters The size of the quadratic playground is $1000\,\text{m}^2$ in both scenarios. For Manhattan grid each square obstacle is of size $78\,\text{m}^2$ and streets between these obstacles are 20 m wide (Figure 3.17(b)). This playground size sufficed for statistical significant results without effects at the playground margins. We vary the number of nodes to study P^o for various node densities, i.e., the mean number of neighbors in the propagation domain of the sender.

To account for path loss, we use the same model and parameters as in the previous studies of this chapter (Section 3.3.1). Rayleigh fading averages out over time and is, thus, not modeled. For symmetry, we assume that all nodes transmit at the same power. The SNR thresholds are $th_S = 4.5$ dB and $th_D = 6$ dB according to a typical IEEE 802.11a/g WLAN transceiver specification [Ath07]. Here, the chosen th_D value corresponds to a transmission rate of 6 Mbits/s at 20 MHz signal bandwidth.

Discussion

Figure 3.19 shows the occurrence rate P^o of the studied flow networks in the unobstructed and Manhattan grid scenario.

The figures show the effect of a varying mean SNR on P^o for a limited number of nodes (i.e., fixed network density). For both scenarios, we observe that P^o exponentially increases with the SNR until it saturates. On the other hand, the occurrence probability of all other networks decreases for higher SNR. This can be explained by considering the limit $\Gamma \to \infty$. In the unobstructed scenario (Figure 3.19(a)), any node can hear any other node at such high SNR. Since all nodes are fully connected, $P^o_{\text{SFD}} \to 1$ and the P^o of all sparser networks approaches zero. Naturally, this is different in the Manhattan grid scenario (Figure 3.19(b)). Here, even at asymptotic high SNR paths will be still obstructed and full connection

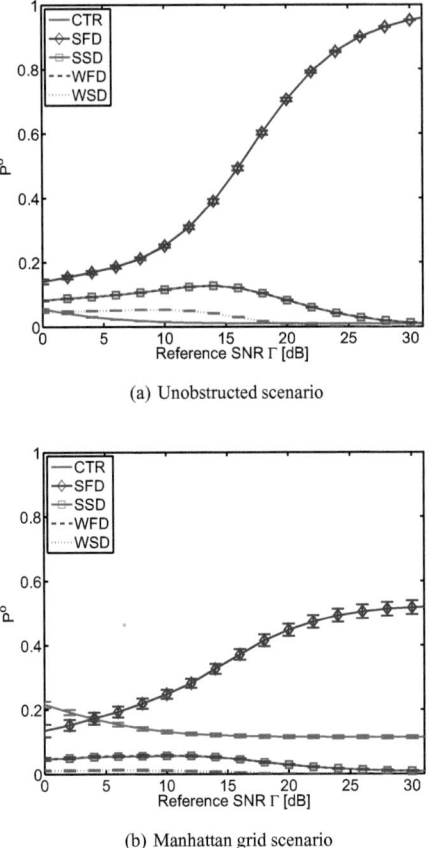

(a) Unobstructed scenario

(b) Manhattan grid scenario

Figure 3.19: Occurrence probability P^o of studied flow networks vs. reference SNR. Simulation results for 100 nodes in the unobstructed and Manhattan grid scenario. The results for the WFD and SSD are equal.

is impossible. Consequently, at high SNR only $P^o_{\text{SFD}} < 1$ is reached which makes the results in Figure 3.19(b) a "damped" variant of Figure 3.19(a).

Summing up, at high SNR, the SFD is 97% more likely than the CTR in an unobstructed scenario (due to an absolute difference of two orders of magnitude), and only 52% more likely in a Manhattan scenario.

3.4.3 Occurrence-conditioned outage capacity

We now summarize our above results on the outage capacity and occurrence probability for the most interesting cases. To this end, we degrade the ideal outage capacity C^{out} of PSR and of CSR by the occurrence probability P^o of all flow networks that a protocol can use (3.24). The resulting occurrence-conditioned outage capacity $C^{\text{out},o}$ takes into account that even a capacity-maximizing protocol is not practical if it relies on flow networks which almost never occur. We further degrade the outage capacity of PSR as in (3.23) to account for limited CSI feedback. We compare PSR and CSR for the two relay case and study all four node flow networks that PSR and CSR can use (cp. Figure 3.10 and 3.11).

Figure 3.20 includes plots for two levels of ε and two propagation scenarios. Each figure shows C^{out} as a solid line and the corresponding $C^{\text{out},o}$ as a dashed line. First, we compare the results for the unobstructed scenario to the corresponding Manhattan grid case at the same ε, i.e., Figure 3.20(a) vs. 3.20(c) and Figure 3.20(b) vs. 3.20(d). This shows clearly that without obstruction all relaying protocols achieve higher $C^{\text{out},o}$ than in Manhattan grid scenarios. Naturally, without obstacles the connectivity increases with the SNR which, consequently, increases $C^{\text{out},o}$. This is not the case in the Manhattan grid where links are permanently shadowed.

Second, we compare different values of ε in the same propagation scenario, i.e., Figure 3.20(a) vs. 3.20(b) and Figure 3.20(c) vs. 3.20(b). In both scenarios ε has the same effect. At high ε, PSR reaches higher $C^{\text{out},o}$ than CSR. At low ε and medium or low SNR this situation reverses. Here, PSR suffers from the low outage capacity of the feedback channel and is outperformed by CSR. This is even the case if the SFD cannot be always established, e.g., in a Manhattan scenario.

Interestingly, in Figure 3.20(b), the outage capacity of PSR only slightly degrades for limited connectivity. Unlike CSR, PSR reaches its largest outage capacity in multiple flow networks making it less vulnerable to the occurrence of a particular flow network. This benefit of PSR is strongest at low ε and without obstacles. In these cases, the outage capacity of PSR suffers less from the occurrence condition than the capacity of CSR.

3.5 Summary of contributions and future work

Starting with an overview of cooperation diversity techniques, we discussed two types of cooperative relaying protocols: Selection relaying with network path allocation (PSR) and selection relaying with combining (CSR).

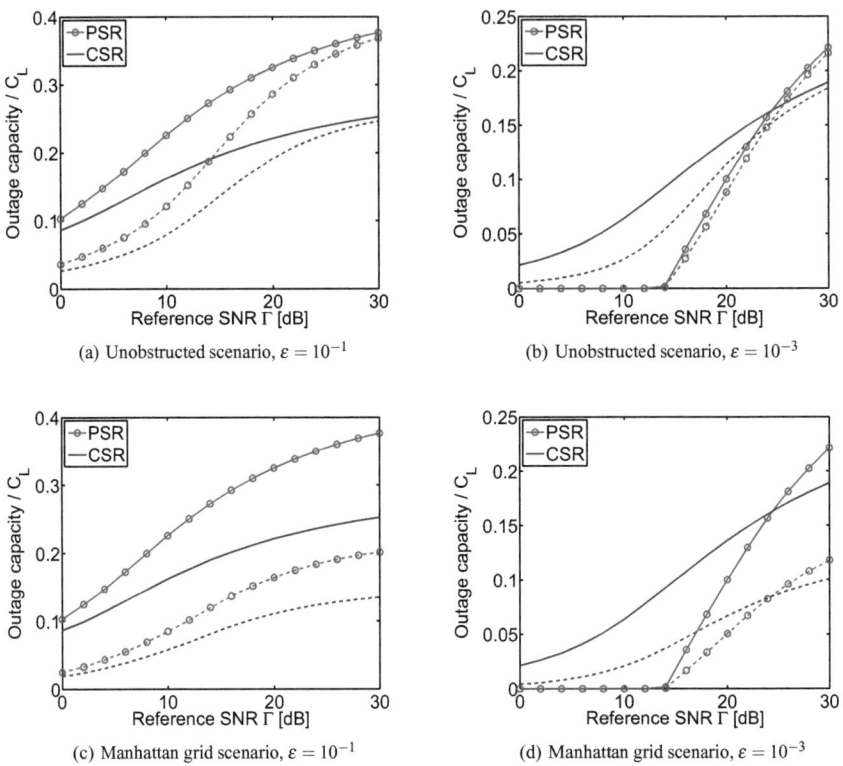

Figure 3.20: Comparing the *ideal C^{out} (solid lines)* to *occurrence-conditioned outage capacity $C^{\text{out},o}$ (dashed lines)* for unobstructed and Manhattan-grid scenario and two levels of ε. Outage capacities C^{out} and $C^{\text{out},o}$ shown as a fraction of AWGN capacity C_L vs. reference SNR Γ.

Contributions

Unified performance analysis For both protocol types, we derived the diversity order and the outage probability in a unified manner using cut set analysis. By extending this method, two approximations for the outage capacity were derived; both matching well with simulation results at medium and high SNR.

The analytical performance results are useful for general cooperative networks with any number of relays. The outage capacity approximation clearly shows how (1) the error rate constraint and (2) the employed links degrade the capacity of an ideal multi-antenna system. In effect, this analytic framework captures the required robustness (typically imposed by traffic demands) and how efficiently a cooperative relaying protocol can use the available links under idealistic assumptions on Channel State Information (CSI) and network connectivity.

Degraded performance: Limited channel knowledge Without full CSI the achievable outage probability and outage capacity of PSR protocols degrade. Accounting for the fact that in many practical fading scenarios transmitter CSI (CSI_{tx}) has to be obtained via wireless feedback channels, we provide the outage capacity of PSR degraded by feedback transmission errors and overhead. This allows a fair comparison to CSR which only employs CSI at the receivers but not at the transmitters. With CSI feedback, the outage capacity of the feedback channel limits the end-to-end outage capacity of PSR if a low error rate is required. Here, PSR performs poorly and CSR succeeds. This situation reverses under a relaxed error rate constraint and at high SNR. Here, feedback errors have only a slight effect and PSR reaches higher outage capacity than CSR.

Degraded performance: Limited network connectivity Furthermore, we condition the outage capacity of PSR and CSR protocols on the probability that the flow networks that a protocol employs actually occur. This accounts for the fact that, in practice, even a cooperation protocol with superior outage capacity performs poorly if it relies on a network graph which can be established only rarely (e.g., due to shadowed links or missing relays). Conditioning the outage capacity on the occurrence probability shows a stronger degradation for CSR than for PSR protocols. CSR relies on densely connected network graphs to reach high capacity while PSR reaches its full performance in various sparser flow networks. The degradation further highly depends on the propagation scenario. A substantial degradation is shown in a Manhattan grid. Naturally, the degradation is lower without large obstacles but still significant at low and medium SNR when relays cannot be reliably reached by the initial broadcast.

Application With these results, a protocol engineer can now choose whether CSR or PSR protocols are best suited in a specific scenario. Main factors are SNR, the error rate constraint, and the network connectivity. Put briefly, CSR would be chosen at low SNR or if a low error rate is required. At high SNR and if a high error rate is acceptable, e.g., a PER of 10% as in IEEE 802.11 WLANs [IEE99], PSR is a better choice.

We illustrated the above analytic and simulation-based framework only for four nodes, two propagation environments, and for the basic CSR and PSR variant. Nonetheless, the presented methods are general and can serve as a useful tool to assess the performance of various CSR and PSR protocols in more complex scenarios.

Future work

Join CSR and PSR – Adapting n So far our analysis and most literature focused on three extreme approaches which can be separated by the number n of forwarding relays per hop:

- $n = 0$: No relay forwards, i.e., direct transmission
- $n = 1$: From N available relays per hop, only a single relay forwards, i.e., a PSR protocol with path allocation but no combining
- $n = N$: All N available relays forward per hop, i.e., a CSR protocol with combining but no path allocation

Our analysis shows that each of these approaches performs best under different SNR, error rate, CSI, and connectivity constraints. Future protocols may join these approaches by optimizing $n \in [0, N]$ to the current scenario conditions. An early system concept joining PSR and CSR was analyzed recently [YK08]. It was shown that full diversity can be reached for a single hop but neither a practical single-hop protocol nor optimizing n for multiple hops was studied so far. Developing such protocols that adapt n may be an interesting field of future research.

Join CSR and PSR – Cooperative feedback Furthermore, the above results show that the applicability of PSR protocols is seriously limited by their CSI_{tx} demands. Especially, if the source or each relay obtains CSI_{tx} individually from a single broadcast channel, feedback errors significantly decrease PSR's outage capacity. It seems promising to cope with feedback errors by employing the CSR approach only for feedback and control packets (while PSR may be still employed for data). We will develop such *cooperative feedback* schemes for specific networks in Section 5.2 and in Chapter 6 of this work. Nevertheless, general analyses of the interaction between the feedback scheme and the capacity of the feed-forward channel are rarely found in current literature and are considered as a cornerstone for developing future networks [LHL+08].

Chapter 4

Selection relaying with partial forwarding

So far, we analyzed selection relaying protocols for block fading channels. By assuming quasi-static fading on a per-packet level, we implied that the relay can perfectly follow the channel's variation by making only a single forwarding decision per packet. This quasi-static fading model with perfect adaptation frequency is the leading assumption in theoretical studies on cooperative relaying protocols [LWT04, KGG05, BSW07] and suits well if the channel varies slowly compared to the packet time. However, when the coherence time tends towards the packet time, a deep fade may only *partially* affect a packet. This separates a packet into erroneous and correct parts. Conventional selection relaying protocols lose those correct parts by dropping the complete packet and, consequently, reduce their performance. To solve this problem of packet-wise selection relaying, we propose to detect and forward these correct parts. We call this approach *Partial Forwarding (PF)*, describe it in Section 4.1 and demonstrate its theoretical gains in Section 4.2. These substantial gains motivate the design of a practical PF system (Section 4.3 and Section 4.4) which comes at feasible complexity and negligible signaling overhead. Simulation results show that this system reaches a superior performance that is close to the theoretical ideal case (Section 4.5).

4.1 Partial forwarding

Let us first focus on the channel assumptions and problem leading to the Partial Forwarding (PF) approach. When the channel coherence time T_c is not significantly larger than the packet time T_p, block fading with a single channel coefficient h per T_p (Figure 4.1(a)) is not an appropriate model anymore [SA04, Section 2.1]. Instead, it becomes necessary to model the channel gain as an autocorrelated process using multiple channel coefficients per packet (Section 2.1.2).

The resulting problem for conventional selection relaying is illustrated in Figure 4.1(b). With multiple channel coefficients per packet, a deep fade may occur even during a short part of the packet time. The resulting burst errors separate a packet into erroneous and correct parts. By dropping the complete packet, a packet-wise forwarding decision discards even these correct parts. Thereby, such conventional relaying unnecessarily reduces the number of combined symbols at the destination which, finally, degrades the

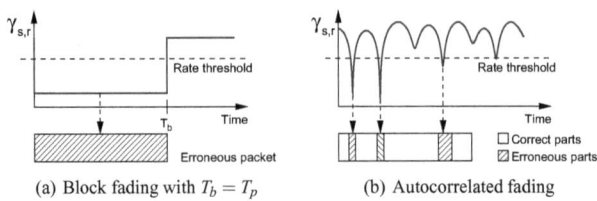

(a) Block fading with $T_b = T_p$ (b) Autocorrelated fading

Figure 4.1: Example instantaneous SNR $\gamma_{s,r}$ and resulting errors with the block and autocorrelated fading model from Section 2.1.2.

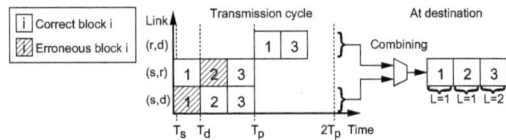

Figure 4.2: PF approach: Transmission cycle, relevant time scales, and resulting packet and diversity order L at destination.

end-to-end Bit Error Rate (BER_{e2e}) between source s and destination d (Section 4.2).

Basic approach This problem of conventional selection relaying protocols is solved by detecting and forwarding the correct parts even if errors occur in the packet. Figure 4.2 illustrates this basic approach of PF. In this example, we focus on the SDF protocol (Section 3.2.2) and assume that each packet is separated into three *decision blocks*. The duration of each decision block T_d is a fraction of the packet time T_p and a multiple of the symbol time T_s. As illustrated, two packets are received from SDF's initial broadcast. The destination d receives a packet from link (s,d) where a deep fade during T_p causes an error in block 1. The relay r receives a packet from (s,r) where block 2 is in error. A conventional SDF relay would now drop this complete packet leaving only an incomplete packet (correct block 2 and 3) at the destination. As illustrated, a PF relay identifies the erroneous block 2 and still forwards the correct blocks 1 and 3 to d. This makes it likely that d can correctly decode the complete packet based on one variant of block 1 and 2 and on two combined variants of block 3.

Region of operation As described in Section 2.1.2, at a higher Doppler frequency f_d the channel coefficients decorrelate in time. Hence, for increasing Doppler frequency it becomes more likely that deep fades affect only small parts of a packet and that gains from PF can be expected. Using the coherence time T_c (2.9) as a rough estimate for the ACF, we can illustrate when the duration of a fade becomes smaller than the packet time in Figure 4.3. The shown f_d region $[8, 350]$ Hz corresponds to a velocity of $v \in [1, 44]$ m/s when the carrier frequency is $f_c = 2.4$ GHz and to $v \in [0.5, 20]$ m/s at $f_c = 5.2$ GHz. We choose a packet time of $T_p = 2$ ms which is needed when a IEEE 802.11a/g[1] system transmits packets

---
[1] We use this shorthand as both IEEE 802.11a and IEEE 802.11g employ the same baseband functions in their OFDM PHY. Using the Direct Sequence Spread Spectrum (DSSS) PHY in IEEE 802.11g is not considered in this work.

4.1. Partial forwarding

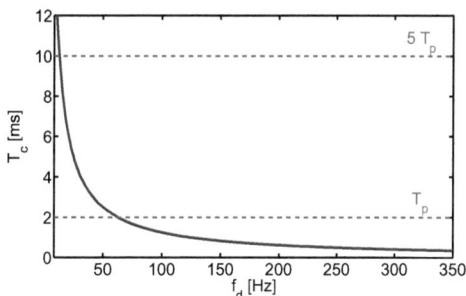

Figure 4.3: Coherence time T_c vs. Doppler frequency f_d for a J_0 ACF. The horizontal lines are multiples of the packet time $T_p = 2\,\text{ms}$.

with 1500 Byte payload at 6 Mbits/s PHY rate. The horizontal lines mark multiples of this packet time.

There are two reasons to consider multiples of T_p. First, many empirical coherence time definitions tend to overestimate T_c (Section 2.1.3). Second, due to the very slow descent of the J_0 ACF a significant autocorrelation is still found for lag times larger than T_c (cp. Figure 2.4). Consequently, engineers often expect fades inside packets even if the coherence time is below multiples of T_p [TV05, Section 5.4.5], e.g, $T_c < 10 T_p$. To account for this fact, we use $5T_p$ as a pessimistic prediction of PF's region of operation.

As illustrated, the coherence time falls below T_p for $f_d \geq 60\,\text{Hz}$ corresponding to $v \geq 7.5\,\text{m/s}$ at $f_c = 2.4\,\text{GHz}$ or to $v \geq 3.5\,\text{m/s}$ at $f_c = 5.2\,\text{GHz}$. Naturally, $T_c < 5T_p$ is reached earlier at $f_d \geq 13\,\text{Hz}$, matching to a velocity of $v \geq 1.6\,\text{m/s}$ at $f_c = 2.4\,\text{GHz}$ or of $v \geq 0.75\,\text{m/s}$ at $f_c = 5.2\,\text{GHz}$. Note that such speeds are common in the propagation environment of cellular, vehicular, and even some Wireless Local Area Networks (WLANs). Here, quasi-static fading per packet cannot be assumed and gains from PF can be expected.

Related approaches Partial Forwarding is strongly related to temporal diversity schemes, particularly to Hybrid Automatic Repeat Request (HARQ) [CC84] and to rateless erasure codes, e.g., Luby's Tornado codes [Lub02] or Raptor codes [Sho06]. Like PF, these schemes retransmit blocks smaller than a packet but there are two major differences. The first difference is obvious. While with HARQ and rateless codes a single source s retransmits its own information, with relaying a different node r forwards the information of s. Due to this spatially separated relay, both cases differ by the employed links and type of diversity. While HARQ and rateless codes gain only from temporal diversity, cooperative relaying can exploit spatial diversity as well [ZV05]. PF is one approach to leverage both types of diversity.

The second major difference is feedback. Unlike HARQ, PF and rateless codes do not demand Channel State Information (CSI) feedback. While each ACK of HARQ can be seen as a feedback of transmitter CSI (CSI_{tx}), a PF relay bases its forwarding decision only on local CSI_{rx}. We compared CSI_{rx} and CSI_{tx}-based relaying in Chapter 3 and showed in Section 3.4.1 that either of these approaches succeeds in a different region of operation. Like PF, rateless codes do not require CSI feedback. Instead, redundancy for a single message[2] is transmitted until the decoder signals the source to stop. Even such occasional feedback is not required if PF is used with SDF protocols where all communication is unidirectional.

System components   PF adds several functions to conventional selection relaying systems. At the relay, the erroneous blocks have to be identified. This requires a *metric* to assess the error probability even for small blocks. To design such a metric, we follow the *soft output decoding* approach that is widely used in iterative decoders [HWR07]. We will describe and compare our metric to other soft output decoders in Section 4.4. Based on this metric, the relay uses a threshold to decide which block to forward. Searching optimal and suboptimal (but practical) thresholds is discussed in Section 4.4.1. Further, PF extends the cooperation protocol. Combining PF with SDF's packet-wise forwarding decision is described in Section 4.4.2 and efficiently signaling the dropped blocks to the destination is covered in Section 4.4.3.

4.2   Forwarding decision frequency

Before designing practical schemes for Partial Forwarding (PF), it is useful to assess the potential gains of this approach. For a first analytic insight, we ignore autocorrelation but use a generalized block fading model where deep fades may affect only parts of a packet (autocorrelated fading is then studied in Section 4.5). Furthermore, we ignore that the practical accuracy of the forwarding decision is limited in the time and in the value domain. Instead, we assume that the relay perfectly knows the CSI_{rx} value and can decide arbitrarily often. These idealistic assumptions allow to derive the minimum BER_{e2e} for PF. This performance bound and the still high BER_{e2e} gains at less frequent forwarding decisions clearly show that designing a practical PF system is promising.

4.2.1   Block lengths and decision frequency

As we perform our analysis at symbol level, we define all block lengths as multiples of modulation symbols. Simply multiplying this length with the symbol time T_s results in the block durations from Figure 4.2. We define each packet to be L_p symbols long. The length of a *decision block*, i.e., the number of symbols between two relay decisions, is denoted by L_d. For block fading channels, the number of symbols per fading block is indicated by L_b.

With these block lengths, we define the *forwarding decision frequency* D of the relay as

$$D := \frac{L_p}{L_d} \left[\frac{\text{forwarding decisions}}{\text{packet}} \right] \qquad (4.1)$$

which is equivalent to the number of decision blocks per packet. With PF, $D > 1$ and packet-wise SDF is expressed by $D = 1$. Even with a high D, the actual accuracy of the forwarding decision depends on channel coherence time T_c. Using this rough estimate of temporal stability, we can state that PF aims

---

[2]To simplify terminology we denote the FEC-uncoded information vector by *message*.

4.2. Forwarding decision frequency

for at least one decision per coherence time. This is reached when the decision block time T_d is equal or shorter than T_c, i.e., $T_c/T_d \geq 1$.

Using this T_c/T_d ratio we can define the decision frequency more precisely for block fading channels. As described in Section 2.1.2, with such channels the fading block time T_b is equivalent to T_c, i.e., $T_b = L_b \cdot T_s = T_c$. Choosing $T_p > T_b$ leads to multiple fading blocks per packet. The number of these blocks is $K_b = T_p/T_b = L_p/L_b$ and also gives the number of fading states per packet. With this explicit value for K_b, we can analyze the performance loss when the relay decides less frequently than the channel varies, i.e., $D < K_b$. We can denote this relationship between D and K_b by the *number of decision blocks per fading block* D_b

$$D_b := \frac{D}{K_b} = \frac{L_b}{L_d} \left[\frac{\text{forwarding decisions}}{\text{fading block}} \right]. \qquad (4.2)$$

With $K_b > 1$, packet-wise SDF reaches only $D_b < 1$ and PF aims to select D such that $D_b \geq 1$.

4.2.2 Analysis for block fading channels

We analyze the end-to-end Bit Error Rate (BER$_{e2e}$) of PF in two steps. First, we derive the average number of symbols forwarded by the relay. From this number and standard BER equations we, then, derive the BER$_{e2e}$.

System assumptions and notation

For an arbitrary link (i,j) the instantaneous SNR per modulation symbol is denoted by $\gamma_{i,j}$. We use the i.i.d. Rayleigh block fading model from Section 2.1.2 where the random variable $\gamma_{i,j}$ follows the exponential PDF $p_\gamma(\gamma_{i,j})$ in (2.6). The Symbol Error Rate (SER) for the AWGN channel is

$$P^s_{\text{AWGN}}(\gamma_{i,j}) = \alpha_M \text{erfc}\left(\sqrt{\beta_M \gamma_{i,j}}\right) \qquad (4.3)$$

with the complementary error function erfc$(\cdot)$ and modulation-dependent parameters α_M, β_M. This general expression for the SER holds for Quadrature Amplitude Modulation (QAM) as well as for Binary Phase Shift Keying (BPSK) modulation [Pro00, Section 5.2]. Taking the mean with respect to the exponentially distributed random variable $\gamma_{i,j}$ yields

$$\begin{aligned} P^s_{\text{Ray}}(\bar{\gamma}_{i,j}) &= \mathbb{E}\{P^s_{\text{AWGN}}(\gamma_{i,j})\} = \int_0^\infty P^s_{\text{AWGN}}(\gamma_{i,j}) p_\gamma(\gamma_{i,j}) \mathrm{d}\gamma_{i,j} \qquad (4.4) \\ &= \int_0^\infty \alpha_M \text{erfc}\left(\sqrt{\beta_M \gamma_{i,j}}\right) \frac{1}{\bar{\gamma}_{i,j}} \exp\left(-\frac{\gamma_{i,j}}{\bar{\gamma}_{i,j}}\right) \mathrm{d}\gamma_{i,j} \end{aligned}$$

as the SER for a single Rayleigh faded link with mean SNR $\bar{\gamma}_{i,j}$. We will employ a closed-form solution of (4.4) for a specific modulation in Appendix A.

Only a single relay r is used in the CTR network (Figure 3.1(b)). PF extends a conventional SDF relay by a block-wise forwarding decision with D_b decisions per fading block. To isolate the effect of

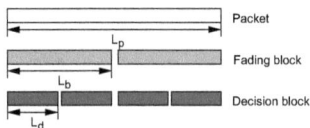

Figure 4.4: Example of the block lengths for Case 1 where $L_d \leq L_b$.

the decision frequency, we assume that the relay bases its decision on ideal CSI$_{\text{rx}}$ and, thus, can perfectly detect errors. To this end, the relay perfectly knows $\gamma_{s,r}$ (i.e., perfect decision in the value domain) but may decide not frequently "enough" (i.e., imperfect decision in the time domain) to follow the fading channel.

Case 1: Decide $D_b \geq 1$ times per fading block

First, we analyze the case illustrated in Figure 4.4. Here, a decision block is shorter than a fading block or has equal length, i.e., $L_d \leq L_b \Leftrightarrow D_b \geq 1$. In this case, PF decides at least once per fading block and, thus, can detect each state change of the block fading channel. The number of fading blocks per packet is L_p/L_b and is assumed to be integer to assure i.i.d. blocks.

With at least one forwarding decision per fading block, the average number of symbols forwarded per packet is equal to

$$N_{p,\text{c}1} = L_p \mathbb{P}\{\text{An arbitrary } \textit{fading} \text{ block is forwarded}\}$$
$$= L_p(1 - \mathbb{P}\{\text{An arbitrary } \textit{fading} \text{ block is not forwarded}\}).$$

Assuming perfect decision in the value domain, the relay does not forward a *fading* block, if at least a single symbol in this fading block is in error. Thus,

$$N_{p,\text{c}1} = L_p(1 - P^s_{\text{Ray}}(\bar{\gamma}_{s,r})) \tag{4.5}$$

where $P^s_{\text{Ray}}(\bar{\gamma}_{s,r})$ denotes the SER for the Rayleigh-faded link (s,r) according to (4.4) with mean SNR $\bar{\gamma}_{s,r}$. The fraction of symbols that are *not* forwarded by the relay is then

$$F_{\text{drop,c}1} = 1 - \frac{N_{p,\text{c}1}}{L_p} = P^s_{\text{Ray}}(\bar{\gamma}_{s,r}) \tag{4.6}$$

and, hence, equivalent to the SER of link (s,r).

Case 2: Decide $D_b < 1$ times per fading block

Second, we analyze the case illustrated in Figure 4.5. Here, a decision block is longer than a fading block, i.e., $L_d > L_b \Leftrightarrow D_b < 1$. This case reflects conventional SDF with multiple fading blocks per packet (Figure 4.5(a)) as well as PF with multiple fading blocks per decision block (Figure 4.5(b)). In either of

4.2. Forwarding decision frequency

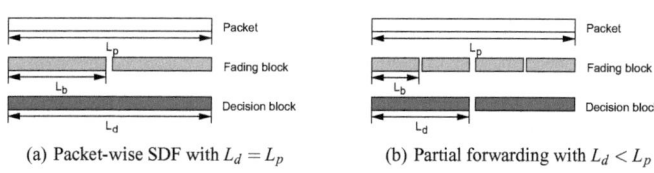

Figure 4.5: Two examples of the block lengths for Case 2 where $L_d > L_b$.

these cases the relay decides less frequently than fading occurs and cannot detect and adapt to each state change of the fading channel. The number of fading blocks per decision block is $1/D_b = L_d/L_b > 1$ and the number of decision blocks per packet is $D = L_p/L_d$. Similar to Case 1, we assume D and $1/D_b$ to be integer to assure i.i.d. blocks.

Deciding once per *decision* block, the relay forwards

$$N_{p,c2} = L_p \mathbb{P}\{\text{An arbitrary } decision \text{ block is forwarded}\}$$

symbols on average. Unlike in Case 1, in this case erroneous *fading* blocks may occur within an arbitrary decision block. The relay cannot locate these erroneous fading blocks and, hence, forwards an arbitrary *decision* block only if all $1/D_b$ fading blocks within this decision block are error free. Put formally,

$$N_{p,c2} = L_p \mathbb{P}\{\text{All } 1/D_b \text{ fading blocks within an arbitrary decision block are error free}\}.$$

and, since the fading blocks are i.i.d.,

$$N_{p,c2} = L_p \mathbb{P}\{\text{An arbitrary } fading \text{ block is error free}\}^{1/D_b}.$$

As for deriving (4.5), we use that an arbitrary *fading* block is in error, if at least a single symbol in this fading block is in error. Thus,

$$N_{p,c2} = L_p (1 - P^s_{\text{Ray}}(\bar{\gamma}_{s,r}))^{1/D_b}. \tag{4.7}$$

where, again, the SER $P^s_{\text{Ray}}(\bar{\gamma}_{s,r})$ is given in (4.4). The fraction of symbols that are *not* forwarded by the relay is then

$$F_{\text{drop},c2} = 1 - \frac{N_{p,c2}}{L_p} = 1 - (1 - P^s_{\text{Ray}}(\bar{\gamma}_{s,r}))^{1/D_b} \tag{4.8}$$

which differs from $F_{\text{drop},c1}$ by the exponent $1/D_b$. Note that at $D_b = 1$ the results for Case 2 are equal to Case 1, i.e., $N_{p,c1} = N_{p,c2}$ and $F_{\text{drop},c1} = F_{\text{drop},c2}$. This allows to express $D_b \leq 1$ only by the results of Case 2 which summarizes the practical relevant cases where the relay decides not more frequently than fading occurs.

End-to-end Bit Error Rate

Using the above results for F_{drop}, the BER_{e2e} for both cases is given by

$$\text{BER}_{\text{e2e}} = F_{\text{drop}} \text{BER}_{s,d} + (1 - F_{\text{drop}})\text{BER}_{\text{mrc}}. \tag{4.9}$$

Here, $\text{BER}_{s,d}$ is the BER of the direct link (s,d) and BER_{mrc} stands for the BER after MRC was used to combine the symbols received from the source and the relay. Both terms are further elaborated below and in Appendix A. Note that F_{drop} is incorporated into (4.9) as a factor and, thus, affects the BER_{e2e} only by a coding gain but not in terms of diversity.

The rationale behind (4.9) is that the destination can only combine symbols and, thereby, reaches only BER_{mrc}, if the relay forwards. This is done with probability $1 - F_{\text{drop}}$. Otherwise, merely symbols from the direct link are received, resulting in $\text{BER}_{s,d}$.

4.2.3 Discussion

Analytic results From the analytic results for Case 1 we can draw the following conclusions. If the relay decides at least once per fading block, only the erroneous symbols are dropped. At $D_b = 1$, the decision is ideal in the time domain and (assuming ideal decision in the value domain) the number of forwarded symbols is maximized.

In Case 2, the relay decides less frequently than fading occurs. Inserting $D_b < 1$ into (4.7) shows that in this case the number of forwarded symbols is always lower than for Case 1, i.e., $N_{p,c2} < N_{p,c1}$. The more fading blocks occur per decision block, the fewer symbols are forwarded (cp. (4.2) and (4.7)). Equivalently, the shorter the decision block is with respect to the fading block, the more symbols are dropped.

Numerical results For a numerical illustration we focus on uncoded BPSK modulation, with MRC, and i.i.d. Rayleigh fading. For this relevant special case, closed-form expressions for direct and combined links are given in standard literature [Pro00, (14.4-15)]. By inserting these expressions into (4.4) and (4.9) we can easily derive the BER_{e2e} and F_{drop} of our ideal PF system in closed form. This derivation and the results are presented in Appendix A.

Furthermore, we assume a symmetric CTR with the same reference SNR Γ for all links. Since path loss is normalized to unity, i.e., $\Gamma_{a,b} = \Gamma_{a,d} = \Gamma_{b,d} = 1$, the mean SNR $\bar{\gamma}$ is equal for all links and equivalent to Γ (Section 2.1.1). For comparison, we include the BER_{e2e} of direct transmission. All three nodes operate under the total energy constraint (Section 2.3). We choose a packet length of $L_p = 8192$ symbols and study $K_b = 16$ fading blocks per packet. We vary the decision block length L_d to select a forwarding decision frequency D. With $D \in \{1,2\}$ we study Case 2 where the relay decides less frequently than fading occurs. Ideal decision is then studied with $D \in \{K_b, L_p\}$ decisions per packet.

Inserting the above values and a varying $\bar{\gamma}$ into (A.4) to (A.7) provides the results in Figure 4.6. Figure 4.6(a) shows the fraction of symbols not forwarded by the relay F_{drop} for both cases. This number is

4.2. Forwarding decision frequency

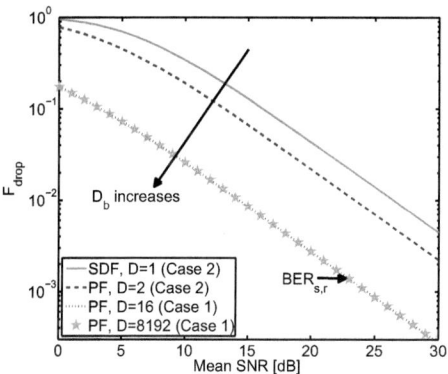

(a) Fraction of symbols not forwarded by the relay F_{drop}

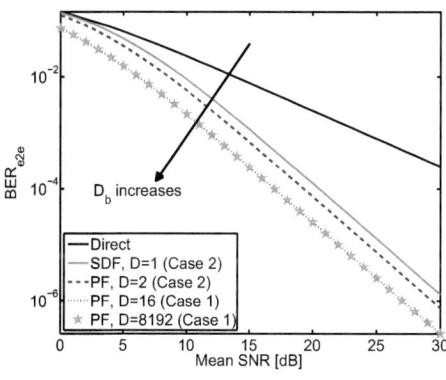

(b) End-to-end Bit Error Rate BER_{e2e}

Figure 4.6: Effect of forwarding decision frequency D on BER_{e2e} and F_{drop}: Shown vs. SNR for an i.i.d. Rayleigh block fading channel with $K_b = 16$ fading blocks/packet. The results for Case 1 are equal.

highest with conventional packet-wise SDF when only a single forwarding decision per packet is made, i.e., only $D_b = 1/16$ decisions per fading block. With $D = 2$, the relay decides once every eighth fading block. This decreases $F_{\text{drop,c2}}$ but is still far from the result of Case 1. This ideal case is reached at $D = 16$ where making one decision per fading block minimizes the number of dropped symbols. Since now F_{drop} is independent on D_b (4.6), further increasing the decision frequency does not improve F_{drop}. Note that $F_{\text{drop,c1}}$ is equal to the BER of link (s,r). This results from the fact that with uncoded BPSK and Case 1 each symbol error corresponds to a dropped bit. This illustrates once more that at $D_b \geq 1$, a PF relay drops only the erroneous bits.

The behavior of F_{drop} directly translates to the BER_{e2e} in Figure 4.6(b). For increasing decision frequency, the relay forwards a higher fraction of symbols which reduces the BER_{e2e} by an SNR-independent factor. This coding gain increases with D until the relay decides once per fading block ($D = 16$). At this decision frequency, the BER_{e2e} of PF reaches its theoretical minimum for the given fading block time and, once Case 1 is reached, no improvement is shown by further increasing the decision frequency. This is a consequence of the block fading model where each fading state can be detected as soon as $D_b = 1$ is reached, i.e., once the decision block time matches the (perfectly known) coherence time T_c. This is different if more-realistic autocorrelated fading is assumed where T_c becomes a poor estimator of the channel stability (Section 2.1.3). In this case, deep fades may occur even within T_c and, thus, multiple forwarding decisions per coherence time can still provide gains. We will demonstrate this in Section 4.5 and discuss in Section 4.3.4 that such high decision frequencies are realistic even with the constraints imposed by practical CSI measurement, coding, and signaling.

From these results, we can expect high BER_{e2e} gains for PF above conventional SDF when multiple fades per packet are likely. Therefore, it seems worth to design practical schemes for PF. Such schemes – namely, CSI measurement, protocol and signaling functions – are described next.

4.3 Forwarding decision metric

So far, we made the idealistic assumption that the relay perfectly knows the channel state even if a frequent forwarding decision is made. Designing a practical scheme to provide such frequent estimates at high accuracy is non-trivial. With conventional CSI_{rx} metrics – like SNR or CRC – more frequent estimation reduces the number of training symbols on which each estimate is based and, thereby, the estimation accuracy. Compensating for this lack of training information by extensive training would considerably decrease the data rate. After describing such shortcomings of conventional metrics in Section 4.3.1, we focus on a decoder-based metric called Minimum Path Difference (MPD) in Section 4.3.2. Similar to *soft output* decoders [BCJR74, HH89], MPD provides frequent CSI_{rx} estimates by observing the FEC decoding process. This metric requires no further training overhead, and, thus, allows frequent estimation without decreasing the data rate. We describe an MPD-extended Viterbi decoding algorithm [Vit67] which imposes significantly lower calculation complexity than other soft output decoders (Section 4.3.3) but accurately expresses the true BER by MPD (Section 4.3.4).

4.3.1 Related work and terminology

In current literature, a relay bases its forwarding decision either on CRC error detecting codes, soft output FEC decoders, or channel state measurements. Which of these methods can be employed depends on the used code.

In uncoded systems, the relay can use channel state measurements. In [HZF04], Herhold, Zimmermann, and Fettweis propose to use SNR as decision metric and to perform a threshold-based forwarding decision at the relay. This SNR-based approach provides a valuable theoretical framework to analyze the relay's local forwarding decision but cannot be directly applied to PF. Measuring SNR comes at the cost of training symbols which reduces the data rate. Therefore, many systems measure SNR only once per packet using a short training sequence in the packet's preamble [OP99, Chapter 12]. Moreover, as measured prior to decoding, SNR cannot accurately account for the coding gain in practical FEC decoders. With these limitations, SNR cannot accurately identify erroneous parts within the message and is, thus, not an ideal candidate for PF.

In many papers, the relay uses error detecting codes for its forwarding decision [SE04, LWT04, HSN06, LTN[+]07]. Typically, a single Cyclic Redundancy Check (CRC) is used per packet which does not rely on a potentially suboptimal threshold. Per packet, such CRC-based forwarding decision reliably prevents error propagation and the overhead due to the added Frame Check Sequences (FCS) is acceptable. However, this procedure becomes inefficient for short blocks [Wil04]. First, block-wise error detection requires one FEC codeword per block, thereby reducing the length of the codeword and FEC performance. Second, detecting burst errors requires a large FCS in many systems, e.g., 32 bit in IEEE 802.11 [OP99]. With small blocks such long FCS imposes high overhead. Consequently, CRC-based decision is inefficient for PF.

With FEC codes, the relay can estimate CSI_{rx} following the soft output approach. In addition to the decoded bit – the so-called *hard decision* – a soft output decoder returns the probability of a correct decoding decision [Pro00, Section 8.2.7]. This CSI_{rx} estimate is referred to as *soft output* or, more precisely, as *A Posteriori Probability (APP)*. Here, *a posteriori* denotes that the decoder has already used all available information for its decoding decision. To produce such soft output, two fundamental decoder designs are known in literature. Maximum A Posteriori (MAP) decoders [BCJR74, RVH95] calculate APP per decoded symbol while the Soft Output Viterbi Algorithm (SOVA) algorithm [HH89] provides APP per symbol *sequence*.

Soft output decoders are often used at an intermediate stage in iterative decoders (e.g., turbo decoders [HWR07]) and only few applications to cooperative relaying are known. Sneessens and Vandendorpe described relaying as an iterative decoding process where the relay forwards its soft output [SV05]. Protocols that followed this *soft Decode-and-Forward (DF)* approach either rely completely on soft information [BL07, DM09] or exploit soft channel side information to refine SDF's hard decision [RF09]. Soft DF is similar to the fundamental Compress-and-Forward (CF) protocol [CG79] but can profit from a coding gain at the relay. Like CF, a soft DF relay minimizes BER_{e2e} by delegating the hard decision to the destination where decoding can employ the CSI of all channels. On the other hand, CF and most soft DF approaches forward real-valued CSI for each received bit, whose overhead significantly decreases data rate.

In this section, we use a different approach than CF and soft DF. Instead of forwarding soft output, we use soft information only at the relay to improve the forwarding decision. Keeping the decoder's soft output local limits overhead and enables gains due to Partial Forwarding. Using soft output for this partial decision has two benefits above other CSI_{rx} metrics. First, soft output assesses the actual coding gain. Second, a decoder returns soft output frequently per packet and requires no more training information than the redundancy bits. Thus, even a high forwarding decision frequency does not reduce the data rate. A drawback of the soft output approach is the significant complexity of SOVA and MAP decoding algorithms [RVH95, Wu01].

To avoid an infeasible complexity increase at the relay, we use a simplified soft output metric called MPD. The calculation and complexity of this metric is described next.

4.3.2 Calculating Minimum Path Difference

The MPD metric estimates the BER by comparing the decoding decision to the received codeword. In essence, MPD expresses the distance between decoding decision and the received symbols. For a large distance (i.e., a large MPD value) a high BER is assumed. This metric is based on the idea that the larger the distance between decoding decision and the received symbols is, the more errors are corrected by the FEC decoder, and the lower the decoder certainty for each corrected bit. We now detail the calculation of MPD and provide a simple example.

MPD definition and example for hard decision Viterbi decoding

With the Viterbi Algorithm (VA), the decoding decision is made as soon as the *minimum-weight path* $V_{\min}$ through the decoding trellis is found [Pro00, Section 8.2.2]. Each edge of $V_{\min}$ is associated to coded and uncoded symbols. A standard Viterbi decoder returns the uncoded symbols during its traceback of $V_{\min}$, which results in the decoded message $X_{s,r}$.

Additionally, an MPD-extended Viterbi Algorithm (MPD VA) returns the distance between (1) the *coded* symbols along $V_{\min}$ and (2) the symbols in the received codeword $c_{s,r}$. During the traceback, this provides the MPD vector $\text{mpd}_{s,r}$. More formally, we can define the MPD value for the ith coded symbol as

$$\text{mpd}_{s,r}[i] = \text{dist}(c_{s,r}[i], \text{codesymbol}(\text{edge}[i])) \tag{4.10}$$

where edge[i] is the respective edge of $V_{\min}$ and the function codesymbol() returns the coded symbol at this edge.

The distance calculation in function dist() depends on the form of the symbols in $c_{s,r}$. With hard decision decoding, all symbols in $c_{s,r}$ are binary decision variables. In this case, dist() computes the Hamming distance and $\text{mpd}_{s,r}[i]$ represents the number of corrected errors for the ith symbol. Figure 4.7 illustrates this case where one integer MPD value is returned for each edge of $V_{\min}$. With soft decision

4.3. Forwarding decision metric

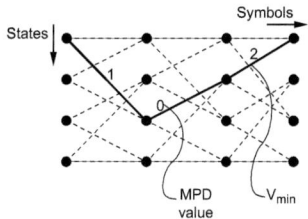

Figure 4.7: Example decoding trellis for hard-decision decoding of $u = 3$ symbols: Each edge of the surviving minimum-weight path $V_{\min}$ contains an MPD value. Finally the metric vector $\text{mpd}_{s,r} = [1,0,2]$.

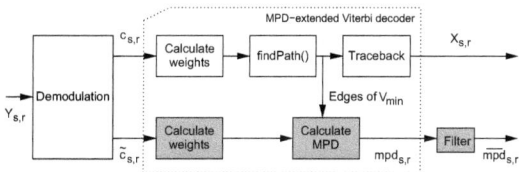

Figure 4.8: Basic functions of an MPD-extended Viterbi Algorithm (MPD VA). The shaded parts illustrate extensions to the standard VA.

decoding, the demodulator passes real-valued soft decision variables (aka *soft bits*) to the decoder. To rate each of these soft bits by a real-valued MPD index we extend the VA as follows.

MPD-extended Viterbi algorithm

We will now generalize the above example to an MPD-extended Viterbi Algorithm (MPD VA) which supports hard and soft decision decoding. Figure 4.8 summarizes the extensions to a standard Viterbi decoder. As shown, the demodulator maps the coherent modulation symbols in $Y_{s,r}$ to the two vectors $c_{s,r}$ and $\tilde{c}_{s,r}$. The codeword $c_{s,r}$ contains conventionally demodulated hard or soft bits and is used for standard Viterbi decoding of message $X_{s,r}$. Additionally, vector $\tilde{c}_{s,r}$ provides CSI for calculating MPD. An example of constructing $\tilde{c}_{s,r}$ for BPSK is described on Page 76. Based on $\tilde{c}_{s,r}$ and on the edges of the minimum-weight path $V_{\min}$, the MPD VA calculates the soft output vector $\text{mpd}_{s,r}$. This MPD vector contains one real-valued CSI_{rx} estimate per symbol and is, finally, smoothed by a statistical filter, e.g., a moving average, which returns $\overline{\text{mpd}}_{s,r}$.

The decoding process is described more formally in Algorithm 1. To focus on the extensions, the standard VA operation is abbreviated. In particular, we summarize the VA's path search by function findPath() in line 1, and omit standard functions like weight calculation and quantization. A detailed description of the full VA is provided in standard literature, e.g., [Pro00, Section 8.2.2].

The algorithm returns message $X_{s,r}$ that was encoded at rate $R_c = k/n$ with n coded bits per k (uncoded) *message bits*. In total, message $X_{s,r}$ consists of $u = l/k$ message symbols or l message bits. This message is decoded from codeword $c_{s,r}$, which consists of u code symbols or l/R_c *coded bits*. Based on these u symbols, standard Viterbi decoding is performed in three steps: First, the weights are cal-

---
Algorithm 1: MPD-extended Viterbi Algorithm (MPD VA).

Input: Codeword $c_{s,r}$ with u code symbols: $c_{s,r}[1], \ldots, c_{s,r}[u]$;
Codeword $\tilde{c}_{s,r}$ with u code symbols: $\tilde{c}_{s,r}[1], \ldots, \tilde{c}_{s,r}[u]$
Output: Message $X_{s,r}$ with u message symbols: $x_{s,r}[1], \ldots, x_{s,r}[u]$;
Metric values $\text{mpd}_{s,r}$ per code symbol: $\text{mpd}_{s,r}[1], \ldots, \text{mpd}_{s,r}[u]$

```
   // Search minimum-weight path V_min
1  edge[1,...,u] = findPath(c_{s,r});
   // Traceback over V_min
2  for i = u,...,1 do
3      x_{s,r}[i] = messagesymbol(edge[i]);
       // MPD calculation adds line 4
4      mpd_{s,r}[i] = dist(c̃_{s,r}[i], codesymbol(edge[i]));
5  end
6  return X_{s,r}, mpd_{s,r}
```
---

culated for each branch and state of the trellis (not shown in Algorithm 1). Second, the path $V_{\min}$ is searched which minimizes the accumulated weight (function findPath() in line 1). Third, for all u edges of this path, a traceback is performed (line 2–5) and one message symbol is returned per edge (function messagesymbol() in line 3). Finally, the decoded message $X_{s,r}$ is returned.

As discussed above, calculating $\text{mpd}_{s,r}$ can be integrated into the traceback of the VA. During this final step, the algorithm iterates over the complete path $V_{\min}$ and uses (4.10) to calculate MPD per code symbol (line 4). With hard decision decoding, function dist() is given by the Hamming distance. In this case $\tilde{c}_{s,r} = c_{s,r}$, i.e., no additional CSI vector $\tilde{c}_{s,r}$ is required. With soft decision decoding dist() uses the Euclidean distance as a standard function of many decoders. In particular, dist() calculates

$$\text{dist}(a,b) := ||a - b|| = \sqrt{\sum_{j=1}^{n}(a_j - b_j)^2} \qquad (4.11)$$

as the Euclidean distance in the n-dimensional coding space. Here, a_j stands for one of n soft bits in symbol a of the CSI vector $\tilde{c}_{s,r}$ and b_j corresponds to one of n soft bits in code symbol b from the trellis edge (as returned by function codesymbol() in line 4). In this case the demodulator has to pass $\tilde{c}_{s,r}$ with CSI to the decoder (cp. Figure 4.8).

Additional CSI with BPSK

The vector $\tilde{c}_{s,r}$ provides additional CSI in terms of carrier phase mismatches. Although we assume coherent detection, such synchronization errors are common in practical receivers where limited CSI_{rx} can inhibit perfect compensation of complex fading and noise [SA04, Section 3.2].

As illustrated in Figure 4.8, both vectors $c_{s,r}$ and $\tilde{c}_{s,r}$ originate from the same symbol stream $Y_{s,r}$. The difference between $c_{s,r}$ and $\tilde{c}_{s,r}$ is twofold. First, a soft bit in codeword $c_{s,r}$ contains the real part of a complex modulation symbol in $Y_{s,r}$ but a soft bit in $\tilde{c}_{s,r}$ represents the angle $\varphi \in [-\pi, \pi[$ of such a symbol. If $\varphi \neq 0$, $\tilde{c}_{s,r}$ expresses a carrier phase mismatch. The second difference is that soft bit values in $c_{s,r}$ are

4.3. Forwarding decision metric

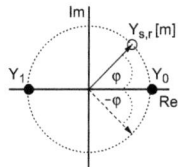

Figure 4.9: BPSK constellation example: Representing a received symbol $Y_{s,r}[m]$ by $-\varphi[m]$ or $\varphi[m]$ does not affect the distance between $Y_{s,r}[m]$ and the reference symbols Y_0, Y_1. Thus, $|\varphi[m]|$ can be used to represent $Y_{s,r}[m]$.

unbounded but $\tilde{c}_{s,r} \in [-1,1]$. Limiting $\tilde{c}_{s,r}$ to this interval assures that $\tilde{c}_{s,r}$ can be used as a norm for the channel quality.

Based on φ we obtain the soft bits for an mth symbol by

$$\tilde{c}_{s,r}[m] = \frac{2|\varphi[m]|}{\pi} - 1. \qquad (4.12)$$

This maps $\varphi \in [-\pi, \pi[\to \tilde{c}_{s,r} \in [-1,1]$ and fulfills two properties. First, dividing by π normalizes the values in $\tilde{c}_{s,r}$ to unity. Second, $|\varphi|$ treats both directions of the synchronization error equally. This is sufficient with BPSK where the sign of φ is not relevant to distinguish symbols in the angular domain and, thus, both directions of the synchronization error equally affect the distance to the reference symbol (cp. Figure 4.9).

Due to the two operations in (4.12), MPD can be simply used as an unsigned real-valued index without having to account for signed special cases. With this mapping, the minimum Euclidean distance between two soft bits is $||1-1|| = 0$ and the maximum is $||-1-1|| = 2$. Hence, MPD can take values $\text{mpd} \in [0,2]$.

Using the CSI vector $\tilde{c}_{s,r}$ to account for synchronization errors leads to very high estimation accuracy (Section 4.3.4) but limits the application of MPD. So-far only the above mapping for coherent BPSK is known. Mappings for higher order modulation, where information symbols and synchronization errors blend in the angular domain, are not obvious. To use MPD for higher order modulation, either hard decision decoding (where high accuracy is also found without CSI [VVA+08a]) or a different soft output method has to be used.

4.3.3 Decoder complexity and implementation remarks

Calculating MPD changes the standard Viterbi Algorithm (VA) only slightly. Unlike the SOVA and the MAP algorithm, this adds only insignificant computational complexity and no further constraints to decoder implementation.

Computational complexity

Although the exact computational complexity highly depends on implementation details, MPD's additional effort can be approximated by expressing and aggregating the basic operations in terms of *Equiva-*

Table 4.1: Computational complexity of several soft output decoding algorithms.

Decoding algorithm	Function of M and n [EA]	Example $M=6, R_c = 1/2$ [EA]	Factor over VA
VA	$(4n+2)2^M + 6$	646	1
MPD VA	$(4n+2)2^M + 15Mn - 5M + 12$	802	1.24
Log-MAP	$(4n+50)2^M - 19$	3693	5.71
SOVA	$(4n+9)2^M + 75M^2 + 35M + 5$	4003	6.2

lent Additions (EAs) [Wu01, CRWC07]. This approximation depends only on the basic coding parameters n, *memory order* M, and *truncation depth*. The memory order stands for the total number of input symbols stored at the decoder and is also known as *constraint length* [Pro00, Section 8.2]. The truncation depth defines the size of the path memory, i.e., the number of symbols the decoder looks back during its traceback. Many practical Viterbi decoders truncate their path memory to $5M$ symbols to limit delay and complexity [Pro00, Section 8.2.8]. This value is also used in the study below.

With these parameters we can now compare the complexity of MPD VA and the standard VA. With function codesymbol() in Algorithm 1, MPD calculation adds 1 table lookup to the traceback of the VA. Per memory order M, 1 additional calculation of the Euclidean distance (4.11) is required. Each call of this function adds 1 multiplication and 1 subtraction per n symbols as well as 1 addition per $n-1$ symbols to the VA. As in [Wu01] we count 6 EA per table lookup, 1 EA per multiplication, and 1 EA per subtraction. This leads to

$$\text{Complexity(MPD VA)} = \underbrace{(4n+2)2^M + 6}_{\text{VA}} + \underbrace{15Mn - 5M + 6}_{\text{MPD adds}} \text{ [EA]} \quad (4.13)$$

for the computational complexity of the MPD VA.

Table 4.1 compares this result for MPD VA to the computational complexity of VA [Vit67], SOVA [HH89], and of the Log-MAP algorithm [RVH95] which represents a feasible example of a MAP decoder. The results for these standard decoding algorithms are given in [Wu01]. With respect to M, all complexity functions have order $\mathcal{O}\{2^M\}$. However, within this exponential regime two terms cause large complexity differences between the algorithms.

First, compared to VA and MPD VA, Log-MAP and SOVA increase the factor in front of 2^M. With Log-MAP, this results from several calls of the max() function per path node to compute the soft output. Although Log-MAP computes this function in the logarithmic domain, the complexity increase is still substantial. SOVA increases the factor to 2^M by generating the path metric difference between survivor path and discarded path for each branch. This is not done by any other of the above decoding algorithms which consider only the surviving path.

Second, by taking even the discarded paths into account, SOVA performs an extensive traceback which adds term $75M^2$ to the complexity function. Note that, at the usually small n and M, this quadratic term contributes more to SOVA's complexity than the 2^M term. Based on these two terms, we can conclude that the complexity of Log-MAP and SOVA grows substantially faster in M than the complexity of VA and MPD VA.

Besides providing complexity as a function of M and n, Table 4.1 shows an example for $M = 6$ and $R_c = 1/n = 1/2$. Both parameters match the common $g_0 = 133_8; g_1 = 171_8$ code used in IEEE 802.11a/g WLAN systems [OP99]. While Log-MAP or SOVA are approximately 5.71 or 6.2 times as complex as the VA, respectively, MPD adds only 24 % computational complexity to the VA. This highlights the insignificant computational burden of MPD compared to SOVA and feasible MAP algorithms.

Implementation remarks

Regarding the implementation of MPD-extended Viterbi Algorithm (MPD VA) two observations can be made.

Parallel soft output MPD VA decodes and calculates MPD within a single iteration of the standard VA traceback (cp. Algorithm 1). This has two benefits over SOVA and MAP. First, implementations of MPD VA can decode and compute soft output in parallel. Second, no trellis iterations are added to the VA. Hence, calculating MPD adds only marginal decoder complexity and delay to the VA.

Pipelining A further important observation is that MPD VA does not constrain the stream processing of the standard VA. During the traceback, one MPD value can be returned per symbol and can be continuously processed by the smoothing filter and subsequent functions (Figure 4.8). This allows to profit from pipelining on a per-symbol basis, reducing decoder delay and memory demands.

Note that this unconstrained pipelining is a large benefit of MPD VA over SOVA and MAP decoders. To generate soft output, these algorithms have to take the minimum (SOVA) or maximum (MAP) over a large number of branch metrics. Computing and storing all these metrics beforehand, serializes the soft output calculation and, thus, increases memory demands and delay.

4.3.4 Accuracy study

A CSI_{rx} estimation has not only to be feasible, it also has to be accurate. We now study how accurately MPD estimates the true BER of a direct transmission and compare this accuracy to other metrics. We focus on slow and fast autocorrelated fading channels and use IEEE 802.11a/g standard PHY assumptions.

System model and parameters

To study the accuracy of MPD it suffices to focus on the direct link. We consider direct transmission from the source node s to the relay node r, i.e., link (s,r). We assume that s transmits a constant message flow with 512 Bytes payload per message X. For the transmitter chain, we make standard IEEE 802.11a/g physical layer assumptions. In particular, we assume that message X is FEC encoded using a convolutional code with generator polynomial $g_0 = 133_8; g_1 = 171_8$ and code rate $R_c = 1/2$ [OP99, Chapter 12]. This results in codeword c of 8192 coded bits which is then transmitted as a single packet. BPSK modulation leads to a packet length of $L_p = 8192$ symbols which are then passed to OFDM multi-carrier modulation. As in IEEE 802.11a/g, $S = 48$ modulation symbols are transmitted per OFDM symbol time of $T_s = 4\,\mu\text{s}$ which results in a packet time of $T_p = T_s \cdot L_p/S = 0.68\,\text{ms}$. In total 16×10^3 packets are transmitted per simulation.

Apart from MPD calculation, the receiver operates as in the standard IEEE 802.11a/g PHY. For each PHY packet, the received signal is coherently detected using the $16\,\mu\text{s}$ Physical Layer Convergence Procedure (PLCP) preamble [OP99, Chapter 12]. Due to this limited CSI_rx, complex channel coefficients may still cause carrier phase mismatches. OFDM demodulation returns the symbol vector $Y_{s,r}$ and BPSK demodulation maps each complex symbol value to a coded bit in codeword $c_{s,r}$. From this vector, finally, soft decision Viterbi decoding returns the received message $X_{s,r}$.

Like the above PHY functions the channel is modeled in the digital baseband at symbol level as described in Section 2.1. Per symbol time T_s, a single frequency-flat channel gain $|h|^2$ is calculated. Instead of assuming uncorrelated block fading, we use the autocorrelated fading model from Section 2.1.2. From the examples in Figure 2.3, we study two cases of the Doppler frequency f_d. At $f_d = 17.34\,\text{Hz}$ the channel gains $|h|^2$ are highly autocorrelated and the channel can be considered as *slow* compared to the packet time. This corresponds to low mobility in the propagation environment, e.g., an indoor WLAN with carrier frequency $f_c = 5.2\,\text{GHz}$ and relative velocity of $v = 1\,\text{m/s}$ between s and r. With this f_d, the coherence time of $T_c = 7.2\,\text{ms}$ (2.9) is 11 times longer than the chosen packet time T_p and, thus, deep fades in small parts are not very likely but may still occur (cp. Figure 4.3). The second case represents relatively *fast* fading where $f_d = 350\,\text{Hz}$ decorrelates the channel gains. Such f_d is typical at high mobility and, e.g., corresponds to a vehicular scenario with $v = 20\,\text{m/s}$ at $f_c = 5.2\,\text{GHz}$. In this case, T_p spans two coherence times.

Simulation results

We study two cases of MPD calculation. First, MPD is averaged over a complete packet. This provides a single CSI_rx estimate per packet and allows us to compare MPD to conventional SNR-based estimation methods. Nonetheless, PF requires multiple CSI_rx estimates per packet. This is studied as a second case.

Single CSI_rx estimate per packet To study how accurate a CSI_rx metric estimates the BER of a packet we compare three metrics to the true BER of the received code word $c_{s,r}$. Our first metric reflects the unrealistic case where the true value of the instantaneous SNR $\gamma_{s,r}$ is known for each modulation symbol. Based on all symbols, one SNR average is calculated per packet. Symbol-wise SNR measurement requires to use each symbol for training and, thus, does not allow any data transmission. We call this unrealistic metric *ideal* $\gamma_{s,r}$. Compared to this idealistic channel assessment, the second metric is closer to practical SNR measurement. This so-called *realistic* $\gamma_{s,r}$ is measured only over the PLCP preamble [OP99, Chapter 12]. Thus, only the first $16\,\mu\text{s}$ of the packet are observed and one realistic $\gamma_{s,r}$ value is returned as a time average over all preamble symbols. As third metric, we calculate MPD over all code symbols of $c_{s,r}$

4.3. Forwarding decision metric

as described in Section 4.3.2. The resulting mpd$_{s,r}$ vector is averaged over the complete packet, finally, providing one $\overline{\text{mpd}}_{s,r}$ value per packet.

To compare their accuracy, each of these metrics is shown as a function of the true BER of the corresponding packet which is, obviously, only available in simulation. To study this function for a large region of the true BER, we vary the mean SNR in $\bar{\gamma}_{s,r} \in [0, 30]$ dB. For each metric and each studied Doppler frequency, this results in one scatter plot shown in Figure 4.10 and 4.11. Each point represents a metric/BER mapping for one packet and a line illustrates the metric's mean over all packets. An important indicator for a metric's accuracy is the variance on the x-axis. With an ideal metric, this variance would be zero such that all points fall onto a single line expressing a distinct BER value only by a single distinct metric value. Note that, in these scatter plots, the varied mean SNR is only implicitly shown as the average true BER but that we explicitly study the effect of $\bar{\gamma}_{s,r}$ in Figure 4.12.

The results for the SNR metrics are shown in Figure 4.10. For both values of f_d, the ideal $\gamma_{s,r}$ values fall into a structure similar to a typical BER vs. SNR curve. Although the variance of $\gamma_{s,r}$ increases for lower BER, still a close match of ideal $\gamma_{s,r}$ to the true BER is shown. The accuracy increases when, due to higher f_d, the channel gains decorrelate in time (Figure 4.10(b)). This situation changes completely with more realistic SNR measurement. In Figure 4.10(c) and 4.10(d) the realistic $\gamma_{s,r}$ metric shows no clear structure. For both values of f_d, the high variance of the metric values impedes an accurate mapping to the true BER. Consequently, the realistic $\gamma_{s,r}$ metric cannot serve as an accurate indicator for the BER. This is different for MPD. The scatter plots in Figure 4.11(a) and 4.11(b) fall into a very small region. As for ideal $\gamma_{s,r}$, the variance improves with f_d and with the BER. This results in an injective mapping of the mean MPD to the true BER.

While the scatter plots provide a first overview, we can quantify the accuracy of the CSI$_{rx}$ metrics by taking the pairwise *correlation coefficient* ρ between the metric value and the true BER value of the corresponding packet. Precisely, we take the Pearson product-moment correlation coefficient $\rho(X, Y) \in [-1, 1]$ which is a standard measure for the linear dependency between two random variables X and Y. The results are shown in Figure 4.12. A high absolute value of ρ stands for a close linear expression of the true BER by the channel estimation metric. Vice versa, a correlation coefficient close to zero stands for poor channel estimation. The sign of ρ does not serve as a measure for metric accuracy. Naturally, the SNR metrics and BER are negatively correlated since SNR $\sim 1/$BER while, due to MPD $\sim$ BER, ρ is positive for MPD.

Both plots in Figure 4.12 clearly demonstrate the high accuracy of the MPD metric and the dependency on the mean SNR. With increasing mean SNR, all metrics lose estimation accuracy since the number of deep fades per packet (and, thus, the number of measured error events) decreases. However, while this statistic drawback highly affects the accuracy of ideal and realistic $\gamma_{s,r}$, MPD can take full advantage of the decoding memory and is, thus, only marginally affected. The accuracy of realistic $\gamma_{s,r}$ is further decreased at higher Doppler frequency f_d (cp. Figure 4.12(a) and Figure 4.12(b)). With increasing f_d, the channel gain decorrelates in time and the probability of deep fades inside a packet's payload increases. By observing only the packet preamble, realistic $\gamma_{s,r}$ cannot account for these events. While this results in an unacceptable accuracy for realistic $\gamma_{s,r}$, decorrelation even slightly improves the CSI estimation of ideal

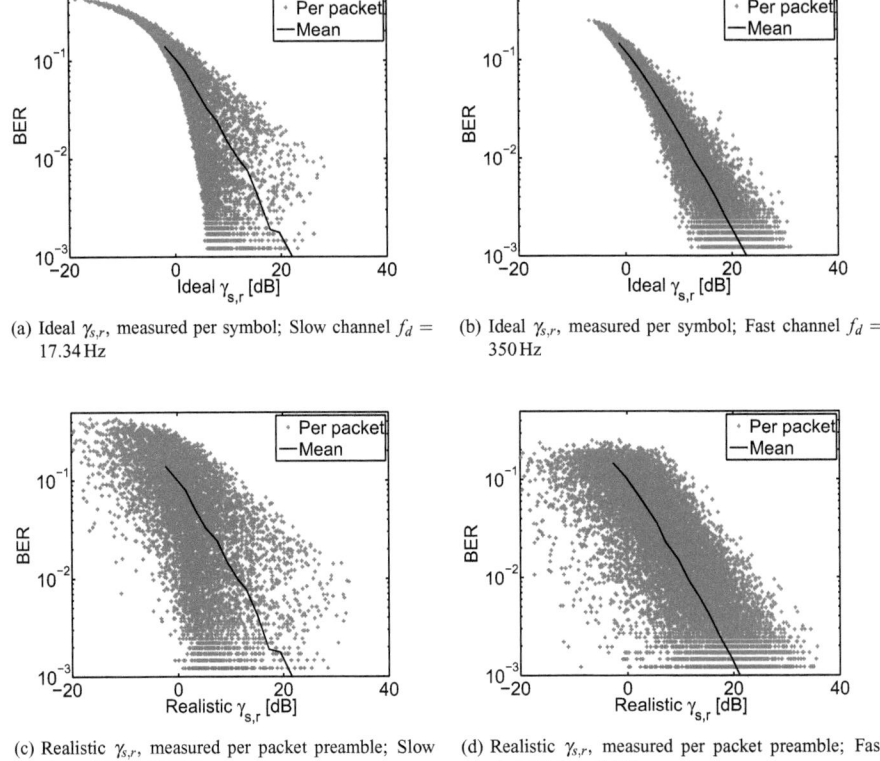

(a) Ideal $\gamma_{s,r}$, measured per symbol; Slow channel $f_d = 17.34\,\text{Hz}$

(b) Ideal $\gamma_{s,r}$, measured per symbol; Fast channel $f_d = 350\,\text{Hz}$

(c) Realistic $\gamma_{s,r}$, measured per packet preamble; Slow channel $f_d = 17.34\,\text{Hz}$

(d) Realistic $\gamma_{s,r}$, measured per packet preamble; Fast channel $f_d = 350\,\text{Hz}$

Figure 4.10: Accuracy of realistic and ideal SNR measurement: Scatter plot matching true BER of $c_{s,r}$ to the corresponding SNR measurement. Shown for two values of the Doppler frequency f_d. Each plot is based on 1000 packets.

4.3. Forwarding decision metric

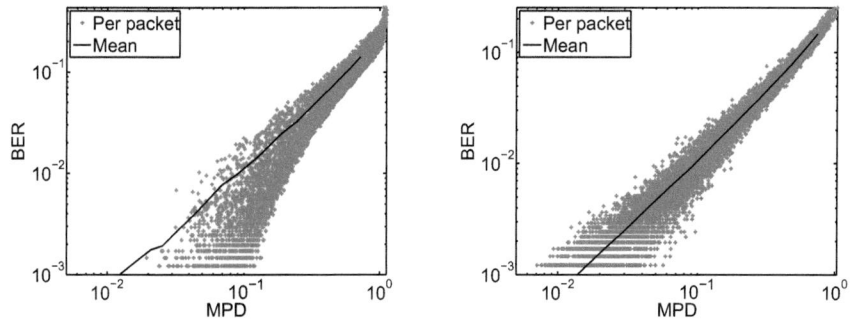

(a) MPD measured per packet; Slow channel $f_d = 17.34\,\text{Hz}$

(b) MPD measured per packet; Fast channel $f_d = 350\,\text{Hz}$

Figure 4.11: Accuracy of MPD: Scatter plot matching true BER of $c_{s,r}$ to the corresponding MPD value averaged over all symbols of $c_{s,r}$. Shown for two values of the Doppler frequency f_d. Each plot is based on 1000 packets.

$\gamma_{s,r}$ and MPD. This improvement is already known from the scatter plots in Figure 4.10(b) and Figure 4.11(b), and highlights the benefit by observing all symbols per packet.

From these simulation results we can conclude that MPD is an excellent BER estimator. Unlike realistic preamble-based SNR measurement, MPD takes all code symbols within a packet into account which, first, leads to a statistical benefit. Second, unlike ideal (yet unrealistic) measurement of the instantaneous SNR, MPD profits from the observation of the actual decoder certainty. Let us now study MPD's estimation accuracy if we compute this metric more frequently than once per packet.

Multiple CSI_{rx} estimates per packet Computing MPD more frequently reduces the number of symbols on which a single metric value is based. This statistical drawback reduces the metric's accuracy but, on the other hand, allows to adapt to the channel's variation more often. This tradeoff between adaptation frequency and accuracy is interesting for applying MPD to Partial Forwarding (PF). Only if MPD allows the relay to decide frequently and accurately "enough", this metric is feasible for PF.

To quantify this tradeoff, Figure 4.13 shows MPD values for various block lengths. Each shown MPD value is averaged over all L_d symbols of a decision block. As shown, the accuracy improves with the block length. If MPD is averaged over $L_d = 8$ symbols, no clear structure is shown. Choosing $L_d = 2048$ symbols already provides an accuracy that is similar to the packet-wise MPD in Figure 4.11. With the above packet length of $L_p = 8192$ symbols, this block length allows $D = 4$ forwarding decisions per packet.

Selecting the decision block length If a higher decision frequency is desired, L_d is decreased (4.1). We can define a practical minimum for L_d based on the truncation depth of the decoder. As mentioned in Section 4.3.3, many practical Viterbi decoders use a truncation depth of at least $5M$ input symbols or,

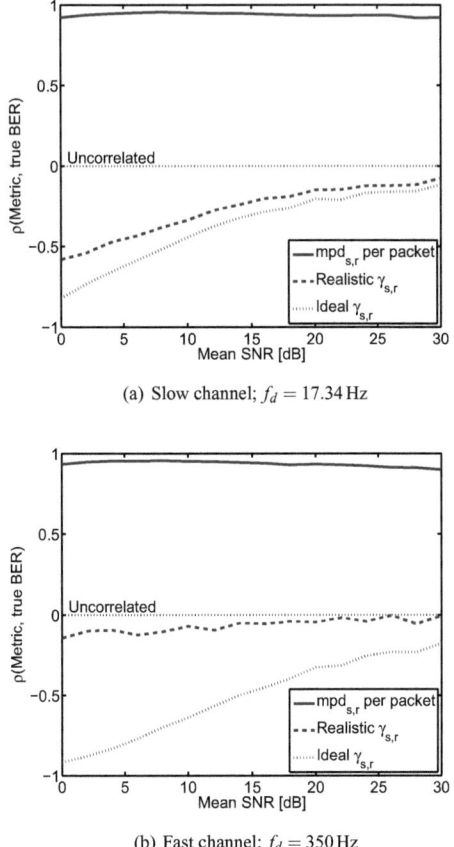

Figure 4.12: Accuracy of the CSI_{rx} metrics shown by the pairwise correlation coefficient ρ of metric and true BER. Shown vs. mean SNR for two values of the Doppler frequency f_d. Each value of ρ is based on 3000 packets.

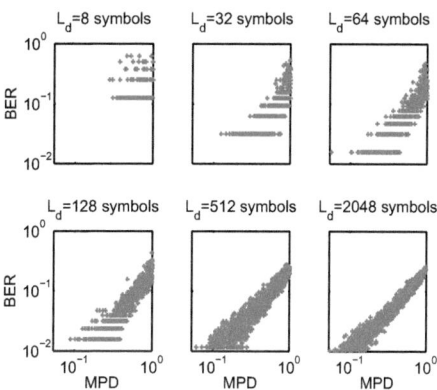

Figure 4.13: Effect of block length on MPD accuracy: True BER of $c_{s,r}$ vs. MPD averaged over an arbitrary block within $c_{s,r}$. Shown for 6 block lengths L_d and $f_d = 350$ Hz. The axes of all plots are scaled equally. Each plot is based on 1000 packets.

equivalently, $5Mn$ coded bits. It is a common rule of thumb that after this period the decoding decision has stabilized such that the path memory can be truncated at negligible performance loss [Pro00, Section 8.2.8], [Moo05, Section 12.3.3]. Hence, to observe MPD for a stable decoding decision, a block length of $L_d \geq 5Mn$ coded bits is required. With the IEEE 802.11a/g FEC parameters $M = 6$ and $n = 2$, this leads to $L_d \geq 60$ coded bits (equivalent to 60 BPSK symbols) and allows to choose $L_d = 64$ symbols from the block lengths in Figure 4.13. This block length shows still a clear MPD-to-BER mapping while providing $D = 128$ forwarding decisions per 8192 symbol packet or, equivalently, one decision per 4 Byte block in a 512 Byte message.

4.4 Protocols for partial forwarding

Having discussed MPD's feasibility and accuracy, we will now use this metric to build a practical PF system. We describe two extended SDF protocols, discuss how to choose an MPD threshold, and study necessary signaling functions.

4.4.1 Single forwarding decision

A simple integration of PF into SDF is illustrated in Figure 4.14. Here, the relay's receiver chain from Figure 4.8 is extended by a single decision stage based on an MPD threshold. For the current decision block i in message $X_{s,r}$, the relay simply compares the average MPD value $\overline{\text{mpd}}_{s,r}[i]$ to an *MPD threshold* θ. If $\overline{\text{mpd}}_{s,r}[i] < \theta$ the relay forwards the current block. Otherwise, the block is passed to the transmitter chain and forwarded. This forwarding decision is repeated for each block.

Even this simple single-stage forwarding procedure already requires to select two free parameters.

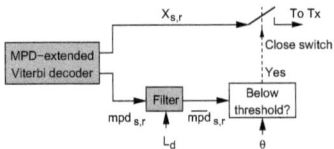

Figure 4.14: Basic functions of an SDF relay using a single MPD threshold. The shaded parts illustrate the extensions to conventional threshold-based SDF.

First, in the time domain, the forwarding decision frequency D (4.1) has to be defined by the window size L_d of the smoothing filter. Here, we employ a simple moving average to accurately capture deep fades that cross block boundaries. Nonetheless, also other smoothing operations (e.g., low pass filters) can be used. The block length can be chosen according to the truncation depth of the decoder. We described this choice and provided typical values for L_d and D in Section 4.3.4. The second free parameter – the MPD threshold θ – affects the forwarding decision in the value domain and has to be carefully selected to avoid decision errors.

Forwarding decision errors

The error events for a threshold-based forwarding decision are summarized in Table 4.2. Event $\mathcal{E}_1$ occurs when the current forwarding decision is too optimistic and erroneous blocks are forwarded. In this case, errors from link (s,r) propagate to destination d. At event $\mathcal{E}_2$, the decision is too pessimistic and correct blocks are dropped. Similar to packet-wise SDF this unnecessarily reduces the number of symbols that d can combine.

When the optimal threshold θ_{opt} is chosen, the probability that either of the events $\mathcal{E}_1$ and $\mathcal{E}_2$ occurs is minimized. This optimal choice minimizes the $\mathrm{BER}_{\mathrm{e2e}}$ which is shown in Figure 4.15 for the symmetric CTR network and the IEEE 802.11a/g assumptions from Section 4.3.4. If the chosen threshold θ is equal to θ_{opt}, a clearly shaped $\mathrm{BER}_{\mathrm{e2e}}$ "valley" is shown. Left and right from $\theta = \theta_{\mathrm{opt}}$ the $\mathrm{BER}_{\mathrm{e2e}}$ increases significantly. At $\theta < \theta_{\mathrm{opt}}$, $\mathcal{E}_1$ occurs and error propagation increases $\mathrm{BER}_{\mathrm{e2e}}$ by up to 1.5 orders of magnitude. At $\theta > \theta_{\mathrm{opt}}$, $\mathcal{E}_2$ has a less degrading effect on the $\mathrm{BER}_{\mathrm{e2e}}$ than $\mathcal{E}_1$. Hence, reducing the number of combined symbols is less severe than forwarding errors to d.

Table 4.2: Error events $\mathcal{E}$ for threshold-based forwarding decisions.

	Block IS erroneous	Block IS correct
Threshold-based decision $\Rightarrow$ Erroneous	Correct decision	$\mathcal{E}_2 := \{\text{Drop correct block}\}$
Threshold-based decision $\Rightarrow$ Correct	$\mathcal{E}_1 := \{\text{Forward erroneous block}\}$	Correct decision

4.4. Protocols for partial forwarding

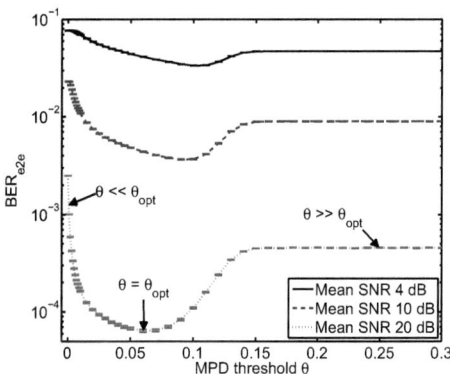

Figure 4.15: Effect of the chosen MPD threshold θ on BER_{e2e}: Shown for $f_d = 350\,\text{Hz}$ and various levels of the mean SNR and θ.

Selecting the MPD threshold

From the results in Figure 4.15 we can draw three conclusions for selecting the MPD threshold θ. First, PF requires a careful threshold selection since choosing $\theta \neq \theta_{\text{opt}}$ has a large effect. Second, if a suboptimal threshold has to be chosen, the pessimistic choice $\theta > \theta_{\text{opt}}$ is preferable. In this case the large drawback of error propagation is avoided at the cost of dropping correct blocks. Third, the optimum MPD threshold is a function of the mean SNR $\bar{\gamma}$. As shown in Figure 4.15, θ_{opt} decreases with increasing $\bar{\gamma}$. Thus, θ_{opt} has to be chosen for each $\bar{\gamma}$ which complicates the threshold choice. We denote this SNR dependency by $\theta_{\text{opt}}(\bar{\gamma})$. On the other hand, the effect of an suboptimal threshold choice diminishes for increasing $\bar{\gamma}$. This effect can compensate for the dependency on $\bar{\gamma}$ and is further elaborated below.

So far, selecting the optimal forwarding threshold was only studied for packet-wise SDF protocols with SNR thresholds [HZF04]. In [OAF+08] several approximations of θ_{opt} either based on the mean SNR or on instantaneous SNR knowledge were derived. However, these approximations are only valid for BPSK without FEC coding and for block fading channels. For systems with FEC coding, autocorrelated fading channels, or a combination of both, no analytic solution for optimal SNR thresholds is known so far.

Unfortunately, this is also the case for MPD where soft decision decoding further complicates analysis [HWR07]. Instead of deriving the theoretical optimal threshold, we perform an empirical study. By transmitting many training packets for different $\bar{\gamma}$ and θ we establish a large set of MPD values. From this set, the BER_{e2e}-minimizing threshold is chosen which provides an empirical optimum $\theta_{\text{opt}}(\bar{\gamma})$ for a given scenario.

The result of this threshold search is illustrated in Figure 4.16 which can be seen as a 3D variant of Figure 4.15. For a clear graphical presentation, the contour lines show

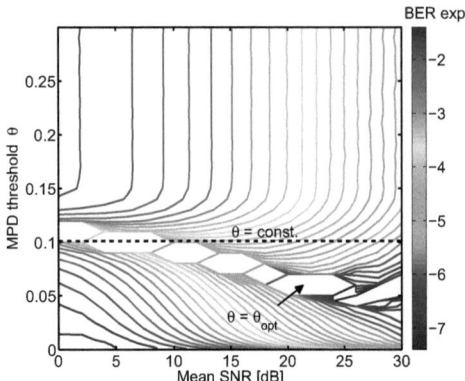

Figure 4.16: Effect of the MPD threshold θ on BER_{e2e}: Contour plot of $\text{BER}_{\text{e2e}}^{\Delta}$ vs. SNR and vs. θ for $f_d = 350\,\text{Hz}$. The line color represents the BER exponent.

$$\text{BER}_{\text{e2e}}^{\Delta} = \text{BER}_{\text{e2e}} - \min_{\forall \theta}(\text{BER}_{\text{e2e}})$$

and the optimal threshold $\theta_{\text{opt}}(\bar{\gamma})$ is chosen when $\text{BER}_{\text{e2e}}^{\Delta} = 0$. As expected from Figure 4.15, choosing $\theta = \theta_{\text{opt}}(\bar{\gamma})$ causes a clearly shaped BER_{e2e} "valley" and the threshold value decreases for increasing $\bar{\gamma}$.

Figure 4.16 provides further insight in choosing *suboptimal* thresholds. As shown by the flattening contour lines, the "valley" around $\theta_{\text{opt}}(\bar{\gamma})$ becomes wider if the SNR increases. At high SNR (here, $\bar{\gamma} \geq 15\,\text{dB}$), this allows to choose a large set of different suboptimal thresholds without significantly degrading BER_{e2e}. Even if an $\bar{\gamma}$-independent threshold is chosen, the widening BER_{e2e} "valley" only negligibly decreases the performance (cp. $\theta = \text{const.}$ in Figure 4.16). This simplifies the practical threshold selection. Based on the approximate mean SNR (which is easily obtained in many systems), a practical system can use Figure 4.16 as a lookup table to select θ for an $\bar{\gamma}$ interval or even independent of $\bar{\gamma}$. Neither accurate knowledge of the mean SNR nor knowing the instantaneous SNR is required.

4.4.2 Two decision stages

In systems where FEC as well as error detecting codes are used, we can decrease the probability of $\mathcal{E}_2$ by combining MPD with error detection. The resulting, so-called *Two-stage SDF (2SDF)* protocol extends the relay's receiver chain from Figure 4.8 by two decision stages (Figure 4.17). After the MPD VA returns message and MPD vector, the FCS is extracted and used in the first decision stage. This stage tests the complete message by an error detecting code, e.g., a CRC. If the message passes this test, it is considered to be correct and forwarded completely. If the message fails this test, packet-wise SDF would drop this message. This is not the case with the 2SDF protocol. Here, in a second stage, an MPD threshold-based decision is made for each message block as in Section 4.4.1. Hence, each block with an MPD sufficing the threshold is forwarded.

4.4. Protocols for partial forwarding

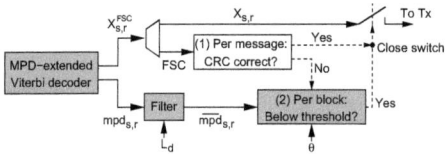

Figure 4.17: Basic functions of an Two-stage SDF (2SDF) relay. The shaded parts illustrate the extensions to a conventional CRC-based SDF.

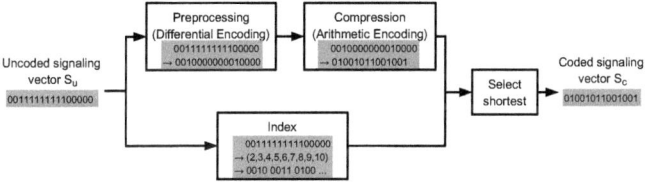

Figure 4.18: Source encoding scheme reducing PF's signaling overhead and example vectors (shaded).

By combining packet and block-wise decision, 2SDF provides the following benefits. By its first stage, 2SDF decreases the probability of ε_2. Even if the chosen threshold is too pessimistic, correct blocks are not dropped if the complete message passes the CRC test. If the CRC test fails, MPD is used to inspect the message at higher temporal resolution. In this second stage, an MPD threshold is used to find and forward correct blocks. This keeps the benefits of Partial Forwarding (PF) but can outperform a single threshold-based decision with suboptimal thresholds. We will demonstrate these gains in Section 4.5.

4.4.3 Transmitting control information

To not fragment the medium access, a PF relay does not forward each decision block separately. Even if blocks are dropped, still one packet is forwarded per cooperation cycle. This packet includes the remaining blocks and additional control information to indicate the removed blocks to the destination d. This indication is crucial to assure that d combines the remaining blocks with the appropriate blocks from the direct link but, naturally, adds overhead. To avoid that this overhead substantially decreases the data rate we use the following signaling scheme.

Per packet, the relay performs D binary forwarding decisions. Representing each decision by a single bit leads to a *signaling vector* S_u of D bits per packet. Since with fading channels decoding errors usually result from burst errors, it is likely that S_u contains long runs of zeros and ones. Such data can be well compressed by standard lossless source coding which is illustrated by the upper branch in Figure 4.18. First, preprocessing reduces the uniform distribution of zeros and ones in S_u. This improves the rate of the actual compression scheme that is applied in the second step. We employ *differential coding* [Pro00, Section 3.5.1] for preprocessing and use *arithmetic coding* for compression [CT91, Section 5.10]. Although other schemes can be used, these standard schemes readily support pipelining and arithmetic coding is efficient for small code alphabets (such as the binary values in S_u).

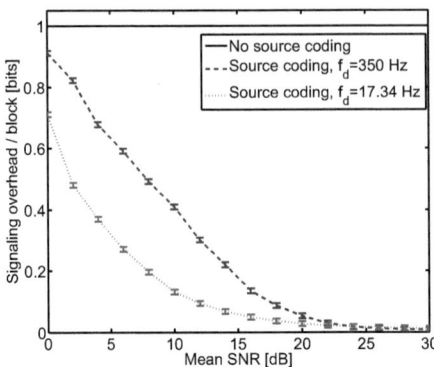

Figure 4.19: Signaling overhead per block. Shown with and without source coding for two values of the Doppler frequency f_d.

However, for a very large number of ones or zeros, compression can be less efficient than directly signaling the block indices. In this case, the signaling scheme selects the lower branch in Figure 4.18 and sends $L_{\text{sig,b}} = \lceil \log_2(D) \rceil$ bits per index plus one additional bit stating if the signaled indices refer to forwarded or dropped blocks. Which of the branches in Figure 4.18 is chosen depends on D and on the current S_u. By running both methods in parallel and choosing the shorter output vector (Figure 4.18), the more efficient signaling scheme is automatically selected.

We illustrate the resulting signaling overhead per block in Figure 4.19. Again, we assume the above IEEE 802.11a/g system with $D = 128$ blocks per packet, each block is $L_d = 64$ symbols long (Section 4.3.4). Without compression, the signaling overhead per block is 1 bit. As shown, source coding significantly reduces this overhead. The compression gain is higher for lower Doppler frequency f_d where the channel gains are highly autocorrelated and, thus, longer runs occur in the signaling vector. Similarly, the run length increases at higher SNR where a larger number of blocks can be forwarded. Consequently, only little signaling overhead is required at high SNR and at low f_d.

Note that D can be chosen such that PF's signaling overhead does not decrease the data rate. Each dropped block "frees" $L_d R_c$ uncoded bits per message but requires at worst $L_{\text{sig,b}}$ bits of signaling information. In the above example, a $L_d R_c = 32$ bits block requires only a maximum signaling information of $L_{\text{sig,b}}(D = 128) = 7$ bits. Here, only up to 22 % of the block length is spent for signaling. Generally speaking, if D is chosen such that $L_{\text{sig,b}}(D) \leq L_d R_c$, the forwarded packet is never longer than the original packet. Since the signaling overhead is shorter than the length of a dropped block, each removed block reduces the time spent for forwarding. This even increases the end-to-end data rate of standard selection relaying.

4.5 End-to-end performance study

Now all components of the Partial Forwarding (PF) system are described and we can study its end-to-end performance. First, we study the effect of the decision metric and threshold on the BER_{e2e}. Second, we focus on the BER_{e2e} and data rate differences due to the above PF protocols. As expected from the theoretical results (Section 4.2), high gains are shown for the BER_{e2e} of PF. Moreover, even a practical PF system closely reaches the BER_{e2e} of the ideal case. In terms of data rate, PF can significantly improve the rate of SDF at medium and low SNR when relaying (under the orthogonality constraint) becomes relevant. These gains are even reached if overhead is included and with suboptimal thresholds.

4.5.1 System model and parameters

To study PF's BER_{e2e} and data rate by simulation, we use the standard IEEE 802.11a/g PHY assumptions from Section 4.3.4. Each message is 512 Bytes long, which leads to a packet length of $L_p = 8192$ symbols. An included FCS allows one CRC test per message. Due to the very high error detection rate of CRC-32 we assume this test to be ideal. Cooperative relaying is studied in the symmetrical CTR network (Figure 3.1(b)) with a single relay and equal mean SNR $\bar{\gamma}$ for all links. Each node operates under the per-node power constraint that reflects IEEE 802.11 medium access (Section 2.3). If the relay employs SDF (Section 3.2.2), either the complete packet (repetition coding) or no packet is forwarded. If PF is used, a block length of $L_d = 64$ symbols and, thus, a forwarding decision frequency of $D = 128$ is selected according to the truncation depth of typical IEEE 802.11a/g decoders (Section 4.3.4). Finally, the destination combines the received signals using MRC. A MAC scheme perfectly assures an orthogonal channel (e.g., a separate time slot) for each transmission.

As in Section 4.3.4, we select a Doppler frequency of $f_d = 17.34\,\text{Hz}$ or $f_d = 350\,\text{Hz}$ to study slow and fast autocorrelated frequency-flat fading, respectively. The effect of this parameter on the employed fading model is described in Section 2.1.2. The Doppler frequency and, thus, the relative velocity v, is equal for all transmitters and receivers. Correlation is modeled only in the time domain, i.e., the channel coefficients are frequency-flat and different links are statistically independent. All BER_{e2e} results are shown prior to decoding which allows comparison to studies for uncoded cooperation systems, e.g., [LWT04, HZF04, OAF+08]. Each shown value for the BER_{e2e} and for the mean data rate is based on 10^5 transmitted packets, i.e., $8.192 \cdot 10^8$ modulation symbols.

4.5.2 Effect of the decision metric

First, we study the effect of the forwarding decision metric, decision frequency D, and threshold selection on the BER_{e2e} performance of SDF protocols. In particular, we study the following cases. *CRC* and *realistic* $\gamma_{s,r}$ represent an ideal or inaccurate CSI_{rx} measurement once per packet ($D = 1$), respectively. *Ideal* $\gamma_{s,r}$ allows symbol-wise decision ($D = 8192$) but is a suboptimal metric in coded systems. With *MPD* the relay decides per block using the above parameters ($D = 128$). All these metrics are studied using the simple single-stage SDF protocol, i.e., conventional SDF for CRC and threshold-based decision for SNR and MPD. The SNR and MPD thresholds are selected by numerical search as described in Section 4.4.1. For MPD, we study if choosing an SNR-dependent threshold $\theta(\bar{\gamma})$ is worth the effort by comparing it to the SNR-independent MPD threshold θ.

Furthermore, we include *Direct* transmission and *Genie* SDF in our study as an upper and lower BER_{e2e} bound, respectively. *Genie* denotes the ideal PF system from Section 4.2 that is now studied for autocorrelated channels. In this idealistic case, the relay knows and forwards only the correct symbols. As ideal $\gamma_{s,r}$, Genie uses highest decision frequency ($D = 8192$) but differs by the decision metric. While Genie always makes a perfect local forwarding decision, the decision of ideal $\gamma_{s,r}$ may be suboptimal since SNR-based decision neglects the gains of FEC decoding.

For all these cases, the BER_{e2e} results are shown in Figure 4.20. Interestingly, even for the slowly varying channel in Figure 4.20(a), packet-wise decision leads to poor performance compared to higher D. Even an ideal decision metric (CRC) cannot compensate for $D = 1$ and the relay drops correct parts of a packet. This results from the quasi-periodic nature of the J_0 Autocorrelation Function (ACF) where the channel decorrelates quickly after T_c (thus, changing channel state) but then correlates again (Figure 2.4). A further degradation results from the decision metric itself. As SDF with realistic $\gamma_{s,r}$ bases its decision only on a short part of the packet, it achieves lower accuracy (cp. Figure 4.10) and, thus, significantly higher BER_{e2e} than CRC and ideal $\gamma_{s,r}$. Although ideal $\gamma_{s,r}$ decides most frequently, it is outperformed by the MPD metric which accounts for the actual decoder certainty. Hence, from all studied metrics, MPD achieves a BER_{e2e} closest to the Genie case although its D is 64 times lower than with ideal $\gamma_{s,r}$. This is even the case with SNR-independent thresholds.

Similar results are obtained for a fast channel (Figure 4.20(b)). Again, both MPD cases reach best performance; the gain for SNR-dependent threshold selection can be neglected. Compared to the slow channel, the results for realistic $\gamma_{s,r}$ and CRC are interesting. Realistic $\gamma_{s,r}$ profits if the channel coefficients decorrelate in time (Section 4.10). This statistical benefit increases the accuracy of this most inaccurate metric and, thereby, the BER_{e2e}. The results for CRC-based SDF clearly demonstrate the drawback of packet-wise decision at high Doppler frequency. While for high SNR a large diversity gain is shown, the gain quickly diminishes for lower SNR until, at 10 dB, merely the performance of direct transmission is reached. In this case, the number of dropped packets is so high that almost no symbols are forwarded anymore. That still a significant number of correct symbols can be forwarded is shown by the significant gains for ideal $\gamma_{s,r}$ and MPD at low and medium SNR.

For slow and fast autocorrelated fading, MPD outperforms all studied feasible metrics. Even with a practical decision frequency and SNR-independent thresholds, MPD-based PF closely reaches the BER_{e2e} of the ideal case. This shows that PF's high BER_{e2e} gains, promised by the theoretical results in Section 4.2.2, can actually be reached for autocorrelated fading and with practical methods.

4.5.3 Effect of the protocol and signaling functions

We now study how the Two-stage SDF (2SDF) protocol and the signaling scheme affect the end-to-end Bit Error Rate (BER_{e2e}) and the data rate.

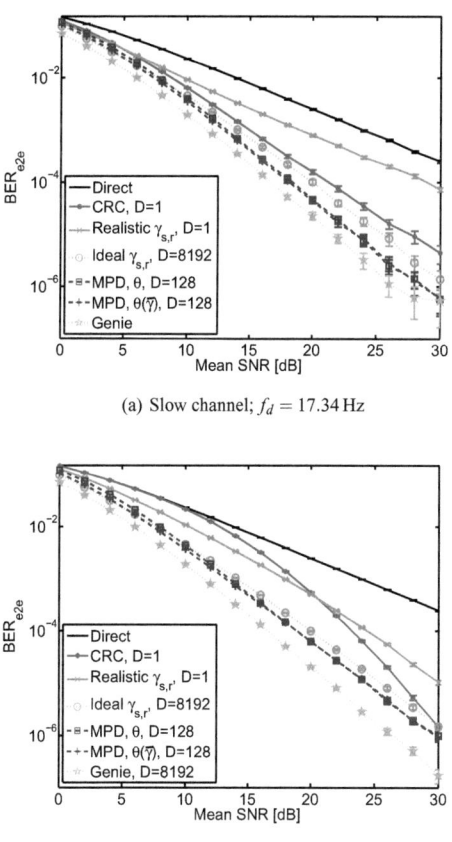

(a) Slow channel; $f_d = 17.34\,\text{Hz}$

(b) Fast channel; $f_d = 350\,\text{Hz}$

Figure 4.20: Effect of forwarding decision metric on BER_{e2e}: Shown vs. SNR for two values of the Doppler frequency f_d.

Bit error rate

The BER$_{e2e}$ results for the slow and fast fading scenario are shown in Figure 4.21. All results other than for 2SDF are equivalent to Figure 4.20 and included here for comparison. Conventional SDF with a single packet-wise decision (i.e., $D = 1$) is called *SDF, CRC*. PF with a single block-wise decision (i.e., $D = 128$ using an SNR-independent MPD threshold) is called *PF, MPD*. 2SDF's decision frequency is $D = 1$ if the first packet-wise stage suffices but is increased to $D = 128$ if its second block-wise decision stage is required (Section 4.4.2). Note that only this second MPD-based stage introduces decision errors since an ideal CRC is assumed for stage one. Thus, 2SDF cannot have a larger BER$_{e2e}$ than a single MPD threshold-based decision.

While 2SDF's end-to-end Bit Error Rate (BER$_{e2e}$) shows no significant improvement at $f_d = 17.34$ Hz, at higher Doppler frequency a clear benefit over the single-stage cooperation protocols is found. This gain demonstrates that 2SDF's first decision stage avoids that the relay pessimistically discards correct messages. More formally, 2SDF's CRC decision decreases $\mathbb{P}\{\mathcal{E}_2\}$ for all blocks of a message. As with increasing SNR correct messages occur more frequently and are, thus, more likely to be dropped by an erroneous forwarding decision, the BER$_{e2e}$ gain of 2SDF increases with the SNR. Nonetheless, the gain is comparably small which indicates the high quality of the chosen MPD threshold. For larger thresholds $\mathbb{P}\{\mathcal{E}_2\}$ increases and a higher improvement can be expected from 2SDF.

Effective data rate

To account for all symbols which are (1) discarded at the relay, (2) lost due to fading or noise, and (3) occupied by signaling overhead, we define

$$R_e = \frac{\text{Total number of correctly received payload bits}}{\text{Total number of transmitted bits}} = \frac{N_{\text{correct}}}{N_{s,d} + N_{r,d} + N_{\text{sig}}} \quad (4.14)$$

as the *effective data rate*. Here, $N_{s,d}$ and $N_{r,d}$ denote the sum of uncoded bits sent over the respective link and N_{correct} stands for the sum of correctly received payload bits. Note that $N_{\text{correct}} \leq N_{s,d}$ and that for direct transmission the relay forwards $N_{r,d} = 0$ bits. With relaying, $N_{r,d} \in [0, N_{s,d}]$ captures different forwarding decisions. Finally, N_{sig} represents the length of the signaling vector S_c (Section 4.4.3) accounting for the overhead due to PF. Overhead due to other protocol functions is not considered in this study. From the MPD-based protocols we focus only on SNR-independent thresholds and on the succeeding protocol 2SDF.

Counting $N_{\text{correct}}, N_{s,d}, N_{r,d}$, and N_{sig} during simulation results in the effective data rate shown in Figure 4.22. Independent of f_d, the multiplexing loss dominates R_e at high SNR. While with increasing SNR the effective rate for direct transmission tends to one, R_e approaches only $1/2$ for the relaying protocols. As discussed in Section 3.3.4, this multiplexing loss is a consequence of repetition coding under the orthogonality constraint.

However, SDF protocols can exceed this rate when (1) the relay forwards only $N_{r,d} < N_{s,d}$ bits but (2) the destination still receives an N_{correct} high enough such that $N_{\text{correct}} > (N_{s,d} + N_{r,d})/2$. CRC-based

4.5. End-to-end performance study

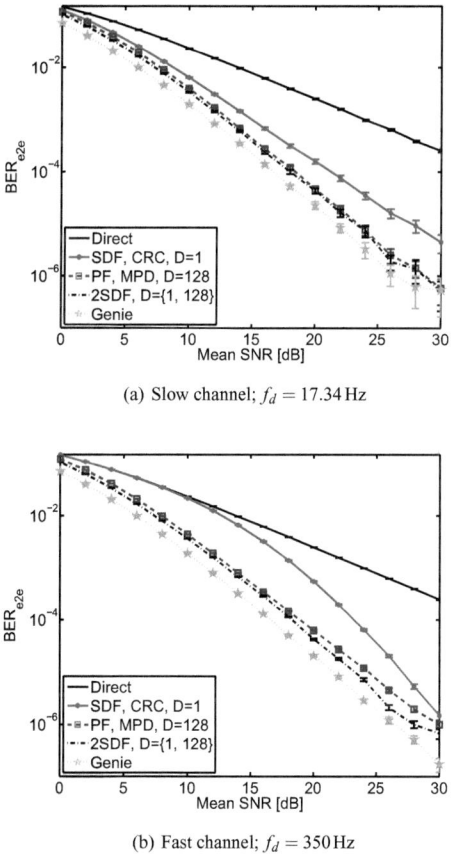

(a) Slow channel; $f_d = 17.34\,\text{Hz}$

(b) Fast channel; $f_d = 350\,\text{Hz}$

Figure 4.21: Effect of selection relaying protocol on BER_{e2e}: Shown vs. SNR for two values of the Doppler frequency f_d.

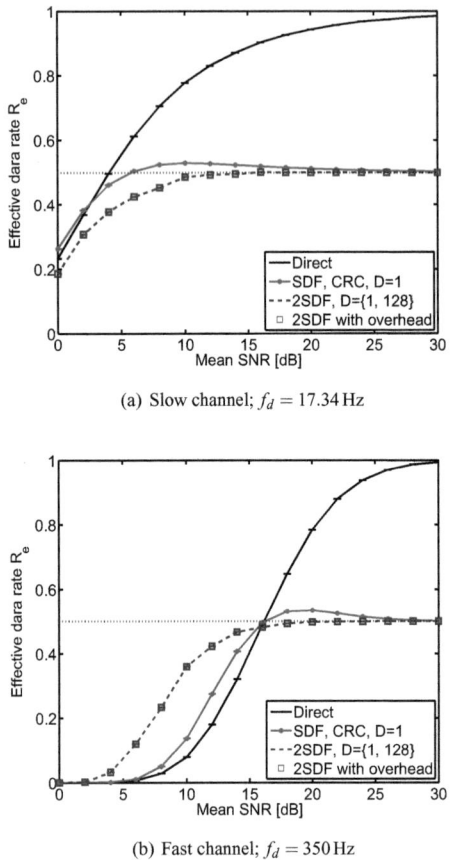

(a) Slow channel; $f_d = 17.34\,\text{Hz}$

(b) Fast channel; $f_d = 350\,\text{Hz}$

Figure 4.22: Effect of selection relaying protocol on mean effective data rate: Shown vs. SNR for two values of the Doppler frequency f_d.

SDF achieves this at $\bar{\gamma} = 10$ dB and at $\bar{\gamma} = 18$ dB for low and high f_d, respectively. However, in either of these cases direct transmission succeeds and relaying is not needed. Due to its high number of forwarded bits, MPD-based relaying does not achieve $R_e > 1/2$ but improves its BER_{e2e}. While none of the relaying protocols can outperform direct transmission at high SNR and low f_d, 2SDF substantially improves the data rate when deep fades during the packet time become more likely. This is the case at high f_d and low to medium SNR and shown in Figure 4.22(b). For instance, at $f_d = 350$ Hz and at 10 dB, 2SDF's BER_{e2e} gain suffices to reach a 2.6 times higher data rate than conventional SDF. This is even the case when overhead is taken into account. Consequently, instead of conventional SDF protocols, one would employ direct transmission (at high SNR, low f_d) and 2SDF (at low to medium SNR, high f_d) to reach a high data rate.

4.6 Summary of contributions and future work

Contributions

Basic approach and analysis With Partial Forwarding the relay may decide to forward parts of a packet. This approach generalizes the forwarding decision of the SDF protocol from an optimization in the value domain only to an optimization in the value *and* time domain. With PF the relay has not only to find the best threshold for its forwarding decision [HZF04, OAF⁺08] but also has to decide frequently enough to follow the variation of the fading channel.

Due to their low forwarding decision frequency, even SDF with ideal thresholds reaches poor end-to-end Bit Error Rate (BER_{e2e}) if several fades per packet occur. For this case, analysis shows substantial coding gains for PF over packet-wise SDF and provides a lower BER_{e2e} bound. Simulation results for autocorrelated fading confirm that even at low mobility several fades per packet occur and high gains for PF can be reached.

Frequent channel state estimation Implementing PF requires the relay to estimate the channel state for small parts of a packet. Following the soft output approach, we described the decoding-based metric Minimum Path Difference (MPD) as an extension of the Viterbi decoder.

The resulting MPD-extended Viterbi Algorithm (MPD VA) estimates the channel state for small blocks of a codeword. While this method reaches similar estimation accuracy as instantaneous SNR, it even captures the decoder certainty. Unlike other estimation schemes, no additional training symbols are needed and the decoder complexity is only insignificantly increased.

Although this channel estimation method is completely independent of cooperative relaying, it can be efficiently employed in our practical PF system design.

System design and performance Employing soft information only for the relay's local forwarding decision but still forwarding hard bits is a new system concept which stands between the classic SDF strategy (hard bit-based forwarding decision at the relay, forwarding hard bits) and recent soft DF approaches (no decision at the relay, forwarding soft bits).

To profit from this new concept, a practical PF system requires more extensions to SDF than channel state estimation. Starting with a simple threshold-based forwarding decision, we show that MPD-based PF pays only a marginal performance penalty even if suboptimal, constant thresholds are selected. By combining this threshold-based decision with conventional SDF, forwarding decision errors for complete packets can be further avoided. Finally, an efficient source coding scheme is introduced to compress the necessary signaling information.

Altogether, these functions provide a feasible PF system which is studied for IEEE 802.11a/g system assumptions, practical PF parameters, and with autocorrelated fading channels. Even under these realistic assumptions, the PF system shows a performance that is close to the theoretical ideal case. These substantial BER_{e2e} gains come at feasible complexity and negligible overhead. The data rate is not decreased but even increased when fades during the packet time are likely.

Future work

Generalization to M-QAM   Although the MPD metric is simple and efficient it needs to be generalized for higher order modulation types in addition to BPSK, i.e., M-QAM. This is not straightforward since MPD exploits the angular domain to assess carrier phase mismatches. Nevertheless, PF can be already implemented for M-QAM by using other soft output approaches which, however, significantly increase the relay's complexity.

Effect of interleaving   Interleaving is not considered in the above studies and system design. Nonetheless, the effect of interleaving can be assessed by the above results for high Doppler frequency. In both cases, the channel decorrelates in time decreasing the length of burst errors. The above results show that for such lower autocorrelation the accuracy of MPD and, thus, the end-to-end performance of the practical PF system significantly improve. Nonetheless, performance studies for practical interleavers are still necessary.

Combination with temporal diversity schemes   PF provides spatial diversity gains even when the channel changes within a packet. It targets an intermediate situation between slow and fast fading where diversity gains can be provided by selection relaying as well as by temporal diversity schemes (e.g., interleaving, HARQ, and rateless codes). These schemes and PF are not mutually exclusive but perform best with different channel statistics and impose different constraints on feedback and delay. Combining PF with temporal diversity schemes can point to interesting tradeoffs and beneficial system designs that obtain high diversity gains with slow, intermediate, and fast mobility.

Chapter 5

Applying selection relaying to resource allocation

We have seen that selection relaying can improve the performance of a single wireless transmission. Let us now focus on more complex communication systems where multiple packet streams of different importance are transferred between the nodes. Prioritizing these streams by *resource allocation* is a common approach to improve the overall performance [BBKT96, WCLM99]. In this chapter, we will focus on two promising approaches to improve resource allocation by cooperative relaying. Both approaches use selection relaying to provide diversity gains. By providing these gains only for the highly relevant packets the overall performance is improved but the multiplexing loss due to relaying is limited.

Our first approach, called *Asymmetric Cooperation Diversity (ACD)*, joins resource allocation and selection relaying at scheduling level. To improve the quality of media streaming, ACD prioritizes packets by asymmetrically allocating the cooperation diversity branches among the users. In Section 5.1 we describe this prioritization approach, verify it by outage analysis and simulation, and demonstrate substantial improvements of the video quality.

In our second approach, called *Cooperative Feedback (CFB)*, resource allocation and cooperative relaying do not interact during scheduling. Instead, cooperative relaying decreases the error rate for CSI feedback packets. This improves the performance of a scheduled downlink since most resource allocation schedulers perform poorly if accurate CSI is not available [PM07, KK08]. We demonstrate the resulting error rate and sum capacity gains in Section 5.2 for a simple cellular scenario with Multiuser Diversity (MUD).

All in all, we will demonstrate two beneficial schemes that apply selection relaying to resource allocation. Let us now detail how relaying can be applied and which performance gains can be expected.

5.1 Asymmetric cooperation for media streaming

Transmitting media streams at high quality *and* in real time is still a challenge for many wireless systems. If the high error rate of fading channels meets the strict delay constraints of media streams, even up-to-date error correction techniques, e.g., Turbo codes and HARQ, may be pushed to their limits [ADF+09].

Improving diversity gain is a key approach to deal with such scenarios but often requires additional redundancy. A diversity scheme, such as cooperative relaying, has to carefully invest this redundancy where it is needed to assure that an improved error rate does not result in unacceptable delay or throughput. As high streaming quality requires error rate, throughput, and delay to be in balance [HTL+06], it is not sufficient to improve only the error rate. Although this objective differs significantly from the previous chapters it can be still achieved with selection relaying as follows.

5.1.1 Approach and scenario

Our basic approach *diversity branch allocation* assigns a larger number of diversity branches to the more important packets of a media stream. These branches are provided by cooperation. In its simplest form, users cooperate only for the most relevant packets and transmit all other packets directly.

Diversity branch allocation with selection relaying

At a first glance, this approach may look like a conventional traffic-aware resource allocation scheme with cooperation on top of it. This is not the case. To support different priorities, diversity branches are allocated and not channel resources. Thus, two packet streams can receive different priorities even if the same share of channel resources (but with different diversity order) is allocate to both streams.

Although diversity branches can be allocated with any diversity scheme, realizing this approach with selection relaying has several benefits. First, after its forwarding decision, a relay knows if it will retransmit the packet that was received from link (s,r). Thus, at an intermediate stage of a transmission, the relay predicts the diversity order that is realized at the destination. This is not possible with conventional diversity schemes (e.g., frequency or temporal diversity) where only the source can assign diversity branches prior to transmission.

Second, knowing the state of link (s,r), a relay can use further stages of the forwarding decision depending on the packet priority. If the current priority can be extracted from the received packet, no further communication is required to make this decision. This enables a distributed prioritization without communication overhead. Consequently, its forwarding decision makes selection relaying very appealing to integrate prioritization by diversity branch allocation.

We separate our contribution in two functions called Asymmetric Cooperation Diversity (ACD) and Traffic-Aware Cooperation Diversity (TACD), illustrated in Figure 5.1. Details of these functions are described in Section 5.1.3 and 5.1.5.

ACD is a selection relaying protocol which asymmetrically allocates diversity branches among the cooperating users to prioritize packets. ACD's operation is independent of the actual traffic type and can assign static priorities to the packets of cooperating users. While such a permanent prioritization may be already useful on its own, it can also be employed to dynamically adapt the diversity branches to the current traffic demands. This is done by TACD, which is a control algorithm to define ACD's priorities.

5.1. Asymmetric cooperation for media streaming

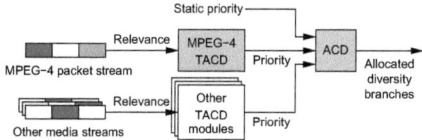

Figure 5.1: Basic structure of the proposed traffic-aware diversity allocation system. Shaded functions are described in this work.

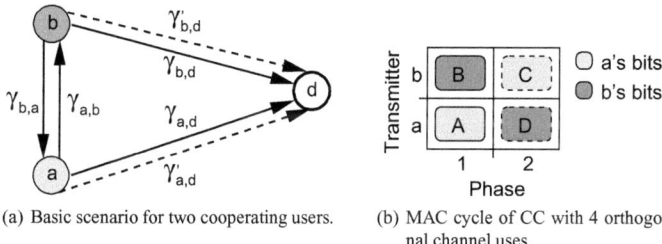

(a) Basic scenario for two cooperating users.

(b) MAC cycle of CC with 4 orthogonal channel uses.

Figure 5.2: Basic scenario and MAC cycle of Coded Cooperation (CC) if user a and b cooperate to reach destination d. The figure shows the instantaneous SNR values γ for all transmissions during phase 1 (solid line) and phase 2 (dashed line) of the MAC cycle.

TACD defines priorities according to the relevance of the current media packet. Unlike ACD, TACD is traffic-aware and many different traffic-specific variants may be used (e.g., for various voice or video codecs). We will describe a variant for MPEG-4 video streams below. TACD's traffic-aware prioritization is completely distributed among the users, comes at no communication overhead, and does not add delays, e.g., due to re-scheduling packets or sorting queues. All this makes TACD most suitable for *real-time* streaming.

Assumed scenario and protocol

ACD generalizes the Coded Cooperation (CC) protocol that symmetrically allocates the diversity branches among the cooperating nodes. We described CC in Section 3.2 and now detail the parts which ACD manipulates as well as the scenario assumptions.

An example of CC with two cooperating nodes is illustrated in Figure 5.2. The two nodes a and b are called *users* and may cooperate to reach the destination d. A cooperating user is called *partner* and may act alternatively as source and relay. As each partner transmits its own and forwards its partner's data, two users split the MAC cycle into the four slots A, B, C, D illustrated in Figure 5.2(b). As in the previous chapters, we assume that a MAC scheme which assures that these slots represent orthogonal subchannels. As common for selection relaying protocols, CC separates each protocol cycle into a source phase (phase 1) and a relay phase (phase 2). Between both phases the relay makes a forwarding decision. If both users forward, user a transmits in slots A, D and user b transmits in B, C.

Unlike other selection relaying protocols, CC integrates cooperation into FEC coding and puncturing

(Section 3.2). We assume that both users employ ideal convolution FEC codes which support various code rates, e.g., the well-known RCPC codes [Hag88]. For generality, we express the code rate as spectral efficiency R in bits/s/Hz. For more specific systems, the transmission rate in bits/s can be easily derived by multiplying R with the modulation order and the signal bandwidth.

We assume the coding procedure described in Section 3.2. Per cycle, each user transmits k information bits coded at rate $R = k/n$ to n transmitted bits. Puncturing removes n_2 bits from n which are saved for phase 2, while the remaining n_1 bits are transmitted in phase 1. After phase 2, for each user $n = n_1 + n_2$ bits may be available at d. In this case d, combines the n_1 and n_2 bits by de-puncturing. If d receive multiple phase 2 signals for a user, d employs MRC to combine these signals prior to de-puncturing. As described in Section 3.2, n_1 and n_2 can be adjusted by choosing a puncturing matrix according to the cooperation level $\beta = n_1/n$. For simplicity, we assume $\beta = 1/2$ which sets both phases to equal length. Consequently, $n_1 = n_2 = n/2$ leading to the code rates $R_1 = R_2 = 2R$ for both phases.

The links (a,d) and (b,d) in Figure 5.2 towards the destination are called *uplinks*. The links (a,b) and (b,a) between the users are called *inter-user links*. As CC is a selection relaying protocol, the states of the links (a,b) and (b,a) define if a user relays its partner's n_2 bits. With two users this leads to four modes of cooperation. In the *symmetric* modes, either both users can decode and forward each other's packets or or none of the users can forward. In the *asymmetric* modes, only one of both users can decode and forward and the other user transmits its own packet.

For all links, i.i.d. Rayleigh block fading channels are modeled as described in Section 2.1.2. By choosing a fading block time $T_b = T_p$, we assume that a channel may fade only once per packet time T_p. We denote the instantaneous SNR of the inter-user links during phase 1 by $\gamma_{a,b}$ and $\gamma_{b,a}$ (Figure 5.2). The instantaneous SNR for the uplinks is denoted by $\gamma_{a,d}, \gamma_{b,d}$ for phase 1 and $\gamma'_{a,d}, \gamma'_{b,d}$ for phase 2. We assume a symmetrical network geometry where both partners experience the same mean SNR $\bar{\gamma}_u$ in the uplink, i.e., $\bar{\gamma}_u := \bar{\gamma}_{a,d} = \bar{\gamma}_{b,d} = \bar{\gamma}'_{a,d} = \bar{\gamma}'_{b,d}$, and the same mean SNR $\bar{\gamma}_i$ during the *initial* data exchange in phase 1, i.e., $\bar{\gamma}_i := \bar{\gamma}_{a,b} = \bar{\gamma}_{b,a}$. As in Chapter 4 we normalize path loss to unity. Hence, the mean SNR $\bar{\gamma}$ is equivalent to the reference SNR Γ (Section 2.1.1).

5.1.2 Related work

Unlike many media-aware cooperation protocols, ACD and TACD do not allocate a higher source coding rate [GE04, XGEW05, KHL05] or more channel resources [LCSK07, LSC07] to increase the priority of highly relevant parts of a media stream. Instead, our approach allocates diversity branches which are provided by a selection relaying protocol.

On top of our approach, resource allocation [LCSK07] or retransmission schemes [LSC07], which are customized to cooperative media streaming, can be still applied. Some of these schemes rely on perfect feedback from the destination which cannot be guaranteed in many systems. One example is [LSC07], where the relay repeats a video packet if its ACK has not been received in time. If, with erroneous feedback, even an ACK for a *correctly* received packet may be lost, source and relay waste channel capacity. This is not the case with TACD which does not rely on feedback from the destination and does not rely on any control packets.

Exchanging control packets is also required if source coding is combined with cooperation [GE04, XGEW05, KHL05]. As cooperating users have to negotiate their code rates, such schemes are more vulnerable and less general than ACD and TACD. Furthermore, unlike these schemes, our approach is not limited to a particular source codec and traffic type. ACD and TACD's coordination scheme can operate with any traffic type as long as a priority is given or can be derived from the packet.

5.1.3 Asymmetric diversity branch allocation (ACD)

We now describe how the ACD protocol allocates diversity branches to the users' transmissions. To realize priorities, ACD exploits the high effect of cooperation diversity on the end-to-end error rate. As true diversity order L is only known after a transmission, ACD bases its allocation on the *estimated diversity order* $\tilde{L} \approx L$ that is known after the relay's forwarding decision.

Based on $\tilde{L}$, ACD lets users asymmetrically allocate their diversity branches to their current packet. Assuming uncorrelated fading channels in time and space, one diversity branch is reached per slot A,B,C,D (Figure 5.2(b)). Hence, diversity branches can be allocated by slots.

Initially, slots A,B are fixed since each user transmits its own packet at least once. Hence, only the $\tilde{L} = 2$ diversity branches in slots C,D can be allocated freely. Per user, this leaves ACD three possibilities of allocation and provides three priorities. First, symmetrical CC can be used to allocate $\tilde{L} = 2$ diversity branches per user. In this case, user a receives the slots A,C while user b receives B,D. Since both users receive equal $\tilde{L}$, this case is called *equal priority*. Second, asymmetric CC can be used to assign $\tilde{L} = 3$ to one user. This user (e.g., a employing the slots A,C,D) receives *high priority*. Third, the partner of a high-priority user can only employ a single phase 1 slot and, thus, receives *low priority* by $\tilde{L} = 1$. For instance, if a receives high priority, user b can only employ slot B.

Nevertheless, the actually reached L depends on the forwarding decision of each user. With ACD, no spatial diversity is reached for a user a if its partner b fails to decode a's n_1 bits. Due to this dependency, ACD allocates diversity branches between phase 1 and 2 of the MAC cycle. Here, the result of the forwarding decision is known and each user knows which $\tilde{L}$ it can provide for its partner.

If one or both users cannot cooperate, equal priority cannot be provided by cooperation. Instead, ACD still provides equal priority by falling back to direct transmission. In this case a and b still receive $\tilde{L} = 2$ temporal diversity branches in slots A,D and B,C, respectively.

Direct transmission is also employed as a fallback option when the neighbor of a high priority user cannot cooperate. Without a partner, high priority cannot be provided and both users realize equal priority by direct transmission. We will detail this discussion in the following outage analysis.

5.1.4 Outage probability and diversity order

ACD's prioritization only works if its diversity branch allocation has a significant effect on the error rate. We now confirm this large effect and detail ACD's description by outage probability and diversity order

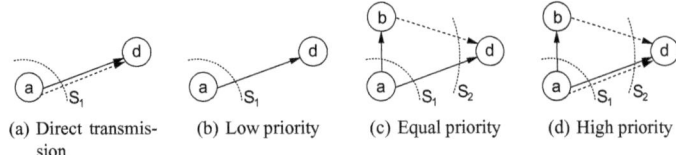

(a) Direct transmission (b) Low priority (c) Equal priority (d) High priority

Figure 5.3: Flow network of each ACD transmission mode for $a \to d$. The cut sets S_1, S_2 are defined over all links which ACD can use during phase 1 (solid line) and phase 2 (dashed line).

analysis.

Method and assumptions

As discussed in Chapter 3, deriving the exact outage probability for multi-channel systems is not trivial. For CC, an approximation is provided in [HSN06] assuming high SNR and i.i.d. Rayleigh fading channels. Unlike in [HSN06] and in parts of this work, we will not use numerical integration and Taylor approximation to obtain the outage probability P^{out} for asymptotically high SNR. Instead, we will derive the conditional probability terms from the flow networks as in Section 3.3 and provide results for high and low SNR by simulation.

While this method joins generality and exact results, it neither provides the diversity order L nor $\tilde{L}$. Instead, L has to be derived asymptotically (Section 2.2). We do so by applying cut set analysis in the high SNR regime. The applied method is similar to the approach in Section 3.2 but now we separate the phases to account for an asymmetric allocation of the phase 2 slots. Note that at high SNR and without correlation, cut set analysis even provides the exact diversity order L. This quantity provides an upper bound for the practical estimate $\tilde{L}$.

To isolate the effect of ACD's allocation we focus on a simple scenario with static priorities and only two cooperating users (Figure 5.2). Note that it suffices to derive P^{out} only for a single user. Although ACD is an asymmetric scheme, its function depends only on the priority and not on the user. Hence, we study only user a. For user b, identical expressions and cut sets are obtained with the roles of both users reversed.

Outage and cut set analysis

We now apply these methods to direct transmission and to each of ACD's three priorities. We start by decomposing Figure 5.2(a) into one flow network for each transmission mode of user a. For the resulting flow networks in Figure 5.3, we define all N unidirectional cut sets $S_1, \ldots, S_N$ as described in Section 3.3.1.

Equal priority by direct transmission Let us start with direct transmission to d as a simple example. Both users receive the same number of slots and diversity branches. User a utilizes slots A, D for its own data and leaves B, C to b (Figure 5.2). During each slot the link fades independently in time, thus, the

5.1. Asymmetric cooperation for media streaming

link has to fail in both time slots to cause an outage. Consequently, a temporal diversity order of $L = 2$ is reached.

In Figure 5.3(a), this result is reflected by the two edges in cut set S_1. If the instantaneous SNR $\gamma_{a,d}$ as well as $\gamma'_{a,d}$ of these two statistically independent phases drop below the corresponding rate-dependent threshold $\hat{\gamma}_1 = 2^{R_1} - 1$ and $\hat{\gamma}_2 = 2^{R_2} - 1$, direct transmission fails. Hence, the outage probability of this event (5.1) depends on the code rates $R_1 = k/n_1$ and $R_2 = k/n_2$ for both phases.

$$P_{\text{di}}^{\text{out}} = \mathbb{P}\{(\gamma_{a,d} < \hat{\gamma}_1) \cdot (\gamma'_{a,d} < \hat{\gamma}_2)\} \tag{5.1}$$

Low priority With low priority user a employs only the single slot A. Hence, only $\gamma_{a,d}$ needs to fall below threshold $\hat{\gamma}_1$ to cause an outage. This reduces S_1 to a single link, i.e., $L = 1$, and leads to

$$P_{\text{low}}^{\text{out}} = \mathbb{P}\{\gamma_{a,d} < \hat{\gamma}_1\}. \tag{5.2}$$

Note that (5.2) is always larger than (5.1) since with direct transmission each user obtains a higher L and transmits at lower code rate than with low priority.

Equal priority by cooperation In this case both users cooperate to symmetrically share their antennas during phase 2. This allows each user to distribute n bits over two antennas. In Figure 5.3(c) both cut sets S_1 and S_2 contain two links. Thus, the diversity order L of this priority is two.

Such symmetric cooperation, however, only works if *each* user correctly decodes the partner's n_1 bits. This is represented by the first case in (5.3). Here, $\gamma_{a,b}$ as well as $\gamma_{b,a}$ exceed $\hat{\gamma}_1$, allowing both users to cooperate. In the three remaining cases in (5.3), at least one user fails to cooperate and cannot provide spatial diversity to its partner by cooperation. In each of these remaining cases, both users fall back to direct transmission leading to a P^{out} similar to (5.1).

$$\begin{aligned}
P_{\text{eq}}^{\text{out}} = & \ \mathbb{P}\{\gamma_{a,b} \geq \hat{\gamma}_1\} \cdot \mathbb{P}\{\gamma_{b,a} \geq \hat{\gamma}_1\} \cdot \mathbb{P}\{\gamma_{a,d} < \hat{\gamma}_1\} \cdot \mathbb{P}\{\gamma'_{b,d} < \hat{\gamma}_2\} \\
& + \mathbb{P}\{\gamma_{a,b} < \hat{\gamma}_1\} \cdot \mathbb{P}\{\gamma_{b,a} \geq \hat{\gamma}_1\} \cdot \mathbb{P}\{(\gamma_{a,d} < \hat{\gamma}_1) \cdot (\gamma'_{a,d} < \hat{\gamma}_2)\} \\
& + \mathbb{P}\{\gamma_{a,b} \geq \hat{\gamma}_1\} \cdot \mathbb{P}\{\gamma_{b,a} < \hat{\gamma}_1\} \cdot \mathbb{P}\{(\gamma_{a,d} < \hat{\gamma}_1) \cdot (\gamma'_{a,d} < \hat{\gamma}_2)\} \\
& + \mathbb{P}\{\gamma_{a,b} < \hat{\gamma}_1\} \cdot \mathbb{P}\{\gamma_{b,a} < \hat{\gamma}_1\} \cdot \mathbb{P}\{(\gamma_{a,d} < \hat{\gamma}_1) \cdot (\gamma'_{a,d} < \hat{\gamma}_2)\}
\end{aligned} \tag{5.3}$$

High priority by cooperation If user a receives high priority it employs the slots A,C,D. Consequently, the cut sets S_1 and S_2 include three links and the diversity order for user a is three (Figure 5.3(d)). In this case, user b obtains only low priority by $L = 1$.

As a does not help b, only b needs to decode correctly, i.e., transmission (a,b) must not be in outage during phase 1. We incorporate this condition in the first probability term of (5.4). The second term includes two events due to de-puncturing, where $\gamma'_{a,d} + \gamma'_{b,d}$ represents MRC of the phase 2 signals (Section 2.2.3). If the first condition (5.4) fails, high priority cannot be provided for a, direct transmission is used

Table 5.1: Diversity order for two users.

Tx scheme/ Priority of user a	Diversity order L of user a	b
Direct	2	2
Low	1	3
Equal	2	2
High	3	1

as fallback option, and P^{out} is similar to (5.1).

$$\begin{aligned} P_{\text{hi}}^{\text{out}} &= \mathbb{P}\{\gamma_{a,b} \geq \hat{\gamma}_1\} \cdot \mathbb{P}\{(\gamma_{a,d} < \hat{\gamma}_1) \cdot (\gamma'_{a,d} + \gamma'_{b,d} < \hat{\gamma}_2)\} \\ &+ \mathbb{P}\{\gamma_{a,b} < \hat{\gamma}_1\} \cdot \mathbb{P}\{(\gamma_{a,d} < \hat{\gamma}_1) \cdot (\gamma'_{a,d} < \hat{\gamma}_2)\} \end{aligned} \qquad (5.4)$$

We summarize our diversity order results in Table 5.1. The table lists the priorities for user a and the according diversity orders for both users. Since the four slots in Figure 5.2(b) are assumed to fade independently, both users can employ a maximum of four diversity branches per MAC cycle. Since each user has to transmit its packet at least once, no user can employ more than three branches.

Note that these diversity orders provide only a first, coarse overview of the order of magnitude of P^{out}. As described in Section 2.2.1, error rates can further differ by a coding gain or different results may be obtained at low SNR. Let us now study such differences in detail.

Simulation results

Inserting the instantaneous SNR from simulation into the probability terms (5.1), (5.2), (5.3), and (5.4) provides the results in Figure 5.4(a). The figure shows P^{out} of user a for direct transmission as well as ACD's three priorities.

In Figure 5.4(a) we study P^{out} vs. the *mean uplink SNR* $\bar{\gamma}_u$ for a high *mean inter-user SNR* $\bar{\gamma}_i$. This corresponds to a situation where the partners are close to each other. Figure 5.4(b) emphasizes the effect of the inter-user links by varying $\bar{\gamma}_i$ at a fixed, medium $\bar{\gamma}_u$.

In both figures, the results clearly separate into three priority groups – one for each diversity order L. In Figure 5.4(a), a higher L results in a steeper exponential decrease of P^{out}. At high SNR, this behavior is well known from the analysis in Section 3.3. However, even at lower SNR the diversity order groups differ significantly. Based on this large difference, ACD can provide its three priorities in the complete SNR region.

As expected, allocating high priority leads to the best performance. This is shown by the steep slope in Figure 5.4(a). Nevertheless, high priority for one user always comes at the cost of low priority for the other user. In this case, only $L = 1$ and the highest P^{out} is reached. Direct transmission employs both phases to reach temporal diversity of order $L = 2$. If equal priority is realized by cooperation, it depends on the inter-user links and, thus, performs slightly worse than direct transmission.

5.1. Asymmetric cooperation for media streaming

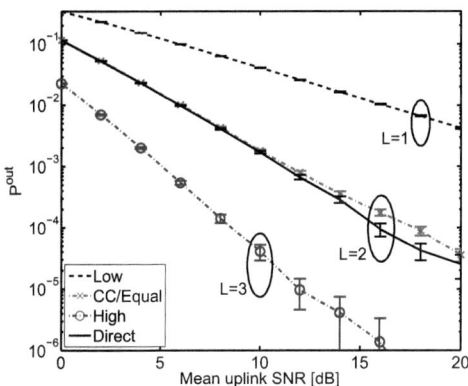

(a) Outage probability vs. mean uplink SNR $\bar{\gamma}_u$ for an mean inter-user SNR of $\bar{\gamma}_i = 20$ dB.

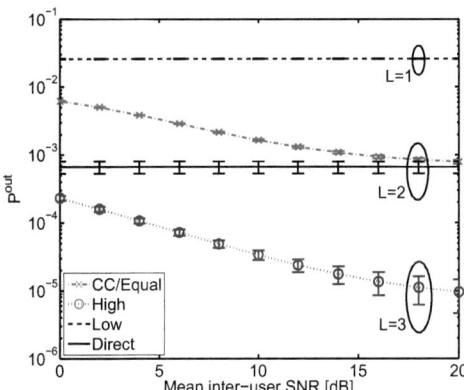

(b) Outage probability vs. mean inter-user SNR $\bar{\gamma}_i$ for an mean uplink SNR of $\bar{\gamma}_u = 12$ dB.

Figure 5.4: Outage probability for $R = 1/4$. Shown for direct transmission, Coded Cooperation (CC), and ACD's three priorities.

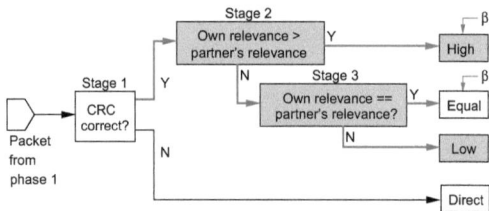

Figure 5.5: TACD's decision stages performed by each user between phase 1 and phase 2; extensions of CC due to TACD are shaded.

This dependency on the inter-user links is studied in Figure 5.4(b). At low $\bar{\gamma}_i$, both users can only seldom cooperate and realizing equal priority by CC is inefficient. If $\bar{\gamma}_i$ increases, successful cooperation becomes more likely and the performance of cooperative equal priority tends to the direct case. Also high priority depends on the inter-user links and, thus, improves with $\bar{\gamma}_i$. Low priority and Direct transmission make no use of these links and, naturally, remain static. As in Figure 5.4(a), the diversity order clearly separates the priorities in Figure 5.4(b).

From our analytic and simulation results we can conclude that ACD effectively provides static priorities by diversity branch allocation. At low SNR, different priorities are realized by different coding gains. At medium and high SNR, prioritization is provided by different diversity orders L. The results show that the allocated diversity branches $\tilde{L}$ matches to the actually reached diversity order. For high SNR, this $\tilde{L} \approx L$ was expected from the analytic results in Section 3.3 and 5.1.4. But even at medium SNR, our simulation results show a clear separation of the priorities in terms of outage probability. Let us now use these priorities in the TACD scheme to improve the quality of media streams.

5.1.5 Traffic-aware cooperation diversity

To efficiently improve the quality of real-time media streams with limited resources, TACD increases the diversity order only for the most relevant packets of the stream. This prioritization is dynamic, as it changes over time depending on the current packet's relevance, but can be integrated into cooperative relaying without additional communication overhead. This efficient, distributed prioritization scheme is described next.

Distributed priority selection

TACD chooses one ACD priority per packet. Similar to the 2SDF protocol in Section 4.4, TACD uses multiple decision stages which are illustrated in Figure 5.5. Each user indepently follows this procedure between phase 1 and 2.

In decision stage 1, each user tests if it has correctly decoded the partner's packet by performing a CRC. If this test fails, a user switches to direct transmission and sends its own n_2 bits to d. If the partner's packet passes the CRC test, the user can cooperate and, thus, is able to prioritize the partner's packet.

In stage 2, a user compares its own packet relevance to the relevance of its partner's packet. Without further knowledge, both users perform a distributed diversity branch allocation by following the decision stages in Figure 5.5. If the relevance of its own packet is higher than the relevance of the partner's packet, a user chooses to transfer its own packet at high ACD priority. If the partner can cooperate, it uses the same decision cycle and, thus, makes the opposite decision. Hence, it chooses low priority and provides its second phase to the high priority user. If the partner cannot cooperate, it transmits directly and does not provide its second phase to the high priority user. In this case, even the high priority user can only employ its own diversity branches, i.e., it can only transmit directly. With this fallback to direct transmission both users assure that no part of the second phase is wasted.

While this scheme seems rather straightforward, a conflict occurs if both users cooperate for packets of equal relevance. If both users choose high priority for their packets, they request more than the maximum number of diversity branches. If both users choose low priority, the second phase is wasted. Fortunately, this conflict occurs only when both users are able to cooperate and, thus, can be easily detected as follows. After phase 1, each user knows its own *and* the partner's packet (if not, cooperation is not possible for this user anyway). In stage 3, each user compares the relevance of these packets (Figure 5.5). If the relevance of both packets is equal, the conflict is detected and solved by falling back to equal priority.

As an example, consider that user a and b transmit a packet of the same relevance. We denote the relevances of these packets as ρ_a and ρ_b. If both users correctly decode the partner's packet (stage 1), user a extracts ρ_b from the packet of user b and compares it to its own relevance ρ_a in stage 2 and 3. Since $\rho_a = \rho_b$, stage 3 detects the conflict and a falls back to equal priority. Extracting ρ_a, user b follows the same decision procedure and falls back to *equal priority* as well.

Note that both users make the same decision without further coordination between them. By falling back to equal priority, both users assure that neither the maximum number of diversity branches is exceeded nor that resources are wasted. With this simple decision scheme, two cooperating users can agree on the mutually exclusive high and low priorities. Direct transmission and equal priority are used as fallback options. All this is performed in a completely distributed manner, without additional communication on top of the relaying process.

Choosing TACD priorities for MPEG-4 video streams

To allow such distributed prioritization without overhead, each cooperating user has to know the relevance of its own and of the partner's packet. In Variable Bit Rate (VBR) source-coded voice or video streams the source coder has already classified the parts of the stream. Here, the relevance can be extracted by inspecting the header of the Real-Time Transport Protocol (RTP) protocol [The03] or by using a packet classification scheme to inspect the payload [CK02, ZLE+05]. Based on the extracted relevance, users can agree on their priorities with TACD as described above. We will now discuss how to customize TACD for MPEG-4 video streams as a simple example.

Let us briefly recapitulate MPEG-4 video encoding. With the MPEG-4 Advanced Video Coding (AVC) codec, video streams consist of at least two types of video frames, the most relevant *I-frames* and

Table 5.2: Parameters of the video quality study.

Parameter	Setting
Channel model	i.i.d. Rayleigh block fading $T_b = T_p$
Mean uplink SNR $\bar{\gamma}_u$	7 dB
Mean inter-user SNR $\bar{\gamma}_i$	20 dB
Maximum packet size	1500 Bytes
Test video sequences	Mobile/Akiyo/Football (MAF) [Vid04]
Test sequence duration	23 s
Video/Color format	CIF/YUV 4:2:0
Video codec	MPEG-4 AVC/H.264 [ISO00]
Mean video bitrate	256 Kbits/s after source encoding
Group Of Pictures (GoP)	IPPPPPPPPPPP [ISO00]

the less relevant *P-frames* [ISO00]. While an I-frame contains a full picture, P-frames only include the so-called *motion vector* encoding differences between two subsequent I-frames. Hence, information in P-frames is always based on the previous I-frame and source-decoding errors within this I-frame would propagate through the shown video stream until the next I-frame occurs.

Our MPEG-4 variant of TACD assigns ACD's priorities according to this relevance. High priority is provided for each I-frame-related packet while for each P-frame packet low ACD priority is assigned. Equal priority and direct transmission are used as fallback options as given in Section 5.5.

5.1.6 Video quality study

We now study the effect of TACD's traffic-aware prioritization and of static priorities on the quality of a transmitted MPEG-4 video.

Scenario and test video sequence

We model the two-user scenario in Figure 5.2 as described in Section 5.1.1. The most important settings are summarized in Table 5.2. Similar to the outage probability study, we choose a scenario with low $\bar{\gamma}_u$ but high $\bar{\gamma}_i$ where cooperative relaying is relevant. Our test video sequence, called *Mobile/Akiyo/Football (MAF)*, is based on three commonly used test sequences [Vid04]. For a representative sample, we combined the low-motion test sequence Akiyo with two high-motion sequences. The resulting MAF sequence is converted to *Common Intermediate Format (CIF)* format, i.e., 352×288 pixels at a frame rate of 25 Hz. As part of the ITU standard H.261 [ITU93], CIF is widely used in video conferencing and supported by many mobile terminals. Also the chosen MPEG-4 AVC codec is common in such scenarios. Standardized in H.264, this VBR video codec was specifically designed for telecommunication [WSBL03]. We encoded the MAF sequence using a typical 12 Group Of Pictures (GoP) defining the I and P-frame placement in the stream [ISO00].

For the resulting MPEG-4 coded stream we simulate cooperative and non-cooperative transmission using a typical maximum packet size (Table 5.2). Within this stream, 26 % of the packets refer to I-frames and 74 % to P-frames. To achieve statistical significant results, each user continuously transmits the video stream until the confidence intervals reach a specified size. In our experiments 434 video transmissions where necessary per user. Inserting a random delay before transmitting the first stream assures that both users do not transmit their videos at exactly the same time. The Evalvid framework [LK08] allows us to emulate erroneous video transmission by inserting transmission errors from the simulation into the video stream. These "received" videos are then decoded and compared to the original, not transmitted video stream according to the video quality metric.

Video quality metrics

We measure the PER separately for I and P-frame packets, to have a first objective estimate of the video quality. Studying the subjective, i.e., perceived video quality with computer-based metrics is challenging since human visual perception cannot be easily formalized [ITU96, LK08, WP09]. We employ two different metrics, each emphasizing different aspects of visual perception. First, we use the widely-accepted Peak Signal-to-Noise Ratio (PSNR) metric to focus on instantaneous quality changes [ITU96].

Our second metric, called Distortion In interVal (DIV) [GKKW04, LK08], accounts for the fact that a viewer might average out very short impairments while still perceiving longer quality impairments. DIV reflects this by counting the percentage of decoded video frames that are worse than the original ones within a certain time interval. Similar to a moving average, this comparison slides over the complete video stream until, finally, the maximum percentage is returned as DIV value. Consequently, DIV represents the worst distortion over all intervals and is a rather pessimistic metric. As interval length, we choose the standard value of 20 s [GKKW04]. DIV is part of the Evalvid framework [LK08]; a detailed description and examples are provided in [GKKW04].

In addition to these formal studies, readers can download our video results at [Val09] and judge them according to their own visual impression.

Results

For a first illustration, we provide visual examples in Figure 5.6 and 5.7. In each figure, we compare a video frame transmitted using either CC or TACD. Both schemes are compared at equal channel states and reach equal diversity order. The only difference is that TACD prioritizes I-frame packets while CC does not. In Figure 5.6 the first I-frame of the MAF sequence is shown. Here, the impact of TACD's prioritization is very clear. While no significant impairments are shown with TACD, with CC the picture is almost completely destroyed due to transmission errors in I-frame packets. Note that this intense impairment will propagate through the video stream until the next I-frame is shown. Although the visual quality difference in Figure 5.7 is less significant, still a large impairment is shown with CC. Unlike in Figure 5.6, this impairment results from errors in P-frame packets. This leads to an erroneous motion vector which can be observed as a blur behind the running football players. In this example, such impairments are not shown for TACD. Nevertheless, these visual examples are only a first snapshot. Further examples are provided along with the video streams at [Val09] and show similar high quality differences between CC

(a) CC (b) TACD

Figure 5.6: Frame 1 of the MAF video sequence; received at equal instantaneous SNR using CC or TACD.

(a) CC (b) TACD

Figure 5.7: Frame 139 of the MAF video sequence; received at equal instantaneous SNR using CC or TACD.

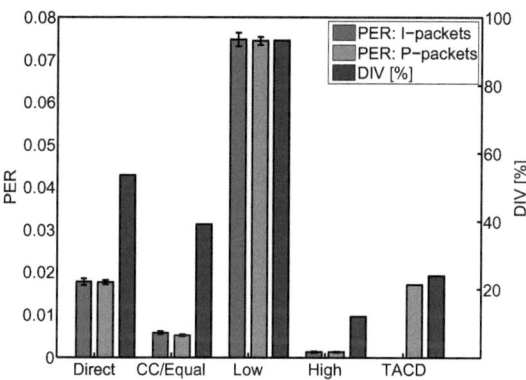

Figure 5.8: Mean PER for I-frame and P-frame packets and DIV for the received MAF video sequence. Shown for direct transmission, CC, static priorities, and TACD.

and TACD.

We now complement these visual examples by statistically significant video quality results observed during many transmissions of the video stream. First, we show PER results separately for I- and P-frame packets in Fig. 5.8. In general, the PER results for direct transmission and for the static priorities reflect the outage probabilities in Figure 5.4. Obviously, static high priority achieves the best performance with PER of 0.13 % for both I-frame and P-frame packets. However, the partner of the high priority user always receives low priority, leading to the worst PER for both packet types. The two temporal diversity branches used by direct transmission lead to a PER of 1.77 % for both I-frame and P-frame packets. CC increases this performance by symmetrically allocating spatial diversity. This decreases the PER to 0.57 % for both packet types. Compared to CC, TACD's traffic-aware allocation pays off by leading to a PER of zero for the important I-frames. For both users *no* I-frame packet error occured over all 434 transmissions of the MAF video. However, TACD can reach this benefit only by penalizing P-frame packets. The resulting PER of 1.71 % is significantly larger than for CC.

Figure 5.8 also includes results for the DIV metric. As expected, with high priority only a slight distortion of 12 % occurs. However, in this case the partner receives low priority leading to an unacceptably high DIV of 93 %. The further results clearly demonstrate that TACD's prioritization of I-frame packets achieves higher video quality than CC, even if this penalizes P-frame packets. While TACD achieves a DIV of 24 %, CC suffers from its symmetric allocation and achieves merely 39 %. This performance of CC is not much better than direct transmission with a mean DIV of 53 %.

To understand how often TACD chooses a particular priority, we counted how often both users transmit a packet of equal or different video frame type per MAC cycle. With two frame types and two users, four cases are possible. The results for these cases are presented in Figure 5.9. In 22.6 % of the MAC cycles, user *a* and *b* transmitted a different frame type. Such an asymmetric case occurs if either user *a* transmits

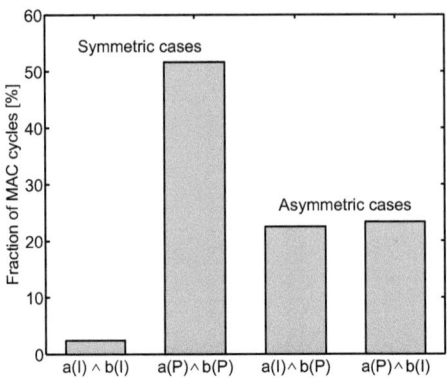

Figure 5.9: Occurrence of video frame types with MAF: Fraction of MAC cycles where the users a and b transmit packets of equal or different video frame type.

an I-frame packet and user b a P-frame packet ($a(I) \wedge b(P)$ in Figure 5.9) or vice versa. In these cases, TACD performs asymmetric prioritization as described in Section 5.1.5, i.e., the user transmitting an I-frame packet receives high and the other user low priority.

In the symmetric cases both users transmit a packet of equal video frame type in the same MAC cycle. In Figure 5.9 this is denoted by $a(I) \wedge b(I)$ and $a(P) \wedge b(P)$. In 51.7 % of the cycles, both users transmitted a P-frame. Here, both users equally gain by receiving equal priority. On the other hand, if two I-frame packets are transmitted per cycle, both packets lose their high priority and receive merely equal priority. Fortunately, such collision happens only in 2.4 % of the cases due to the smaller amount of I-frame packets in the stream. Therefore, I-frame packets suffer significantly less often than P-frame packets gain from TACD's fallback to equal priority.

As an example, Figure 5.10 shows the PSNR of all video frames vs. the play-out time for a single MAF sequence. Apart from an offset due to the three video parts of the MAF sequence, only slight PSNR changes occur in the low motion Akiyo part. Due to the high quality that is reached by TACD, the PSNR curve of the original video is hidden behind TACD's PSNR results. Unlike TACD, conventional cooperation with CC causes long impairments at the beginning of both high motion parts. These impairments result from I-frame errors that propagate through the shown video and lead to a larger DIV for CC than for TACD. Hence, the PSNR and DIV results clearly show that prioritizing the important I-frames with TACD is beneficial in terms of visual quality.

All in all, the above results demonstrate that TACD works as expected. As each applied video quality metric shows substantial improvements reached by neither direct nor conventional cooperative transmission, TACD is a promising approach for media streaming in cooperative wireless networks.

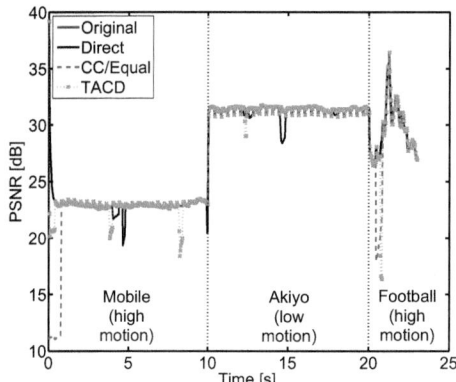

Figure 5.10: Example PSNR for a single MAF video sequence vs. play-out time; Shown before transmission (Original) and after transmission using direct transmission, CC, and TACD.

5.2 Cooperative feedback for multiuser diversity systems

Allocating channel resources according to the users' channel states can significantly improve the performance of multiuser communication. With multiple users, multiple fading channels are present and a scheduler can exploit their variation by resource allocation. This results in a so-called *Multiuser Diversity (MUD) gain*, typically achieved by a central scheduler to improve the capacity of a multiuser downlink (Section 2.2). To perform its allocation, the scheduler requires accurate channel knowledge that has to be available prior to allocation and prior to transmission.

Providing such accurate and timely transmitter CSI (CSI_{tx}) without degrading the MUD gain is a challenge. In most Frequency Division Duplexing (FDD) and some current TDD systems, e.g., IEEE 802.11n [LHL+08], reciprocal channels cannot be assumed. Without reciprocity, the users have to measure their CSI during the downlink and transmit it to the scheduler during the uplink. Such *CSI feedback* introduces overhead and delay and, hence, is always limited in terms of accuracy and redundancy. Therefore, CSI feedback can be a significant source of errors. Beside errors during CSI measurement and quantization, transmission errors during CSI feedback cause inaccurate CSI_{tx}. Using such erroneous CSI_{tx} results in scheduling errors, an inefficient resource allocation, and, consequently, decreases the downlink capacity [PM07, KK08, LHL+08, VK09].

Unfortunately, even protecting the important CSI feedback by sophisticated FEC codes or Automatic Repeat Request (ARQ) protocols is inefficient to assure its reliable and timely transmission. Compared to the few, highly valuable CSI bits, FEC and ARQ introduce significant overhead and delay. Furthermore, FEC and ARQ rely on time diversity, exploiting that a channel improves during a packet's transmission or retransmission. Unfortunately, this is not very likely for the CSI feedback in MUD systems. Typical

CSI packets are very short compared to data packets. Only fading channels with a very short coherence time are likely to improve during the transmission of such a short packet. But on the other hand, MUD systems perform best in low mobility scenarios where long coherence times assure that the probability of outdated CSI is low. This combination of slow channels and short CSI packets highly limits the time diversity gains needed to realize robust feedback with FEC and ARQ. For feedback, FEC and ARQ work best where MUD does not and vice versa.

This problem is demonstrated by the first study in this section. Transmission errors during CSI feedback substantially degrade downlink capacity and error rate even if strong FEC codes are employed. To cope with this problem we do not rely on time diversity gains. Instead we exploit spatial transmit diversity by selection relaying. We introduce the *Cooperative Feedback (CFB)* approach where users cooperate only for the important CSI packets during the uplink. This decreases the error rate of the CSI transmission, directly translates into more accurate CSI_{tx} at the scheduler which, after allocation, improves the performance of the multiuser downlink. As CFB retransmits only small CSI packets, the multiplexing loss is acceptable for a wide range of system parameters and even significant capacity gains can be provided.

We will now describe the assumed multiuser OFDM system, discuss related work, describe the CFB protocol, and study the downlink performance with and without feedback errors and overhead.

5.2.1 Multiuser diversity in OFDM systems

Exploiting multiuser diversity by resource allocation – sometimes referred to as channel-state-dependent scheduling [BBKT96] or opportunistic communication [VTL02] – is a well-known approach which has become practical in many systems. Multiuser MIMO [RJ08, GRTK08], multiuser OFDM [GWAC05, VFK08], or even the combination of both [IEE09b, CLL+07, VHW+08] are well-known examples of such systems.

From the variety of these systems, we focus on a simple multiuser OFDM scenario where a single Base Station (BS) transmits to J users during a point-to-multipoint downlink and where all nodes use only single antennas. In this downlink, OFDM [Cha66] separates the bandwidth W into S mutually exclusive OFDM subcarriers, each carrying a modulation symbol. As typical for OFDM systems, the channel is frequency-selective over full bandwidth W but each subcarrier can be considered as frequency flat [BSE04]. The result are S parallel subchannels, each independently fading in time and frequency.

In point-to-multipoint downlinks, OFDM Multiple Access (OFDMA) signals can be detected [MKP07] which allows the BS to allocate not only power and transmission rate but also OFDM subcarriers to the users [WCLM99, RC00]. By allocating these resources many schedulers aim to optimize the sum throughput over all users with respect to tight delay [LNDX04, VGKW05, GVKW05] or fairness [LL06, VHW+08] constraints. A tutorial on the theory behind these scheduling algorithms and on their design for practical systems is provided in [SL05a, SL05b].

Nevertheless, to isolate the effect of CSI feedback errors and cooperative relaying on the MUD downlink we have to exclude side-effects due to delay and fairness constraints or due to suboptimal resource allocation. To this end, we focus on the simplest optimal resource allocation for OFDM systems – power

5.2. Cooperative feedback for multiuser diversity systems

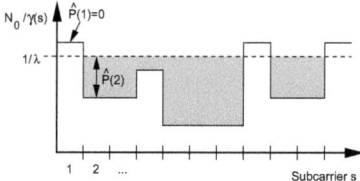

Figure 5.11: Example of waterfilling power allocation over S OFDM subcarriers. Illustration similar to [TV05, Figure 5.11].

allocation by *iterative waterfilling* [TH98].

Waterfilling maximizes the capacity C_S over all S subcarriers by solving the optimization problem

$$C_S(|h|^2) = \max_{P[1],\ldots,P[S]} \sum_{s=1}^{S} \log_2\left(1 + \frac{P[s]|h[s]|^2}{N_0}\right) \text{ [bits/s/Hz]} \tag{5.5}$$

subject to

$$\sum_{s=1}^{S} P[s] = P_d; \quad P[s] \geq 0; \quad s = 1,\ldots,S. \tag{5.6}$$

where P_d denotes the global transmit power constraint for the downlink, $P[s]$ the transmit power at subcarrier s, vector $h = h[1],\ldots,h[S]$ the channel coefficients at these subcarriers in the downlink, and $|h|^2$ the channel gain.

In power, the objective function (5.5) is concave and, thus, can be solved by iterative waterfilling as illustrated in Figure 5.11. The gray area illustrates the power which is "poured" into the depicted function. No power is allocated to a subcarrier s, if its $N_0/|h[s]|^2$ value is above the so-called waterline $1/\lambda$. For all other subcarriers, power is allocated until the optimal power allocation $\hat{P} = \hat{P}[1],\ldots,\hat{P}[S]$ is reached. At this allocation the waterline is chosen such that the power constraint P_d is met.

To derive $\hat{P}$ analytically we can solve (5.5) by Lagrangian methods as described in standard literature [TV05, Section 5.3.3]. Using the operator $x^+ := \max(x,0)$, we can denote the optimal power allocation for subcarrier s by

$$\hat{P}[s] = \left(\frac{1}{\lambda} - \frac{N_0}{|h[s]|^2}\right)^+ \tag{5.7}$$

given that the Lagrange multiplier λ is chosen such that P_d is met. To find λ, the waterfilling algorithm iteratively allocates units of power to the subcarriers as described for Figure 5.11. This algorithm is discussed in detail in [YC06] and the optimality of the waterfilling solution is proven in [LG01].

Note that waterfilling is based on the channel gain $|h|^2$ for each subcarrier. Each user has to provide this CSI to the central scheduler by feedback. Note further that with waterfilling, erroneous values of $|h[s]|^2$ will affect $\hat{P}[s]$ as well as the power that is allocated to subcarriers other than s.

In our simple OFDM system, waterfilling is performed for all J users. For each of the resulting J user-optimal power allocations, the sum capacity is calculated and the user m with the highest sum capacity receives *all* subcarriers. Hence, only the user with the "best" CSI transmits per cycle. Although this "best" user m can change from cycle to cycle, this "the winner takes it all" subcarrier allocation strategy is clearly not fair and may lead to unacceptable delays for other users than m. Nevertheless, this simple power and subcarrier allocation strategy provides the optimal solution in terms of ergodic sum capacity [LG01] and can be used as a simple performance bound in our study.

5.2.2 Related work

Many current and upcoming communication systems require extensive CSI_{tx} and, thus, perform limited feedback. Upcoming 4G standards, e.g., IEEE 802.16m, will include adaptive feedback [LHL+08] and current standard drafts already include [PH09] or consider [ID08] cooperation diversity for data transmission. So far, none of these systems exploits any form of cooperation for CSI feedback.

In particular, there is neither theoretical nor practical literature on employing cooperative relaying to improve CSI feedback. Several papers study the downside of imperfect CSI measurement on general MUD systems [PM07] and for particular OFDMA systems with suboptimal subcarrier and rate allocation [GVKW05]. For such a system, a concise characterization of the CSI estimation errors is provided in [KK08]. As only suboptimal rate allocation and no power allocation was assumed, the SNR and throughput results are limited to a particular type of suboptimal scheduling. Unlike in this section, no performance bounds for optimal resource allocation with feedback errors are provided. Although the above paper takes feedback transmission errors into account, it ignores overhead.

In turn, other work accounts for overhead but ignores feedback errors. Many schemes were proposed to reduce the feedback overhead in multiuser systems either by source coding [NBKL04] or by OFDM subcarrier grouping [GGKW06, CBH08]. Although all these papers mention the high effect of feedback errors, none of them tackles this issue.

The only approach more closely related to our work uses STC to strengthen the feedback channels of a CDMA system by spatial transmit diversity [HW04]. Although our cooperative feedback approach can even work on top of STC, CFB does not require multiple antennas per user. Hence, cooperative feedback differs from STC as follows: STC relies on multiple antennas per user and therefore does not need to repeat overheard packets to gain diversity. On the other hand, each of STC's antennas can employ only a fraction of the per-user-constrained transmission power and the antennas have to be sufficiently spaced apart to achieve spatial diversity gains. As described in Section 3.1, the large coherence distances typically make the design of small wireless devices difficult. This problem does not occur with cooperative relaying where, naturally, source and relay are spatially well separated.

To this end, we introduced CFB and presented a first analysis in [VK09]. Here, we go beyond this paper by detailing the resource allocation strategy and by providing further sum capacity results.

5.2. Cooperative feedback for multiuser diversity systems

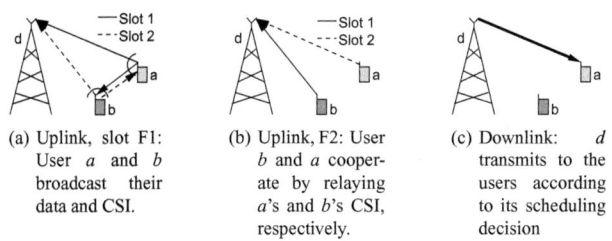

(a) Uplink, slot F1: User a and b broadcast their data and CSI.

(b) Uplink, F2: User b and a cooperate by relaying a's and b's CSI, respectively.

(c) Downlink: d transmits to the users according to its scheduling decision

Figure 5.12: Simple example for cooperative feedback with $J = 2$ users a, b and a single BS d.

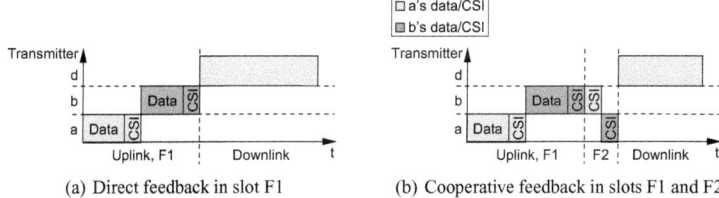

(a) Direct feedback in slot F1

(b) Cooperative feedback in slots F1 and F2

Figure 5.13: MAC cycle for direct and cooperative feedback. Illustration for the example in Figure 5.12 where user a receives all subcarriers.

5.2.3 Cooperative feedback protocol

Figure 5.12 illustrates a simple cooperative feedback protocol in the studied scenario. A single BS serves J wireless users. The MAC cycle is illustrated in Figure 5.13, lasts T_{cycle}, and is separated in an OFDM downlink and TDMA uplink.

During the uplink the users transmit their data and CSI to the BS using separate time slots. The transmission of CSI is called feedback and can be either done directly from each user to the BS (Figure 5.12(a)) or with the help of a cooperating user in an optional cooperation phase (Figure 5.12(b)). Direct feedback employs only slot F1 and leaves F2 to the OFDM downlink (Figure 5.13). In F1, each user is a *source* of its own CSI packet. In F2, each user functions as a *relay* for the CSI packet of another user. Sources are assigned to relays in the preceding downlink by the BS.

Note that this relaying protocol does not differentiate between dedicated Relay Stations (RS) and cooperating users. In fact both relay types are equivalent at capacity level, if equal wireless channels and transmission constraints are assumed for both of them. This allows us to capture RS and cooperating users by the same protocol and analysis.

Based on the relay assignment, our cooperative feedback scheme operates as follows: First, the users transmit their own CSI packets in distinct time slots (TDMA) during F1. In this phase, each user overhears, FEC decodes, and error-tests the feedback packet of its partner. If the packet is erroneous, the relay ignores it and repeats its own CSI packet during F2. If the packet is correct, the relay re-encodes the source's original packet and transmits it during F2. Finally, for each user, the BS combines the CSI packets received during F1 and F2 using Maximum Ratio Combining [Bre03]. This simple cooperation protocol is known as SDF with repetition coding (Section 3.2.2). In the best case, each CSI packet is transmitted twice and a diversity order of two is reached for each CSI packet. On the other hand, if each CSI packet is retransmitted, the total feedback overhead is doubled. Decreasing this overhead either by adapting the cooperation level β according to the quality of a user's feedback channel or by cooperating only for "weak" users is obviously possible but is not considered here.

After the feedback phases, the BS uses the received CSI to allocate the resources of the OFDM downlink as described above. In this example, all subcarriers are allocated to the single "best" user (Figure 5.12(c) and 5.13).

5.2.4 Effects of feedback errors and overhead

We first define the ergodic sum capacity and outage probability of the multiuser downlink for ideal CSI and, then, analyze the degrading effect of CSI feedback errors and overhead.

Multiuser OFDM performance with ideal feedback

The ergodic sum capacity $\bar{C}^{\text{sum}}$ denotes the maximum average throughput that is achieved during the OFDM downlink over all J users. To define this performance bound, we assume that during resource allocation the BS perfectly knows the channel gains $|h_{d,1}|^2, \ldots, |h_{d,j}|^2, \ldots, |h_{d,J}|^2$ for the downlink from d to each of the J users. With OFDM each of these channel gains is a vector over all S subcarriers where S is typically large. Perfectly knowing all these $S \times J$ channel gains neglects error due to the feedback channel as well as errors due to CSI measurement and quantization at the user-side. This is, again, the *perfect transmitter CSI* (CSI$_{\text{tx}}$) assumption which we know from Chapter 3.

Based on these assumptions, we can now define the instantaneous sum capacity reached during a single OFDM downlink phase by inserting the channel gain $|h_{d,m}|^2$ towards the scheduled user m into (5.5). This yields

$$C^{\text{sum}}_{d,\text{ideal}}(|h_{d,m}|^2) = \sum_{s=1}^{S} \log_2\left(1 + \frac{\hat{P}_m[s]|h_{d,m}[s]|^2}{N_0}\right) \text{ [bits/s/Hz]}. \tag{5.8}$$

Note that (5.8) already includes the optimal power allocation $\hat{P}_m[s]$ found by waterfilling (5.7) and implies a subcarrier allocation strategy where *only* the "best" user m in the current downlink phase is scheduled. As discussed in Section 5.2.1, this is assumed to obtain the ergodic sum capacity $\bar{C}^{\text{sum}}_{d,\text{ideal}}$ as a benchmark for the average data rate of the multiuser OFDM downlink with perfect CSI$_{\text{tx}}$.

We can simply obtain this performance bound $\bar{C}^{\text{sum}}_{d,\text{ideal}}$ reached with perfect CSI by time-averaging (5.8), i.e.,

$$\bar{C}^{\text{sum}}_{d,\text{ideal}} = \mathbb{E}\{C^{\text{sum}}_{d,\text{ideal}}\}. \tag{5.9}$$

Similarly, we can define the outage probability reached in the OFDM downlink with perfect CSI by

$$P^{\text{out}}_{d,\text{ideal}} = \mathbb{P}\{C^{\text{sum}}_{d,\text{ideal}}(|h_{d,m}|^2) < R_m(|h_{d,m}|^2)\} \tag{5.10}$$

where R_m denotes the spectral efficiency in bits/s/Hz that the BS assigns to user m according to its CSI. Note that calculating the probability $\mathbb{P}\{\}$ requires no accumulation of the subcarriers since this is already done in (5.8).

While P^out does not capture errors due to fading or noise, it provides the probability of transmission errors only resulting from the erroneous choice of R_m. This so-called rate adaptation is perfect if the BS can employ $|h_{d,m}|^2$ for its decision and this CSI value does not change during the cycle. With this ideal CSI the BS knows $C_\text{d,ideal}^\text{sum}$ and can assign $R_m = C_\text{d,ideal}^\text{sum}$ without rate adaptation errors, i.e., at zero outage probability. But such perfect rate adaptation is indeed not likely with erroneous CSI feedback which is discussed in the next section.

Multiuser OFDM performance with feedback errors

The effect of CSI measurement and quantization errors on the performance of a scheduled OFDM downlink was extensively studied [KK08]. Unlike this study, we isolate the effect of erroneous feedback channels by assuming that each user j perfectly measures and quantizes its channel gains $|h_{d,j}|^2$.

We assume further that the BS perfectly detects feedback transmission errors for each individual user. If feedback errors occur, the BS bases its allocation on the latest correctly received CSI value for the respective user.[1] We denote this (possibly outdated) estimate of the true channel gain by $|\hat{h}_{d,j}|^2 = |\hat{h}_{d,j}[1]|^2, \ldots, |\hat{h}_{d,j}[S]|^2$.

Exchanging $|h_{d,m}|^2$ by $|\hat{h}_{d,m}|^2$ in (5.8) defines the sum capacity $C_\text{d}^\text{sum}(|\hat{h}_{d,m}|^2)$ for possibly erroneous CSI. With (5.10), the outage probability due to allocation errors is given by

$$P_\text{d}^\text{out} = \mathbb{P}\{C_\text{d,ideal}^\text{sum}(|h_{d,m}|^2) < R_m(|\hat{h}_{d,m}|^2)\} \tag{5.11}$$

since now rate adaptation has to be based on the estimates in $|\hat{h}_{d,m}|^2$ whereas the obtained capacity obviously depends on the true channel gain $|h_{d,m}|^2$. Consequently, ideal rate adaptation can only choose $R_m(|\hat{h}_{d,m}|^2) = C_\text{d}^\text{sum}(|\hat{h}_{d,m}|^2)$ which is a wrong decision if $C_\text{d,ideal}^\text{sum}(|h_{d,m}|^2) < C_\text{d}^\text{sum}(|\hat{h}_{d,m}|^2)$, i.e., the true channel gain $|h_{d,m}|^2$ is smaller than its estimate. In this case, the channel is overestimated, the downlink transmission is in outage, and the sum capacity $C_\text{d,ideal}^\text{sum}$ cannot be reached.

Multiuser OFDM performance with feedback errors and overhead

The sum capacity is further degraded by the control overhead to transmit CSI feedback in the uplink and to signal the allocation decision to the users in the downlink.

During the feedback phase, all J users have to transmit their CSI values for each of their S subcarriers to the BS. Assuming that after quantization and source encoding, each of these $S \times J$ CSI values is expressed by N_sig bits, in total

$$L_f(J) = J \cdot S \cdot N_\text{sig} \tag{5.12}$$

---

[1] Alternatively, using the newer but erroneously received CSI value may be preferable in faster fading environments; this is not considered here.

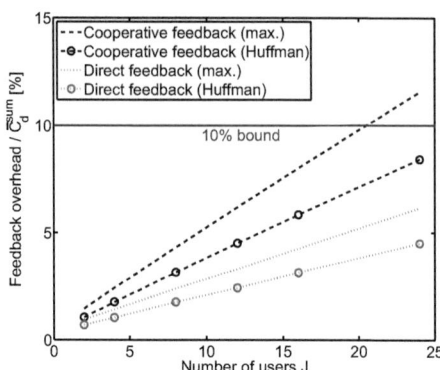

Figure 5.14: Percentage of total overhead on ergodic sum capacity (downlink) vs. number of users for direct and cooperative feedback; with and without Huffman coding; $N_{\text{sig}} = 5$ bits CSI signaling overhead per user per subcarrier.

bits of feedback information are transmitted per cycle. Further, the current resource allocation has to be signaled to the users. As with the above allocation strategy the best user receives all subcarriers, the BS has to broadcast only $\log_2 J$ bits of addressing information to the users to signal its decision.

This uplink and downlink overhead degrades the ergodic sum capacity of the multiuser OFDM to

$$\bar{C}_{\text{d,f}}^{\text{sum}} = \left(\bar{C}_{\text{d}}^{\text{sum}} - \frac{K \cdot L_f(J) + \log_2 J}{R_c \cdot W \cdot T_{\text{cycle}}} \right)^+ \text{[bits/s/Hz]}. \quad (5.13)$$

Here, R_c accounts for the redundancy added by FEC coding, bandwidth W and T_{cycle} express the fact that feedback is only transmitted once per cycle using full bandwidth, and K accounts for the packets repeated by cooperative feedback. If all users transmit their CSI directly to the BS, $K = 1$; the amount of feedback overhead is doubled if a single relay cooperates, i.e., $K = 2$.

Due to $L_f(J)$ in (5.13), the control overhead scales *linearly* in J. On the other hand, the MUD gain lets $\bar{C}_{\text{d}}^{\text{sum}}$ increase only *logarithmically* in J ([TV05, Section 6.6]). Thus, in multiuser OFDM systems, the reduction of $\bar{C}_{\text{d}}^{\text{sum}}$ due to feedback overhead is a serious problem if J, S, or K are large. However, overhead is acceptable for an intermediate number of subcarriers and users per BS [GGKW06], and if cooperative feedback employs only a single relay ($K = 2$). Note that with (5.12) $L_f(J)$ represents the maximum number of feedback bits for the studied OFDM system. It can be significantly compressed by lossless source coding [NBKL04] and by adaptive feedback protocols obtaining $K < 2$ (on the average) by only cooperating for "weak users".

As an example, Figure 5.14 shows the percentage of total overhead on the ergodic sum capacity for the parameters and results in Section 5.2.5. Additionally, $W = 20\,\text{MHz}$, $T_{\text{cycle}} = 2\,\text{ms}$ are assumed as in many IEEE 802.11/16 systems [OP99, GWAC05] and each CSI value is quantized to $N_{\text{sig}} = 5$ bits as with High Speed Downlink Packet Access (HSDPA) [3GP01].

As shown, with direct feedback all 24 users are supported given that the feedback overhead should not reduce $\bar{C}_\mathrm{d}^\mathrm{sum}$ by more than 10 %. This constraint is acceptable in many systems (Example 5.3 in [TV05]). It is even held by cooperative feedback with a single relay and if the well-known Huffmann source coding scheme compresses $L_f(J)$. Consequently, even static cooperative feedback supports a large number of users not increasing the overhead above 10 % of the sum capacity.

5.2.5 Performance study

In this section, we compare the performance of a multiuser OFDM system with cooperative feedback to systems which employ direct or ideal feedback. To this end, we (1) discuss the used method and parameters, (2) describe how cooperation reduces the error probability during feedback, and (3) how this improvement translates into performance gains for the multiuser OFDM downlink.

Method and parameters

To rate the downlink performance, we focus on the ergodic sum capacity $\bar{C}_\mathrm{d}^\mathrm{sum}$ and outage probability $P_\mathrm{d}^\mathrm{out}$ as defined in Section 5.2.4. For ideal feedback, both metrics can be directly calculated using the true channel gain. For erroneous feedback, we simulate the direct and cooperative transmission of CSI, assume that the BS employs old channel gain values in case of an error, and use these estimates $|\hat{h}_{d,1}|^2, \ldots, |\hat{h}_{d,J}|^2$ for ideal power and rate allocation.

We use the following assumptions to clearly point out the consequences of erroneous CSI feedback and potential benefits of cooperation: For the downlink, we assume sum-capacity-optimal resource allocation as described above. A random tie breaker is used and feedback transmission is the only source of errors. Performance losses due to CSI quantization, fading, or noise are neglected. Therefore, we assume that during the downlink, perfect FEC coding is used and model the subcarriers as S parallel, independent block fading channels (Section 2.1.2).

To focus only on MUD gains (and losses due to feedback errors), we fix the reference SNR for the downlink to $\Gamma_d = P_d/(N_0 W) = 0$ dB. This ignores power gains which would only result in a horizontal offset of $\bar{C}_\mathrm{d}^\mathrm{sum}$ and $P_\mathrm{d}^\mathrm{out}$ and simplifies comparison to the literature. Note that a low Γ_d has no negative effect on $P_\mathrm{d}^\mathrm{out}$ since this metric only captures transmission errors resulting from erroneous resource allocation.

In the uplink, all feedback schemes employ reference SNR $\Gamma_u = P_u/(N_0 W)$ and equal MAC time T_cycle and are, thus, compared at equal transmit energy (Section 2.3). We model the non-ideal feedback transmission as a single frequency-flat Rayleigh fading channel using the block fading model from Section 2.1.2. To account for transmission errors, we simulate the symbol-wise transmission at digital baseband level using BPSK modulation and a strong convolutional FEC code with generator polynomial $\{133_8; 171_8\}$ and code rate $R_c = 1/2$. This corresponds to the most robust transmission mode in IEEE 802.11a/g and IEEE 802.16a/d/e systems [OP99, GWAC05].

To sum up, with the above model, the following results show only performance losses due to feedback errors and only gains resulting from MUD and cooperation diversity.

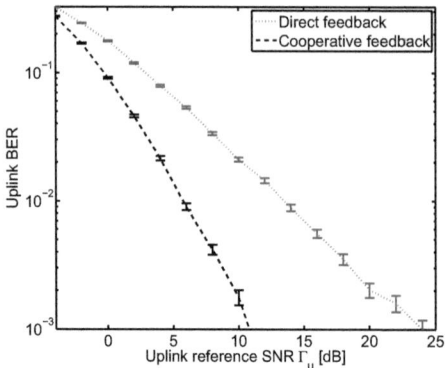

Figure 5.15: BER of the feedback channels vs. uplink SNR for direct and cooperative feedback; $J = 8$ users.

Improving feedback channels and CSI estimation

We now study the post-decoding BER of the feedback transmission. Furthermore, we study the accuracy of the scheduling decision as the Mean Squared Error (MSE)

$$\text{MSE} = \mathbb{E}\{(\hat{\gamma}_{d,\hat{m}} - \gamma_{d,m})^2\} \tag{5.14}$$

between (1) the SNR $\hat{\gamma}_{d,\hat{m}}$ reached for user $\hat{m}$ that was scheduled using the CSI estimate $|\hat{h}_{d,m}|^2$ and (2) the SNR value $\gamma_{d,m}$ reached for the true best user m that was scheduled using the true CSI $|h_{d,m}|^2$. This MSE compares the ideal value $\gamma_{d,m}$ to the SNR $\hat{\gamma}_{d,\hat{m}}$ that the scheduler reaches with limited CSI and, thus, precisely shows how improved CSI affects the scheduler performance.

For MSE and BER, the uplink SNR Γ_u is an important factor as it shows how efficient the feedback scheme can translate transmission power into estimation accuracy and robustness. For this factor, Figure 5.15 shows how cooperative relaying improves the BER of the feedback channels. Compared to direct transmission, cooperative relaying leads to a significant steeper decrease of the error rate for increasing Γ_u. As discussed in the previous chapters, this diversity gain results from combining the spatially independent signals at the BS. Even with the assumed robust modulation and strong FEC codes, cooperation can substantially improve the BER of our feedback channels.

Figure 5.16 shows how these cooperation diversity gains increase the accuracy of the feedback information. To rate the resulting improvement of the scheduling decision, we use the MSE according to (5.14). This metric shows clear improvements for cooperative feedback in Figure 5.16. Decreasing the BER of the feedback channels by cooperation clearly improves the CSI at the scheduler and, thus, its decision accuracy. Cooperative feedback provides this improvement where it is needed most – at low and medium SNR where FEC alone becomes inefficient.

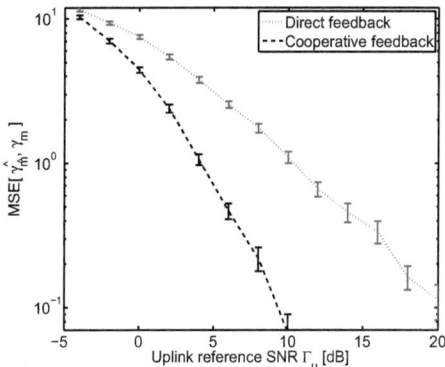

Figure 5.16: MSE comparing the estimated channel gain of the scheduled user to the true value; shown vs. uplink SNR for direct and cooperative feedback; $J = 8$ users.

Improving the multiuser OFDM downlink

As improving the CSI estimation avoids allocation decision errors, it now seems promising to study how the multiuser OFDM downlink profits from cooperative feedback. In particular, we will look at the downlink's ergodic sum capacity $\bar{C}_d^{\text{sum}}$ and outage probability P_d^{out} as functions of the feedback channel's SNR Γ_u and the number of users J. Finally, we derive operating regions for cooperative and direct feedback depending on Γ_u and on an error rate constraint ε.

For a medium number of users, the sum capacity of the downlink is shown vs. the uplink SNR Γ_u in Figure 5.17. In Figure 5.17(a) we neglect feedback overhead and focus only on the effect of feedback transmission errors. These errors substantially degrade the downlink sum capacity at low Γ_u when the feedback channel BER is large (Figure 5.15). For increasing Γ_u, cooperative feedback reaches the ideal sum capacity at 6 dB and direct feedback at 10 dB. Thus, direct transmission requires 4 dB more than cooperative feedback to compensate the degrading effect of feedback errors.

Accounting for overhead as in (5.13) leads to a constant offset for both realistic feedback schemes (Figure 5.17(b)). With overhead neither direct nor cooperative feedback reaches the ideal sum capacity. Decreasing the feedback channel BER by cooperation still slightly outperforms direct transmission for low Γ_u. At 6 dB the situation reverses as the gains of cooperative feedback are exceeded by the multiplexing loss due to relaying. Nevertheless, cooperative feedback forwards only small packets which only slightly decreases the capacity.

This decrease in capacity may be still acceptable as cooperative feedback significantly improves the downlink outage probability (Figure 5.18). If Γ_u increases, the downlink outage probability decreases significantly faster with cooperative than with direct feedback. Consequently, cooperative feedback uses the uplink SNR more efficiently to achieve a given P_d^{out}. For example, if an outage probability constraint of $\varepsilon = 0.01$ should not be exceeded, cooperative feedback realizes this at $\Gamma_u = 9$ dB while 19 dB are

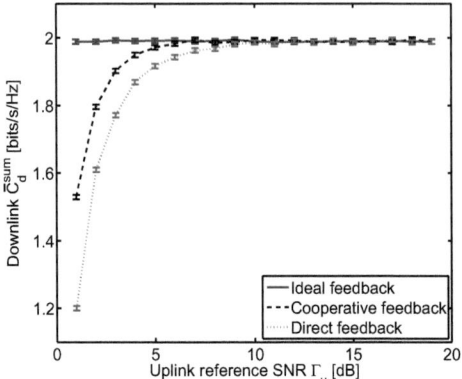

(a) Ergodic sum capacity (downlink): Ideal and degraded by feedback errors.

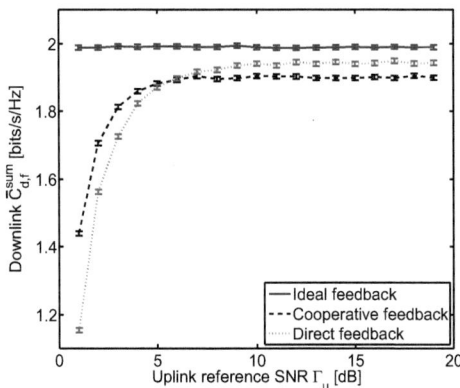

(b) Ergodic sum capacity (downlink): Ideal and degraded by feedback errors and overhead; $N_{\text{sig}} = 5$ bits CSI signaling overhead per user per subcarrier.

Figure 5.17: Ergodic sum capacity (downlink) vs. uplink SNR for ideal, direct, and cooperative feedback; $\Gamma_d = 0$ dB, $J = 8$ users.

5.2. Cooperative feedback for multiuser diversity systems

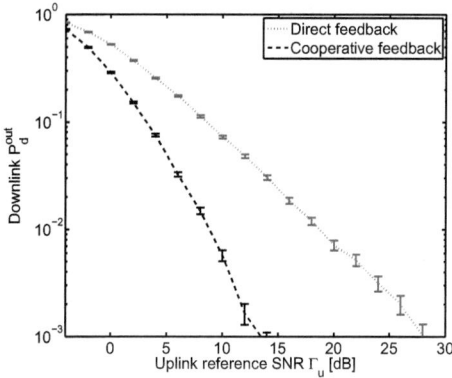

Figure 5.18: Outage probability (downlink) vs. uplink SNR for direct and cooperative feedback; $\Gamma_d = 0\,\text{dB}$, $J = 8$ users.

required with direct feedback. If its SNR cannot be increased by other means, each user with direct feedback wastes 10 dB of transmission power to reach this error rate.

Figure 5.19 provides further insight in this tradeoff between transmission power and error rate constraint ε. For cooperative and direct feedback, it shows the region of Γ_u that is required to reach full downlink capacity given that an outage probability of ε is not exceeded. Below its region, a feedback scheme does not allow the scheduler to reach ε at $\bar{C}_d^{\text{sum}}$. For Γ_u within or above its region, a feedback scheme allows to reach full sum capacity while the error rate constraint ε is held. This allows us to select the appropriate feedback scheme according to Γ_u and ε: In the lowest region, none of the feedback schemes can meet our ε constraint. In the medium SNR region, only cooperative feedback provides feedback channels which are robust enough to meet ε at such low Γ_u. At higher Γ_u, even direct feedback can be used. As shown, for all studied P_d^{out} constraints, cooperative feedback requires a lower Γ_u than direct transmission. This gain even grows for stricter ε. For example, while at $\varepsilon = 0.1$ cooperative feedback requires 6 dB less than direct transmission, the difference increases to 14 dB at $\varepsilon = 10^{-3}$. These high SNR gains can be employed to save the mobile user's transmit power, to increase coverage, or to provide safety margins in channel environments with high mobility.

Finally, we study the ergodic sum capacity of the OFDM downlink for a varying number of users J (Figure 5.20) and account for the degradation due to feedback overhead. To isolate the effect of feedback errors, Figure 5.20(a) shows the ergodic sum capacity which is degraded by feedback errors but not degraded by feedback overhead. Both effects are included in Figure 5.20(b) where the ergodic sum capacity is degraded by the feedback errors *and* the overhead as in (5.13). In both figures, we compare cooperative and direct feedback to the ideal case which includes neither feedback errors nor overhead; we assume a harsh feedback channel by choosing $\Gamma_u = 4$ dB.

For all cases in Figure 5.20(a) and 5.20(b) the sum capacity increases logarithmically with J. This increase results from MUD and is well known from theory; cp. [TV05, Section 6.6 and Figure 6.13]).

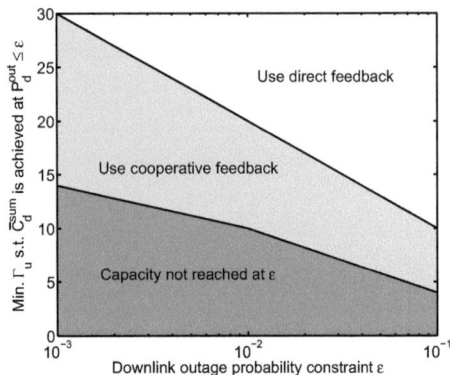

Figure 5.19: Uplink SNR regions required to reach full ergodic sum capacity *while* not exceeding the outage probability constraint ε. Shown vs. ε for direct and cooperative feedback; $\Gamma_d = 0$ dB, $J = 8$ users.

However, both realistic feedback schemes significantly lose sum capacity due to feedback errors. A new observation is that this loss becomes less severe for rising J (Figure 5.20(a)). This reduces the potential gains of cooperative (and other improved) feedback schemes and can be explained by the following symmetry of MUD gains: As for the downlink, a higher number of users improves the probability that a user with a "good" feedback channel exists. Thus, MUD does not only improve downlink capacity but also can compensate for erroneous feedback channels in the uplink.

Nevertheless, at a low and medium number of users J, cooperative relaying can still significantly reduce the capacity loss caused by feedback errors. Compared to direct feedback at $J = 4$, cooperation improves the sum capacity by up to 14 % (Figure 5.20(a) and 5.20(b)). Even with the additional overhead due to relaying (Figure 5.20(b)) significant gains can be provided for a low and medium number of users. For increasing J, the relaying overhead reduces the gain of cooperative feedback until the sum capacity of both realistic feedback schemes converges.

From the above results, we can conclude that MUD systems lose performance due to CSI feedback errors. This is even the case if the feedback channels are protected by robust modulation and strong FEC codes. Strengthening the feedback channels by cooperative relaying increases the resource allocation accuracy, substantially improving the outage probability and sum capacity of the multiuser OFDM downlink. Alternatively, cooperative feedback significantly decreases the SNR required at the feedback channels to operate the multiuser downlink at a given error rate. Compared to the immediate improvements in sum capacity, these SNR gains are very high (6 to 14 dB for the studied cases) and can be exploited in many ways, e.g., to save the mobile users' energy or to increase communication robustness. Naturally, these sum capacity gains are reduced by relaying overhead which makes CFB best suited for systems with limited feedback but poor feedback channels. IEEE 802.16e with mobile users [IEE05] or Long Term Evolution (LTE) with single-bit HARQ [LLM+09] are just two relevant examples of such systems.

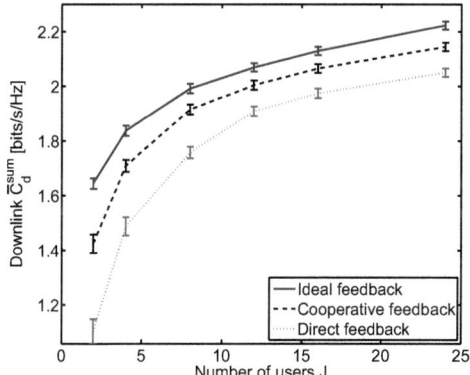

(a) Ergodic sum capacity (downlink): Ideal and degraded by feedback errors.

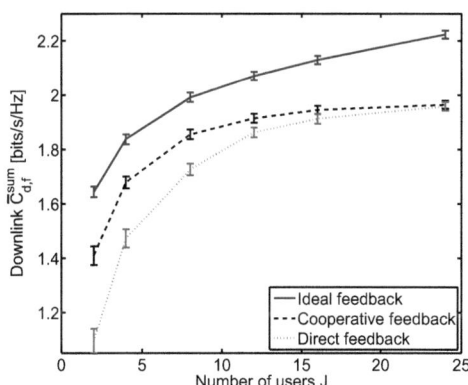

(b) Ergodic sum capacity (downlink): Ideal and degraded by feedback errors and overhead; $N_{\text{sig}} = 5$ bits CSI signaling overhead per user per subcarrier.

Figure 5.20: Ergodic sum capacity (downlink) vs. number of users for ideal, direct, and cooperative feedback; $\Gamma_d = 0\,\text{dB}$, $\Gamma_u = 4\,\text{dB}$.

5.3 Summary of contributions and future work

Contributions

We presented ACD and CFB to improve the performance of resource allocation by selection relaying. Unlike the protocols in the previous chapters, both approaches limit the overhead by retransmitting only highly relevant information. CFB forwards only small CSI packets and ACD only infrequently relays the most relevant packets of media streams. This highly improves scheduling performance but limits the multiplexing loss due to relaying.

Asymmetric Cooperation Diversity (ACD) ACD joins cooperative relaying and resource allocation at scheduling level. The introduced selection relaying protocol prioritizes packets by asymmetrically allocating diversity branches among the cooperating users. With the introduced traffic-aware control scheme, users negotiate their diversity branch allocations. Similar to our Partial Forwarding (PF) approach in Section 4.4, this traffic-aware diversity scheme employs a forwarding decision with multiple stages and requires no centralized coordination. The negotiation does neither add communication overhead nor queueing delays to cooperative relaying.

The resulting system is well suited for real-time streaming. Substantial gains of PER and video quality are shown for MPEG-4 video streams compared to direct transmission and selection relaying without asymmetric cooperation.

Cooperative Feedback (CFB) With this approach, cooperation protects CSI feedback transmission that is crucial in systems with multiuser scheduling. Studying a simple OFDM multiuser downlink has shown that CFB highly improves the CSI accuracy at the scheduler, thus, increasing resource allocation efficiency. Consequently, the outage probability of a scheduled multiuser downlink is highly improved. The resulting SNR gain can be employed for saving the mobile users' energy or for increasing communication robustness. Alternatively, the sum capacity of the downlink can be significantly improved if the multiplexing loss due to relaying is limited. This is the case in multiuser OFDM systems with a medium number of users or in systems with highly limited feedback, e.g., the single-bit HARQ scheme of LTE. As many upcoming communication systems employ feedback channels, the CFB approach is widely applicable.

Future work

ACD and CFB profit from the fact that the amount of relayed information (and, therefore, multiplexing loss and delay) is low but sufficient to improve the error rate of important packets. Focusing on such applications may provide further promising use cases for cooperative relaying. While our above studies and schemes provide first examples, further generalization and practical schemes are required.

Diversity-aware scheduling Using diversity branches as additional criterion to rate an allocated resource is a new, general approach to improve the scheduling efficiency. This has to be further studied.

While early diversity-aware schedulers may only compare the resources' diversity orders for tie breaking, more sophisticated schedulers may improve the overall performance by taking additional constraints into account (e.g., allocating resources with high diversity order to users that demands for a low error rate).

Interaction of cooperative feedback and scheduling CFB was studied in a simple multiuser OFDM scenario to isolate the effects of feedback errors and cooperation. We ignored resource allocation constraints due to OFDMA subcarrier allocation, fairness, and delay. Depending on such constraints and on the scheduling strategy, improved CSI feedback may be required or not. The interaction between scheduler and CSI feedback scheme is not treated in current literature and seems promising for future research.

Practical cooperative feedback We presented CFB as a theoretical approach. Further schemes are required to make it practical. First, the performance of CFB depends on the chosen relay. Especially if mobile users cooperate (instead of dedicated RS), an accurate relay selection can be crucial. Already existing schemes for relay selection [LES06, NH07, HKA08] should be integrated into CFB and the resulting system should be studied. Second, more sophisticated CFB protocols may reduce the multiplexing loss and delay by cooperating only for "weak" users. Such protocols would provide the benefits of CFB to further scenarios.

System integration It remains to integrate these so-far theoretical approaches into upcoming relay-enabled wireless technologies, e.g., IEEE 802.16j [PH09] or LTE-advanced [ID08, ADF$^+$09], and to study the performance of these system designs. This requires to develop system-dependent functions, extensive simulation, first prototypes, and to support the results presented here by actual experiments.

Chapter 6

Cooperative WLANs – A prototype

In the previous chapters, we studied the performance of cooperative relaying protocols in theory based on certain channel and system models. Although these models and the assumptions behind them are widely accepted, we cannot be sure whether – in reality – they apply to a given scenario or if important factors have been overlooked. Moreover, it is not clear whether it is feasible to implement the proposed functions, to which extent theoretically well-performing functions have to be degraded to be implementable, or if optimal schemes can be efficiently replaced by suboptimal but substantially simpler functions.

To answer these practical questions for selection relaying, we use an engineering approach: We implement a transceiver prototype for *cooperative* WLANs and perform extensive field measurements. This experimental approach allows us not only to justify our modeling assumptions from the previous chapters. It also points to important issues that the literature has ignored so far (Section 6.1). In particular, we find that in many cases

1. Maximum Ratio Combining (MRC) can be replaced by *Packet Selection (PS)*. The resulting Physical layer (PHY) is less complex and more flexible than MRC-based systems while, at low mobility, the performance loss is negligible.
2. Cooperative relaying requires a more robust exchange of control information than direct transmission. Such robust signaling may be costly and can complicate the Medium Access Control (MAC) protocol design.

We justify our first observation and describe PS in Section 6.2. We focus on the second problem in Section 6.3 and specify a new MAC protocol with a robust but efficient *cooperative signaling* scheme. Finally, we implement a prototype (Section 6.4) to reinforce our above observations by measurements and to demonstrate the feasibility and high performance of our cooperative PHY and MAC schemes in the field (Section 6.5).

6.1 Scope and related work

As stated above, our objective is a transceiver prototype that enables cooperative relaying in real-world WLANs. To accomplish this task we (1) choose a prototyping platform which allows to implement and study a realistic system in representative scenarios, (2) specify and implement a cooperative MAC protocol for IEEE 802.11 standard WLANs, and (3) implement lightweight extensions to the IEEE 802.11a/g OFDM PHY. Let us now compare our basic approach in each of these fields to the current literature.

Prototyping platform Current prototyping platforms for cooperative relaying are either based on low-cost *Software Defined Radios (SDRs)* [BL06b, KKEP09] or on a combination of off-the-shelf IEEE 802.11 devices and open-source drivers [KNBP06, LTN+07, KKEP09]. Unfortunately, none of these low-cost solutions suffices to fully integrate cooperative relaying into the PHY and Data Link Control layer (DLC) of IEEE 802.11.

Low-cost SDRs use a simple Radio Frequency (RF) frontend and general purpose processors for signal processing [Mit95]. This platform allows to change even PHY functions in software and, thus, provides high programming flexibility. The problem of low-cost SDRs are their low computational power which suffices for high-layer Path allocation-based Selection Relaying (PSR) protocols like Opportunistic Relaying [BL06b] or for testing isolated PHY functions at low data rate [KKEP09]. However, none of the current platforms such as GNU Radio or WARP [GNU09, WAR09] is capable of performing a full IEEE 802.11 stack or even larger parts of the IEEE 802.11b/a/g PHY in real time [VvMK06, KKEP09].

IEEE 802.11 operation is provided by combining off-the-shelf WLAN devices with open-source drivers. Common examples are the HostAP driver [Hos09] used with the IEEE 802.11b-compliant Prism 2/2.5/3 chipset [Int01b, Int01a] or, as a more recent system, the MadWifi driver [Mad09] in combination with the IEEE 802.11a/g-compliant Atheros AR5414 chipset [Ath07]. The problem of this prototyping approach is its limited flexibility. Although MAC functions can be modified at driver level, time-critical DLC functions (e.g., CRC, MAC timers, ARQ) and all PHY functions are implemented in hardware and, thus, cannot be changed. This allows only to implement PSR protocols which, e.g., do not require PHY combining or to change MAC timers. But even the implementation of such high-level cooperation protocols is limited, since fundamental functions cannot be deactivated at driver level. For instance, all Coop-MAC prototypes [KNBP06, LTN+07, KKEP09] suffer from ACKs that are unnecessarily transmitted by the relay. With the chosen Prism/HostAP platform this function cannot be deactivated and measurement results are significantly deteriorated [LTN+07]. In addition to such artifacts of the prototyping platform, no results for IEEE 802.11a/g systems are published so far. Instead of using the Atheros/MadWifi platform, current prototypes of cooperative relaying are either based on IEEE 802.11b cards (driver-level implementation with HostAP) or are far from WLAN operation (low-cost SDRs).

To prototype a cooperative IEEE 802.11a/g transceiver that integrates cooperation into all parts of the PHY and DLC, a platform is required that joins the flexibility of SDRs with IEEE 802.11 operation. This is provided by the SORBAS 101 SDR [SDH+04] which is detailed in Appendix B. Based on a powerful hard/software design, SORBAS runs a complete IEEE 802.11a/g stack in software and in real time. Therefore, it reaches the full transmission rates of IEEE 802.11a/g but allows to modify all DLC and PHY baseband functions in software. With this high programming flexibility a cooperative relaying protocol can be integrated into *all* parts of IEEE 802.11a/g. This is not possible with any other of the above prototyping platforms.

Scenario   As in all previous chapters of this thesis, we focus on mobile scenarios with small-scale fading. Here, the direct link may fail frequently and high cooperative diversity gains can be reached by Combining-based Selection Relaying (CSR) (Section 3.3). We perform our measurements in a standard office environment with low mobility and in a vehicular scenario. Both scenarios are detailed in Section 6.5.1.

For such mobile scenarios, no measurements are published so far in the context of cooperative WLANs. Instead, literature has focused on static environments where PSR protocols such as OR [BL06b] or Coop-MAC [KNBP06, LTN$^+$07, KKEP09] exploit long-term differences among the direct and the relayed link.

Cooperative MAC protocol for IEEE 802.11   By focusing on mobile scenarios with small-scale fading, our so-called *Cooperative Signaling (CSIG)* protocol has two significant differences to CoopMAC [LTP05, LTN$^+$07] and to similar protocols, e.g., [SCTG05, IH07, TWT08, SZW09].

First, CoopMAC follows the PSR approach while CSIG employs CSR. As described in Section 3.2.3, this PSR protocol utilizes only the "best" link towards the destination while a CSR relay transmits each correctly received packet and, thus, spends redundancy in advance. By combining these redundant packets at the destination, CSIG can still reach high diversity gains in mobile scenarios with small-scale fading. By choosing only the (single) link of highest transmission rate, CoopMAC spends less redundancy and is, thus, limited to scenarios where this link state remains static per MAC cycle.

A second important difference between CSIG and CoopMAC is the exchange of control information (so-called *signaling*). Initiating and maintaining a cooperative data transfer requires additional signaling between the related terminals. This information exchange has to be efficient but it also needs to be more reliable than with direct transmission. The reason is simple: Cooperative relaying performs best when direct transmission only reaches a poor data rate, i.e., with fading channels at low SNR (cp. Figure 3.14 and Figure 4.22). Obviously, when direct transmission is weak, cooperation should not rely on *directly* transmitted control frames. With such *direct signaling* the high error rate of the control frames dominates and conditions the end-to-end error rate of the cooperative transmission to the error rate of the direct link. This is the case in CoopMAC which loses a significant number of control frames in mobile scenarios and, thus, only inefficiently improves direct transmission.

This problem of direct signaling is already known from our analysis in Section 3.4.1 and Section 5.2.5, and will be further elaborated below. We will describe CSIG which solves this problem by transmitting even control frames cooperatively. By achieving the same diversity order for control and data transmission, this cooperative signaling process maintains high data rate even at low SNR. Efficiently organizing this process is a challenge which is solved in Section 6.3.

Cooperative PHY extensions   To reach diversity gains, the CSIG protocol employs combining. In most theoretical literature (and up to this point also in this thesis) MRC is assumed for this task. MRC is optimal in terms of SNR but it relies on accurate CSI_{rx} measurements and does not allow to combine signals of different code rates or modulation (Section 2.2.3). This inflexibility highly limits the Degree Of Freedom (DoF) and, thus, performance of rate adaptation. It is solved by so-called *multi-rate* or *code combining* schemes. These schemes allow to combine different modulation levels [SY08] and code rates [Cha85], reach only slightly lower performance than MRC, but significantly increase the system complexity while still relying on accurate CSI_{rx}.

To reduce the complexity of our prototype, we choose a simpler approach. Instead of complex multi-rate combining, we simply select the first correctly decoded packet. We call this method Packet Selection (PS), describe it more formally in the following section and show by analysis, simulation, and measurements that the performance reduction is small and well justified by the simplified transceiver design (Section 6.5).

To sum up Unlike current literature, we integrate a CSR protocol into IEEE 802.11 to profit from cooperation diversity in mobile scenarios. This so-called CSIG protocol cooperates even for control frames and limits transceiver complexity by a simple combining scheme. Using a powerful prototyping platform we integrate CSIG into all layers of IEEE 802.11a/g. Unlike all other current cooperative relaying prototypes, our prototype reaches the full transmission rate of IEEE 802.11a/g in real time and is, thus, close to real cooperative WLAN transceivers.

6.2 Combining versus packet selection

In this section, we describe Packet Selection (PS) as a simple method to combine packets at the destination. We discuss that PS provides large practical benefits above many PHY combining schemes and show by analysis, simulation, and measurement that replacing MRC by Packet Selection (PS) only negligibly increases the error rate at low mobility.

6.2.1 Packet selection

PS simply selects the first correct packet after FEC decoding. More formally, from each of L decoded packets $p_1, \ldots, p_l, \ldots, p_L$ the first packet p_l which passes an error test, e.g., a CRC, is selected. Complexity can be limited by not decoding all later received packets $p_{l+1}, \ldots, p_L$.

By simply selecting the first correctly decoded packet, PS operates similar to Selection Combining (SC) and, thus, cannot reach the high performance of MRC (Section 2.2.3). Nonetheless, it has the following practical advantages:

- Implementing PS is almost trivial since it is based on functions that are already available in the transceiver chain (Section 6.4.1).
- PS considers the coding gain within its combining decision. This is not the case with MRC, classic SC, and some multi-rate combining schemes [SY08] which can weaken their performance [Cha85].
- Unlike MRC and related schemes, the performance of PS does not directly depend on channel estimation quality.
- Unlike MRC, PS does not require s and r to use the same modulation type. Consequently, PS does not limit the choices and performance of adaptive modulation.

Therefore, PS seems very appealing. It does not have the limitations of many PHY combining schemes and, due to its simplicity, reduces implementation time and costs. Nonetheless, PS is only acceptable if it achieves a performance similar to conventional PHY combining.

To show that this is indeed the case in low mobility scenarios we compare PS and MRC in three steps. First, we compare their outage probability for block fading channels. To this end, we extend the outage analysis from the previous chapters (e.g., Section 3.3 and 5.1.4) to selection combining. Second, we study slow and fast autocorrelated fading under IEEE 802.11g system assumptions by simulation. Third, after designing and implementing our transceiver prototype, MRC and PS are compared by measurements in Section 6.5.2.

6.2.2 Outage analysis

We compare the performance of MRC and PS in terms of outage probability. We study the CTR network with source s, a single relay r, and destination d at high SNR. The links between these three nodes are represented by their instantaneous SNR $\gamma_{s,r}$, $\gamma_{s,d}$, and $\gamma_{r,d}$ which are i.i.d. random variables according to the block fading model from Section 2.1.2. Note that in this idealistic model, PS is equivalent to SC (Section 2.2.3) since the channel state does not change within a packet and ideal coding is assumed. Hence, we can write the overall outage event with PS as

$$\mathcal{E}_{PS}^{out} = \left[\{\gamma_{s,r} \geq \hat{\gamma}\} \wedge \{\max(\gamma_{s,d}, \gamma_{r,d}) < \hat{\gamma}\}\right] \vee \\ \left[\{\gamma_{s,r} < \hat{\gamma}\} \wedge \{\gamma_{s,d} < \hat{\gamma}\}\right]. \tag{6.1}$$

where we use the SNR threshold $\hat{\gamma} := 2^{2R} - 1$ for a given spectral efficiency R and denote the logical *and* and *or* operator by $\wedge$ and $\vee$, respectively.

The second line in (6.1) shows the outage event at the destination d when the relay wrongly decodes the source's packet, i.e., $\{\gamma_{s,r} < \hat{\gamma}\}$. Similarly, the first line represents the case when the relay correctly receives the source's packet, i.e., $\{\gamma_{s,r} \geq \hat{\gamma}\}$, and both packets may be combined at d. Here, packet selection is represented by comparing the maximum of the random variables $\gamma_{s,d}$ and $\gamma_{r,d}$ to the threshold $\hat{\gamma}$. This maximum is below $\hat{\gamma}$ if and only if both random variables are below $\hat{\gamma}$. With the probability of this event $\mathbb{P}\{\gamma_{s,d} < \hat{\gamma}\}\mathbb{P}\{\gamma_{r,d} < \hat{\gamma}\}$ we obtain

$$P_{PS}^{out} = \mathbb{P}\{\mathcal{E}_{PS}^{out}\} = \mathbb{P}\{\gamma_{s,r} \geq \hat{\gamma}\}\mathbb{P}\{\gamma_{s,d} < \hat{\gamma}\}\mathbb{P}\{\gamma_{r,d} < \hat{\gamma}\} \\ + \mathbb{P}\{\gamma_{s,r} < \hat{\gamma}\}\mathbb{P}\{\gamma_{s,d} < \hat{\gamma}\} \tag{6.2}$$

as the probability of outage event $\mathcal{E}_{PS}^{out}$ (6.1). Here, each probability term can be solved individually by using the outage probability expression of the direct link (2.11) with threshold $\hat{\gamma} := 2^{2R} - 1$ instead of $2^R - 1$.

Figure 6.1 shows the numerical results for the outage probability of Combining-based Selection Relaying (CSR). We study a symmetrical CTR network with equal mean SNR for all links, i.e., $\bar{\gamma} :=$

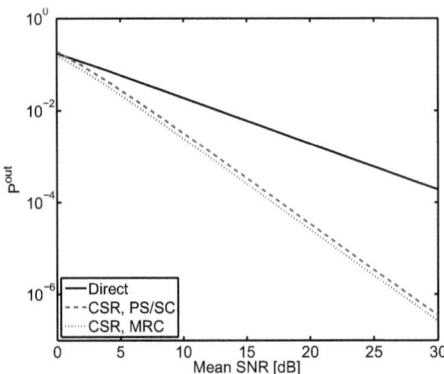

Figure 6.1: Comparing PS and MRC: Outage probability vs. mean SNR. Numerical results for direct transmission and Combining-based Selection Relaying (CSR) for $R = 1/4$ bits/s/Hz.

$\bar{\gamma}_{s,r} = \bar{\gamma}_{s,d} = \bar{\gamma}_{r,d}$. Comparing the results for both combining schemes to direct transmission shows that with MRC as well as with PS a diversity order of $L = 2$ is reached. Comparing the results of both cooperative cases shows that MRC performs only slightly better than PS. This minor difference (found here for ideal channel coding) matches to the results for uncoded systems at low diversity orders in Table 2.1.

6.2.3 Simulation results

To get closer to our measurement results, we compare the PER of PS and MRC under IEEE 802.11g assumptions for autocorrelated fading.

Assumptions As for the numerical results in Figure 6.1 we study CSR at equal mean SNR for all links. Further models and parameters are chosen to correspond to our measurement scenarios in Section 6.5.1. At system level, we assume a standard IEEE 802.11g PHY that is modeled in the digital baseband as described in Section 4.3.4. The symbol time is $4\,\mu s$ at a carrier frequency of $f_c = 2.472$ GHz in 20 MHz bandwidth. The transmission rate is 18 Mbits/s using transmission mode 4 of the OFDM PHY. In this mode, Quadrature Phase Shift Keying (QPSK) modulation and code rate $R_c = 3/4$ are employed.

Autocorrelated fading is modeled as described in Section 2.1.2 and two values of the Doppler frequency f_d are studied. While $f_d = 40$ Hz corresponds to the speed of 5 m/s reached during our vehicular measurements, $f_d = 8$ Hz reflects the quasi-static fading situation in our indoor scenario (Section 6.5.1).

Results For these assumptions, Figure 6.2 shows the end-to-end PER obtained at the link layer of the destination. At low Doppler frequency, selection relaying with both combining schemes behaves as expected. Similar to our theoretic results (Figure 6.1) a large diversity gain is shown and the difference between PS and MRC is insignificant. Like in our outage analysis, this is a consequence of quasi-static

6.3. Cooperative medium access

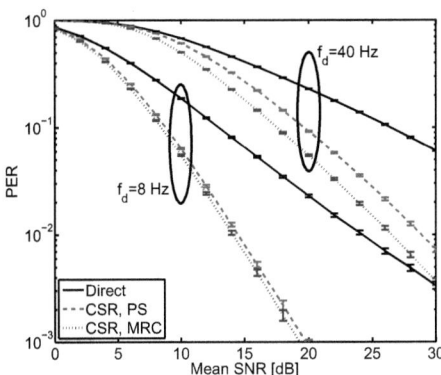

Figure 6.2: Comparing PS and MRC: Packet Error Rate (PER) vs. mean SNR. Simulation results for direct transmission and Combining-based Selection Relaying (CSR) with autocorrelated fading, high and low Doppler frequency f_d, and IEEE 802.11g system assumptions.

fading. In this case, channel state changes during a packet time are unlikely and, thus, symbol-wise combining only slightly outperforms packet-wise combining. At higher f_d, however, the channel gain decorrelates and the channel may change several times per packet. In this case, the error rate of MRC improves compared to PS. Comparing the PER in Figure 6.2 shows that MRC benefits by up to 2 dB at higher mobility.

From these simulation and theoretical results we can conclude that at low mobility replacing MRC by PS comes at negligible performance loss. We will describe in Section 6.5 how PS substantially simplifies the transceiver design and compare both combining schemes by measurements in Section 6.5.

6.3 Cooperative medium access

We introduce the Cooperative Signaling (CSIG) protocol that integrates cooperative relaying into the IEEE 802.11 MAC. Unlike the cooperative MAC protocols discussed in Section 6.1, CSIG employs combining and a cooperative signaling scheme to reach diversity gains even in mobile scenarios. First, we compare CSIG's basic operation to classic direct signaling and data transfer. Second, we describe the protocol's control frames, discuss its overhead, and specify its extensions to the IEEE 802.11 MAC protocol automata.

6.3.1 Signaling for cooperative WLANs

In our CSIG protocol the source node s initiates the cooperative data transfer once per MAC cycle. This initiation requires

1. source s to send a request for a cooperative data transfer to destination d and to potential relays,

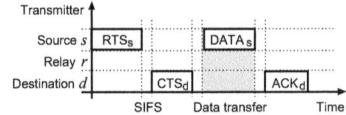

Figure 6.3: MAC cycle for direct IEEE 802.11 transmission with RTS/CTS.

2. a participating relay r to acknowledge the request of s,
3. d to overhear this negotiation to be able to identify the data frames to combine and to acknowledge the request of s to s and r, and
4. nodes nearby s,r and d to overhear these messages for refraining from transmissions during the MAC cycle (i.e., *medium reservation*).

To accomplish these tasks, the nodes have to exchange more control information than the standard IEEE 802.11 MAC protocol. This extended signaling process has to be integrated into IEEE 802.11 in an efficient and robust manner.

RTS/CTS in IEEE 802.11

As a first step, we can integrate this additional signaling into the RTS/CTS handshake. This procedure is already employed in IEEE 802.11 and illustrated in Figure 6.3. In this standard MAC cycle for direct communication, IEEE 802.11 spends a Short Inter-Frame Space (SIFS) time slot to separate two frames; we denote each transmitted frame by its sender index.

By transmitting an RTS_s, node s informs the destination and neighboring nodes. An RTS includes the source and destination address as well as the duration of the transmission. By answering with CTS_d, d negotiates the transmission and retransmits the duration field of the originating RTS_s. This standard procedure avoids interference caused by *hidden nodes* [OP99, Chapter 3] since neighbors of s and d overhear the *duration field* within RTS_s or CTS_d and remain silent for this duration. Each IEEE 802.11 node keeps track of such medium reservations in a local data structure called *Network Allocation Vector (NAV)*.

Direct signaling, cooperative relaying

While RTS/CTS solves the fourth of the above tasks (medium reservation), so far the relay is not included in the signaling procedure. This can be simply incorporated by adding the relay's address to the standard RTS and to the standard CTS. We call these extended frames *cooperative RTS (cRTS)* and *cooperative CTS (cCTS)* and specify their format in Section 6.3.2.

A simple cooperative MAC cycle that employs one cRTS to initiate cooperation is illustrated in Figure 6.4. In addition to the standard RTS/CTS handshake, all potential relays overhear $cRTS_s$ and the addressed relay r answers with an $cCTS_r$ frame that includes its address. Based on this cCTS, relay r is known to s and d, the destination d answers with $cCTS_d$, and the cooperative data transfer starts. As with conventional selection relaying (Section 3.2), r overhears frame $DATA_s$ and, if correctly decoded, retransmits this frame

6.3. Cooperative medium access

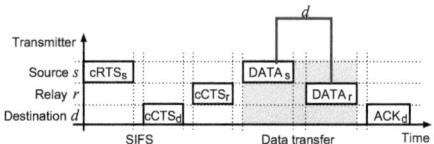

Figure 6.4: MAC cycle for cooperative IEEE 802.11 transmission with direct signaling. The arc marks redundant frames that provide a diversity gain at d.

within DATA$_r$. After correct reception, d acknowledges the cooperative transmission and the next MAC cycle starts.

The arc in Figure 6.4 highlights the redundant transmission of the DATA frame via two spatially independent links. Since both frames DATA$_s$ and DATA$_r$ have to be in error such that the overall transmission fails, d reaches a diversity order of $L = 2$ for the DATA frame (when either of the combining or packet selecting schemes from Section 6.2 are used). This is not the case for the cRTS, cCTS, and ACK. Each of these control frames is received via a single direct link which provides merely $L = 1$. Even if two cCTS frames are overheard at s, the source does not combine these frames. Since only a single *direct* link has to be in error such that the complete signaling process fails, we call this type of control information exchange *direct signaling*. It is the current signaling approach in many cooperative MAC protocols [SCTG05, LTN+07, IH07, TWT08, SZW09].

The direct signaling problem

Due to its discrepancy in diversity orders, direct signaling cannot be efficiently used to cooperate in fading channels. By providing a lower diversity order for control than for data frames, signaling information is exchanged at substantially higher error rate than payload. This mismatch is unacceptable for most MAC protocols (e.g., IEEE 802.11) where correctly received control frames are essential to exchange data.

We know this problem from analyzing the direct feedback channels of PSR protocols and MUD systems (Section 3.4.1 and 5.2.5). We found that loosing signaling information becomes crucial in the low power regime or at strict error rate constraints where direct links fail frequently. Here, a diversity scheme would reach superior gains but direct signaling inhibits a data transfer from even being established – a contradiction which we call the *direct signaling problem*.

That in fading channels this problem cannot be efficiently solved by robust modulation and coding is known from theory (Section 2.2.1) and illustrated by measurement in Figure 6.5. Choosing a more robust modulation and code only introduces a coding gain which cannot cope with a deep fade in case of direct transmission. As shown, even the most robust mode of the IEEE 802.11g OFDM PHY leads to a high error rate for RTS frames. With each lost RTS, a data transfer cannot be established, a full MAC cycle is lost, and spectral efficiency is reduced. Nonetheless, Figure 6.5 also shows the high diversity gain reached by cooperating for control frames. We will utilize this gain in our CSIG protocol.

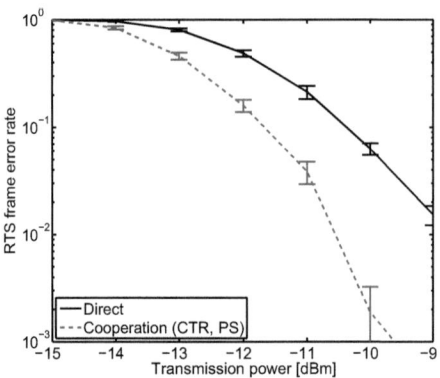

Figure 6.5: RTS control frame error rate vs. transmission power: Measured for direct and cooperative signaling with PS in the indoor scenario (Section 6.5.1) using the most robust IEEE 802.11g PHY mode (BPSK, code rate $R_c = 1/2$).

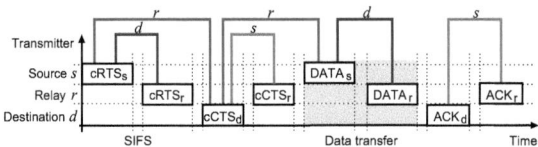

Figure 6.6: MAC cycle for cooperative IEEE 802.11 transmission with Cooperative Signaling (CSIG). The arcs mark redundant frames that provide a diversity gain at the annotated node.

CSIG: Cooperative signaling, cooperative relaying

To overcome the direct signaling problem, the Cooperative Signaling (CSIG) protocol exploits cooperation diversity not only for data, but also for control frames. Therefore, CSIG adds two extensions to the direct signaling cycle (Section 6.4).

The first extension is illustrated by the arcs for d and s in Figure 6.6. After the relay correctly decoded cRTS$_s$ and ACK$_d$, it repeats these two control frames as cRTS$_r$ and ACK$_r$. Collisions between all new frames are avoided since the MAC cycle is fixed and known to all cooperative nodes. Moreover, repeating cRTS silences the neighbors of r and avoids interfering hidden nodes. With these repeated frames, the destination combines cRTS$_s$ with cRTS$_r$, and the source combines cCTS$_d$ with cCTS$_r$ as well as ACK$_d$ with ACK$_r$. To this end, any combining scheme including PS can be used. Consequently, adding cRTS$_r$, ACK$_d$, and combining to direct signaling reaches diversity order $L = 2$ at s and d. This is equal to the diversity order of the data frames.

This diversity order is also reached at the relay by extension two. In Figure 6.6 this extension is marked by the arcs for node r but, unlike for node s and d, it is not based on combining equal control frames. Instead, the relay exploits that the correct reception of some control frames is implicitly acknowledged

6.3. Cooperative medium access

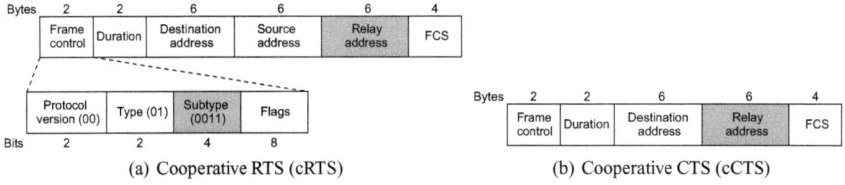

Figure 6.7: Layout of the control frames extended for CSIG: The shaded parts mark changes to the respective IEEE 802.11 standard frame. The *frame control* field is equal for all frames used in CSIG.

by other frames. In particular, the destination transmits $cCTS_d$ if and only if it has correctly received the cRTS (which already origins from two combined frames). By overhearing either $cRTS_s$ or $cCTS_d$, r knows that cooperation is initiated. This information is only *not* transferred to r, if *both* frames ($cRTS_s$ as well as $cCTS_d$) are lost. Hence, a diversity order of $L = 2$ is reached at the relay for initiating the cooperative MAC cycle.

To confirm this initiation, the procedure is similar and marked by the right arc for r in Figure 6.6. The source transmits $DATA_s$ if and only if it has received the cCTS (which, again, is combined from two frames). By overhearing either $cCTS_d$ or $DATA_s$ the relay knows that d has confirmed cooperation and that it should retransmit $DATA_s$. Again two frames have to be in error such that sending the confirmation to r fails and, thus, $L = 2$ is reached at r for this part of the signaling process.

Note that with this procedure the relay increases its diversity order only by overhearing already transmitted frames. No transmission of extra control frames is required. This makes CSIG more efficient than straightforward signaling schemes that would repeat control frames even for r.

To sum up: At each of the participating nodes s, r, and d, CSIG provides the same diversity order for control and data frames. At s and d this is achieved by combining; at r implicit acknowledgments through later frames are overheard at no cost. Let us now specify the frames and MAC protocol for this operation.

6.3.2 CSIG control frames and overhead

The MAC cycle of CSIG (Figure 6.6) is based on extended RTS and CTS control frames that are illustrated in Figure 6.7. These new so-called *cooperative RTS (cRTS)* and *cooperative CTS (cCTS)* frames add the 6 Byte MAC address of the relay to the IEEE 802.11 standard RTS and CTS [IEE99, Figure 15 to 17]. All other frames used in CSIG keep their IEEE 802.11 format but are identified by the subtype field $(0011)_2$. This value is not used in IEEE 802.11 which allows to distinguish the frames of a cooperative MAC cycle from directly transmitted frames at no additional overhead.

The lengths of the data frame and all related control frames are given in Table 6.1. While the lengths of the control frames are fixed, the length of a data frame may vary in IEEE 802.11 systems. As an example, we assume that the DLC payload has a length of 1052 Bytes. This corresponds to a typical packet size of 1024 Bytes payload plus User Datagram Protocol (UDP) and Internet Protocol (IP) overhead. Based on these frame lengths we can simply count the DLC overhead for the three MAC cycles in Section 6.3.1.

Table 6.1: Lengths of MAC frames used in IEEE 802.11 and CSIG.

Frame	Length [Bytes]	Description
RTS	20	Request To Send
CTS	14	Clear To Send
cRTS	26	cooperative Request To Send
cCTS	20	cooperative Clear To Send
ACK	14	Acknowledgment
DATA	1074	Data frame size for 1052 Bytes payload

Table 6.2: Example of DLC and PHY signaling overhead.

Protocol	Overhead w.r.t. payload at	
	DLC [%]	PHY [%]
IEEE 802.11, RTS/CTS	4.5	13.4
Coop. data, direct signaling	7.5	22.4
Coop. data, Coop. signaling (CSIG)	11.2	33.5

For each cycle, we aggregate the lengths of all control frames and then divide this sum by the length of a DATA frame. Naturally, even with cooperative transmission only a single DATA frame is taken as a reference since both transmitted frames are combined at the end.

The DLC overhead with respect to a typical payload size of 1052 Bytes is summarized in Table 6.2. To transmit this payload, CSIG more than doubles the DLC overhead of standard IEEE 802.11 with RTS/CTS. In terms of transmission time, the overhead is even worse when control frames are transmitted at the most robust PHY mode and, thus, at lowest bit rate. This is typically done in IEEE 802.11g which corresponds to a transmission rate of 6 Mbits/s. Assuming that DATA frames are transmitted at 18 Mbits/s leads to the listed PHY overhead.

This example for a typical payload size and typical transmission rates shows that direct and cooperative signaling significantly reduce the spectral efficiency of cooperative IEEE 802.11. Our measurement results in Section 6.5 will show when cooperative diversity gains can compensate for these costs.

6.3.3 CSIG protocol operation

Beside adding control frames, CSIG extends the procedure of the MAC protocol to incorporate the MAC cycle from Figure 6.6. We will now describe these extensions more formally in terms of protocol automata.

The flow charts in Figure 6.8 illustrate how CSIG extends the sender and receiver protocol automaton. In these charts, dashed lines highlight changes to the IEEE 802.11 specification [IEE99, Annex C], edges labeled with incoming frames (e.g., "→ACK") cause a transition when that frame is correctly received, and outgoing frames (e.g., "ACK→") indicate that a frame is sent upon transition. Note that all changes to the standard MAC are *additive*, i.e., direct IEEE 802.11 transmission with the standard RTS/CTS frames or without handshake is still supported. Furthermore, both automata run on each node in a cooperative

6.3. Cooperative medium access

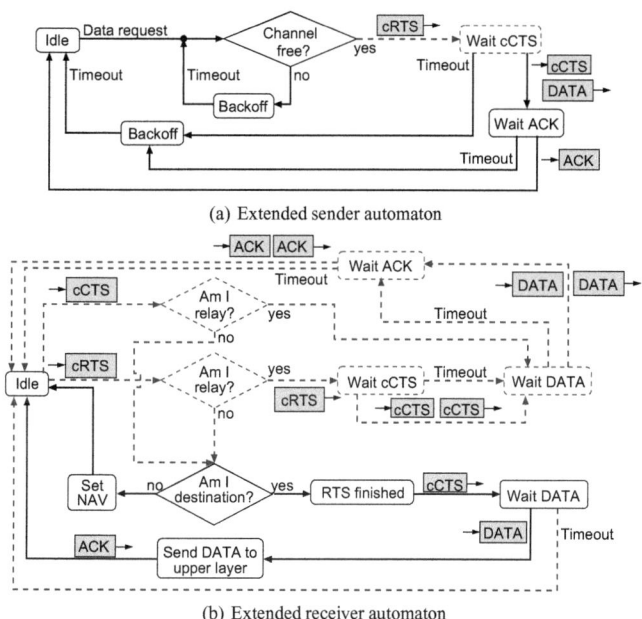

Figure 6.8: Flow chart for IEEE 802.11 MAC protocol automata extended by CSIG. Changes of the standard automata are indicated by the dashed lines.

network. We allow *any* node to take either the role of s, r, or d by integrating the behavior of s into the sender and of r, d into the receiver automaton. Depending on its role, a node operates as follows.

Source s role, Figure 6.8(a): Upon a data request from the upper layer, s contends according to the standard IEEE 802.11 MAC but transmits its cRTS. The cRTS contains the duration of the entire cooperative MAC cycle, so that nearby nodes can set their NAV accordingly. Next, s goes into *Wait cCTS* state awaiting either a timeout or a correctly received cCTS. Although this cCTS is based on the two frames $cCTS_d$ and $cCTS_r$, this is transparent to the MAC automaton since the PHY provides only the combined cCTS. If the cCTS timer expires, s returns to the idle state after a standard backoff. If a cCTS is received in time, s waits a SIFS period and sends its DATA frame. Finally, s sets its ACK timer to perform a backoff if it does not receive the ACK in time. Like the cCTS, this ACK is based on two frames but only the combined variant of ACK_d and ACK_r is passed to the MAC.

Relay r role, Figure 6.8(b): The relay role can be initiated either by $cRTS_s$ or $cCTS_d$. If the MAC address of a node does *not* match the relay address in the cRTS or the cCTS (i.e., the node should not act as relay), the node sets its NAV and returns to the idle state. If the MAC address of node r matches the relay address in the cRTS or cCTS, a node acts as relay. The following operation depends on the frame type that initiated the relay.

If cRTS$_s$ is received, r extracts the MAC address of s and d and uses them to identify the overheard frames. Afterwards, r waits a SIFS, retransmits the cRTS, and sets a timer to wait either for cCTS$_d$ or DATA$_s$. If cCTS$_d$ is received, r repeats this cCTS after a SIFS and sets a timer to wait for DATA$_s$. If cCTS$_d$ is not received, r waits for DATA$_s$. Thereby, the relay uses DATA$_s$ as a reference that the cooperative data transfer has started, which provides $L = 2$ (cp. Page 142).

If no cRTS$_s$ but a cCTS$_d$ initiates the relay, r cannot extract the address of s but only the address of d. After extraction, r goes directly into *Wait DATA* state by setting a timer to wait for DATA$_s$. As soon as DATA$_s$ is overheard, the relay uses the frame control field and the address of d to recognize this frame.

From the *Wait DATA* state onwards, it is irrelevant whether a cRTS or cCTS initiated the relay. After having overheard DATA$_s$, r cancels the previously set timer, repeats this DATA frame after a SIFS, and returns to *Wait ACK* state. If the wait-for-DATA$_s$ timer expires, r immediately returns to the *Wait ACK* state; now ready to repeat ACK$_d$. After repeating this ACK or if a timeout occurs, r returns to the idle state and waits for the cRTS of the next cooperative MAC cycle.

Destination d role, Figure 6.8(b): In case of the destination, the PHY passes a combined version of the cRTS to the MAC that is based on cRTS$_s$ and cRTS$_r$. If the destination address in this cRTS matches to node d, this node replies with cCTS$_d$. Then, d sets a timer to wait for the DATA frame. The PHY combines this frame from DATA$_s$ and DATA$_r$. Upon reception of DATA, d checks if the frame was received correctly. If not, it remains in *Wait DATA* state until the timer expires. If DATA is correct, d sends the payload to the upper layer, waits a SIFS, replies with ACK$_d$, and returns to the idle state.

6.4 A prototype for cooperative WLANs

Having described the PHY and MAC extensions to incorporate cooperative relaying into IEEE 802.11, we can join these functions in a practical transceiver for cooperative WLANs. The result is a prototype that performs Combining-based Selection Relaying (CSR) and cooperative signaling at the full transmission rate of IEEE 802.11g. Designing and implementing this prototype is described below.

6.4.1 Transceiver design

An overview of the cooperative IEEE 802.11g transceiver is given in Figure 6.9. The extensions to a conventional IEEE 802.11g system are marked by the dashed lines.

At the Data Link Control layer (DLC), the sender (Tx) and receiver (Rx) MAC automata are modified as in Figure 6.8(a) and Figure 6.8(b), respectively. Each modified automaton still supports the standard RTS/CTS handshake by the *RTS/CTS block*. The new *cRTS/cCTS Rx block* interprets the received cRTS and cCTS frames and the cRTS/cCTS Tx block constructs the extended frames according to the format in Figure 6.7. In relay role, a node performs a forwarding decision for the received DATA frames and for the control frames. So far, simple SDF operation is assumed that forwards only frames with a correct

6.4. A prototype for cooperative WLANs

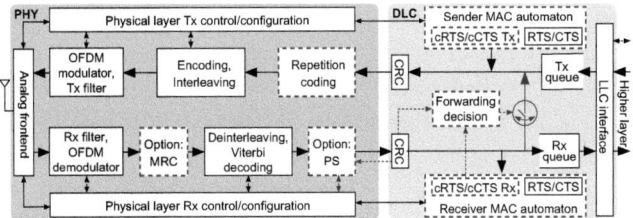

Figure 6.9: Cooperative IEEE 802.11g transceiver design with control (small arrows) and data connections (large arrows). Changes are indicated by dashed lines.

CRC. Figure 6.9 shows this process (1) as a control line from the receiver CRC to the new *Forwarding decision block* and (2) as a switch controlled by this block. Note that this switch passes the forwarded frame directly to the Tx chain to avoid queueing delays at the DLC.

In the current transceiver design, the forwarded frame is transmitted at the same FEC code, puncturing, and modulation as the original frame. This is denoted by the *Repetition coding* block in the Tx chain of the PHY. This block serves as placeholder and can be replaced by improved coding techniques for the retransmitted data.

To compare both combining techniques, Packet Selection (PS) as well as Maximum Ratio Combining (MRC) are added to the IEEE 802.11g Rx chain. The blocks are used alternatively and each of these blocks can be switched on or off during an experiment. If the *MRC block* is used, control or DATA frames are combined prior to decoding. Thus, this block is placed between OFDM demodulation and the FEC decoder. Alternatively, the *PS block* is placed after the FEC which performs Packet Selection (PS) as described in Section 6.2.1. In either case, combining is completely transparent to the DLC functions. Let us now take a closer look at the implementation of these blocks.

6.4.2 Implementing the prototype

The above transceiver design is implemented on the SORBAS 101 prototyping platform. Since SORBAS already provides the IEEE 802.11a/g OFDM PHY and DLC in software, we can implement our prototype by extending this stack. We summarize this implementation below. An extensive description of our prototype implementation is given in [BBF+07, BFK+08]. Details of the SORBAS 101 platform and implementation are provided in Section B.1.

Combining

Both combining blocks are implemented in C and assembler and run on the master Digital Signal Processor (DSP) of the SORBAS. MRC processes the complex modulation symbol stream that is returned from the OFDM demodulation. For each digital symbol, it performs the calculations described in Section 2.2.3 and employs noise and power measurements from the radio frontend to calculate the weights. Since these measurements are provided only once per PHY frame, the weights remain equal for a complete frame. Although suboptimal, such implementation represents the typical case, as in most systems noise and power are measured only once per frame preamble.

The MRC block needs to buffer all modulation symbols of the first received PHY frame in order to combine it with the symbols of the consecutive frame(s). With PS such additional buffering is not required. Here, only a single correct frame passes the CRC and is, thus, selected. If the first received frame passes this test, no delay is added to the Rx chain. Implementing PS is simple, since the CRC block of the DLC can be re-used. Once a frame has passed the CRC, the link layer signals the frame's header to the *PS block* via a control line (cp. Figure 6.9). Then, the PS block drops all received frames with the same header. This operation avoids duplicated frames at the DLC and is performed until the next MAC cycle starts.

DLC extensions

All DLC protocol extensions run on the SMAC card of the SORBAS platform (Figure B.2). Parsing and constructing the new cRTS/cCTS frames as well as the forwarding decision is implemented in C. The MAC protocol automata are specified in the *Specification and Description Language (SDL)* according to Figure 6.8; C code is automatically generated from this specification and compiled for the SORBAS platform.

Beside implementing the CSIG protocol (Figure 6.6), we implement the direct signaling procedure (Figure 6.4) for comparison. Furthermore, the handshake-free direct and cooperative data transfer is implemented that is marked by the shaded phase in Figure 6.3 and Figure 6.6. This allows us to isolate the additional cost of signaling during the experiments.

6.5 Measurement results

Based on our cooperative IEEE 802.11a/g prototype, we perform extensive measurements in indoor and vehicular scenarios.

First, an overview of both scenarios is given in this section. Section B.3 and B.4 detail the parameters of these scenarios and study path loss, link budget, and Signal-to-Interference plus Noise Ratio (SINR).

Second, we present Packet Error Rate (PER) and data rate results that show a good match to theory and clearly demonstrate the high performance and operation areas of Combining-based Selection Relaying (CSR) in cooperative WLANs.

6.5.1 Experimental setup and scenarios

We used 3 SORBAS devices to form the Cooperative Triangle (CTR). In this fundamental cooperation scenario (Figure 3.1(b)), a single relay r assists source s to transmit to destination d. Each of these devices runs the cooperative IEEE 802.11a/g stack described in Section 6.4.2. We choose IEEE 802.11g

6.5. Measurement results

Figure 6.10: Indoor NLOS scenario with 3 SORBAS SDRs (orange) operating as source s, relay r, destination d, and a rotating disc in front of d.

OFDM mode. By selecting a carrier frequency of 2.472 GHz we operate at the upper end of the 2.4 GHz ISM band. Each device employs a single omnidirectional antenna with 5 dBi gain. As common in IEEE 802.11g networks, control frames are sent in the most robust PHY mode at 6 Mbits/s (BPSK modulation, code rate $R_c = 1/2$), whereas data frames are sent at 18 Mbits/s (QPSK, $R_c = 3/4$).

We study two mobile scenarios. The first *indoor scenario* represents a typical office situation with low mobility and NLOS links. The second *vehicular* scenario corresponds to a Line Of Sight (LOS) situation at medium mobility, e.g., WLAN hotspots at urban crossroads or railway stations.

Indoor scenario

The node deployment for the indoor scenario is shown in Figure 6.10. The devices were placed relatively close to each other in an isosceles triangle with distances $D_{s,r} = 1.44$ m between source and relay and $D_{s,d} = D_{r,d} = 2.7$ m between each of the transmitters and the destination. Larger distances are emulated by decreasing the transmission power. The devices itself were not moved during the experiments. Instead, slow mobility was emulated by placing a partially-shielded disc in front of d. The disc rotates at 30 rpm. At the chosen carrier frequency, this corresponds to a tangential velocity of 1 m/s and to a maximum Doppler shift of 8 Hz. By covering the LOS path with the shielding material of the disc and by the metal device cases, an NLOS situation is achieved.

From our measurement results in (B.3), we obtain a path loss exponent of $\alpha = 2.75$. At distance $D_{s,d}$ we obtain a reference path loss of -56.2 dB. The transmission power P_{tx} is varied between -18 and -6 dBm. With these values and with our results from Section B.3, we can expect a mean received power within $[-70.2, -58.2]$ dBm at the RF frontend and the mean SINR to be in $[5.3, 17.3]$ dB. Both are typical values in IEEE 802.11a/g WLANs [Ath07]. Further parameters for the indoor scenario are summarized in Table B.3.

Vehicular scenario

This second scenario was constructed on the RailCab test track [Rai02]; an oval-shaped railroad 600 m long. Figure 6.11(a) illustrates the node deployment. The destination was placed in the center of the track, e.g., representing an access point in the vicinity of a train. The nodes s and r are mounted on the RailCab vehicle with $D_{s,r} = 1.61$ m distance to each other in LOS of d (Figure 6.11(b)).

The RailCab carries s and r around the destination. During each turn, the oval test track causes the distance $D_{s,d} = D_{r,d}$ between the mobile nodes and d to vary between 44 and 90 m. Due to RailCab's linear motor design [Rai02], the nodes always move at *constant* linear velocity of 5 m/s allowing to accurately repeat the circulation along the test track oval during the measurements. At the chosen carrier frequency, this velocity corresponds to a maximum Doppler shift of 40 Hz.

To predict path loss and link budget we assume an ideal LOS situation with path loss exponent $\alpha = 2$. Ground reflection is ignored due to absorption from high grass. The transmission power is varied $P_{tx} \in [-7, -1]$ dBm. With these assumptions we can expect that the mean power received at the RF frontend varies between -82.4 dBm (at $D_{s,d} = D_{r,d} = 90$ m and $P_{tx} = -7$ dBm) and -70.2 dBm (at $D_{s,d} = D_{r,d} = 44$ m and $P_{tx} = -1$ dBm). For the mean SINR we expect values between 14.6 dB and 20.6 dB which includes a safety margin in case of a too optimistic path loss prediction. A more detailed discussion of the scenario and link budget is provided in Section B.3. Further parameters are summarized in Table B.4.

Both scenarios: Metrics and studied cases

We measure PER and data rate at UDP level. By measuring end-to-end, i.e., between source s and destination d, we include the complete overhead and the effect of all links in our measurements. At application layer, a payload size of 1024 Bytes is selected which corresponds to 1052 Bytes IP packets. This packet size is a typical Maximum Transmission Unit (MTU) in WLANs. The packets are passed to the DLC as a continuous flow with constant rate. To saturate the links, the rate of this flow is chosen such that the Tx queue at the DLC (Figure 6.9) is always full.

All compared cooperative relaying protocols perform Combining-based Selection Relaying (CSR) with repetition coding (Section 3.2.2). We compare the performance of our CSIG protocol (CSR with cooperative signaling) to Combining-based Selection Relaying (CSR) with direct signaling and to handshake-free cooperation. This handshake-free case allows to assess the effect of signaling overhead and lost control frames. It can be seen as CSR with ideal out-of-band signaling adding no overhead to data transmission and without errors for control frames.

For direct transmission from s to d, no signaling is considered. This *Direct* case represents conventional IEEE 802.11g operation without RTS/CTS. It allows to isolate the multiplexing loss and errors due to relaying from the effect of signaling. All transmission schemes operate under the per-node power constraint reflecting that in WLANs the MAC cycle is extended when additional nodes participate (Section 2.3). As in the previous chapters, confidence intervals are shown for a level of 95 %.

6.5.2 Indoor scenario results

We start by comparing Packet Selection (PS) with Maximum Ratio Combining (MRC) in Figure 6.12. The figure shows the PER measured at UDP level versus the configured transmission power (excluding antenna gains). The shape of these results is expected from our theoretical results (Section 6.2) as well

6.5. Measurement results

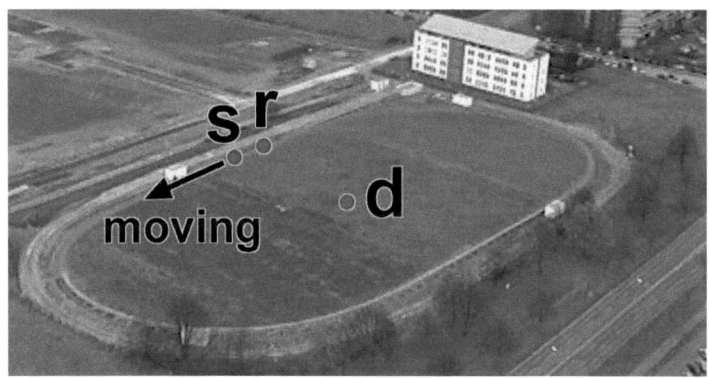

(a) Node deployment at the 600 m RailCab test track; picture from [Rai07]

(b) RailCab vehicle with 2 SORBAS SDRs (orange) operating as source s and relay r to reach destination d in the center of the test track.

Figure 6.11: Vehicular measurement scenario: Node deployment, mobile nodes s and r, and fixed destination d.

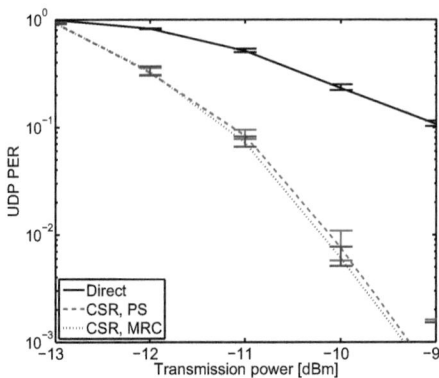

Figure 6.12: End-to-end UDP Packet Error Rate (PER) for the indoor scenario vs. transmission power: Comparing relaying with PS and MRC.

as from our simulation results for low speed (Figure 6.2). The diversity gain of cooperation is clearly shown for both combining schemes. Nevertheless, the performance gains of both combining techniques are equal. No significant difference between PS and MRC is shown by our prototype measurements.

Selecting PS, we now study the performance of cooperative relaying used for data transfer and signaling. Figure 6.13 shows the UDP data rate for the four cases from Section 6.5.1. Note that the instant data rate decrease at -13 and -12 dBm for ideal and cooperative signaling is an experimental artifact. It results from a mismatch between the configured transmission power and the actual power at the SORBAS antenna port. We characterize this mismatch in Section B.2.

At high transmission power, direct transmission clearly outperforms any protocol that employs retransmission and, thus, causes multiplexing loss. At levels below -11 dBm, however, the gains of cooperative relaying begin to show. While for decreasing power the data rate of direct transmission quickly diminishes to zero, cooperation maintains a high data rate even at low power. While with ideal signaling up to 5 Mbits/s are reached, cooperative signaling obtains 3 Mbits/s. Comparing ideal and cooperative signaling at low power shows the combined effect of control frame errors and signaling overhead. Isolating the effect of overhead is possible by comparing the results at high transmission power where the control frame error rate is low (cp. Figure 6.5). At -6 dB the results are similar to Table 6.2. While the data rate of cooperative signaling is 37 % below the ideal case, the costs of direct signaling are less significant.

Nonetheless, relying on directly transmitted control frames makes direct signaling ineffective at low transmission power. In fact, this protocol cannot provide any gains in terms of data rate. At high power this case is outperformed by direct transmission, at low power the data rate is zero. This results from the high error rate for control frames which are transmitted at the most robust PHY mode but directly. Consequently, these measurements justify our above discussion and theoretical results for the direct signaling problem (Section 6.3.1 and Section 3.4.1) as well as our motivation to develop the CSIG protocol.

This finding is further supported by the PER results in Figure 6.14. With ideal and cooperative sig-

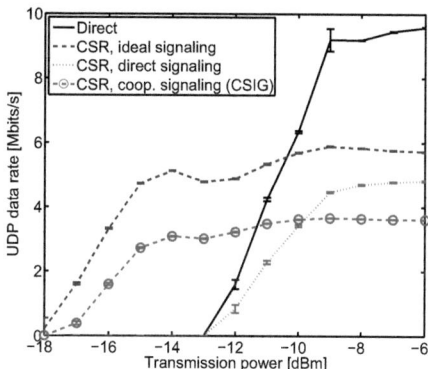

Figure 6.13: End-to-end UDP data rate vs. transmission power: Comparing direct and cooperative signaling for the indoor scenario.

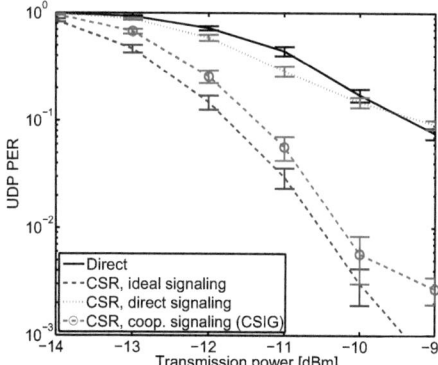

Figure 6.14: End-to-end Packet Error Rate (PER) vs. transmission power: Comparing direct and cooperative signaling for the indoor scenario.

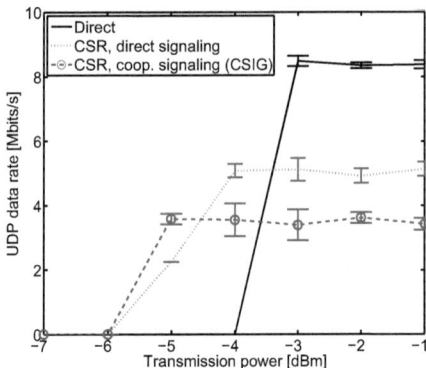

Figure 6.15: End-to-end UDP data rate vs. transmission power: Comparing direct and cooperative signaling for the vehicular scenario.

naling, cooperative relaying outperforms direct transmission by at least one order of magnitude. Hence, the diversity order expected from theory is reached (cp. Figure 3.12). This is not the case with direct signaling. As shown by the matching slope of their PER curves, cooperation with direct signaling reaches the same diversity order as direct transmission. Hence, by transmitting control frames directly, this cooperative MAC protocol cannot benefit from diversity at all. The result is a high PER for the overall transmission if direct signaling is employed.

Naturally, also CSIG loses control frames. The effect of these errors is shown by the PER offset between cooperative and ideal signaling. However, compared to direct signaling this increases the end-to-end PER only slightly.

6.5.3 Vehicular scenario results

Due to the limited availability of the RailCab vehicle, only the most relevant cases were measured. In particular, Figure 6.15 compares the UDP data rate of CSIG to the measurement results for direct signaling and direct transmission.

As in the indoor scenario, direct transmission outperforms cooperative relaying at high transmission power. Again, this is a consequence of the multiplexing loss. At a transmission power below -4 dBm, direct communication is impossible in this scenario. Here, cooperative relaying maintains a considerable data rate but only until -6 dBm is reached. Hence, the power region in which cooperation succeeds is significantly smaller than in the indoor scenario. We can hypothesize that this performance degradation results from the strong LOS component that leads to Rician or Nakagami-like fading [TV05, Section 2.4.2]. In such fading scenarios, the reachable diversity gain is substantially lower than under NLOS conditions where Rayleigh fading can be expected [SA04, Section 9.7].

Comparing the data rate for direct and cooperative signaling at high power shows a clear offset. As in

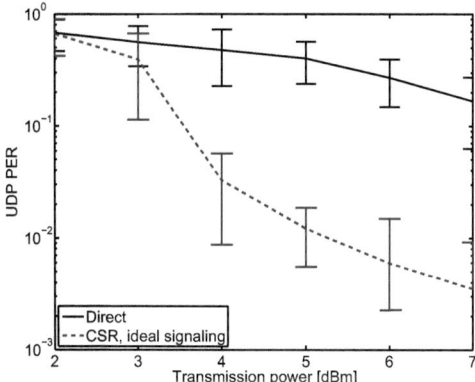

Figure 6.16: End-to-end UDP PER vs. transmission power: Comparing direct and cooperative transmission for the vehicular scenario.

the indoor scenario, this is caused by the overhead added by cooperative signaling. At lower transmission power, the results are interesting. At -4 dBm, even direct signaling provides a data rate gain. This is caused by the varying distance between the moving nodes and the destination. If the moving s and r are close to the destination, even directly transmitted control frames can be transferred at most robust PHY mode. In this case, cooperative relaying can be established and improves the data rate in an intermediate power region. If the power further decreases, even direct signaling is impossible and cooperative signaling is required to maintain communication.

The limited availability of the RailCab vehicle made it necessary to obtain data rate and PER on different days. This required to increase the transmission power for the PER measurements (presumably due to increased air humidity and, thus, higher attenuation). Unfortunately, only the PER for direct transmission and for CSR with ideal signaling could be obtained during the limited measurement time.

Nevertheless, even these basic cases clearly demonstrate the benefit of cooperative relaying in the vehicular scenario. As shown in Figure 6.16, cooperation diversity substantially improves the slope of the PER and, thus, improves the PER by up to one order of magnitude. For CSR with realistic signaling we expect a behavior similar to Figure 6.14 with a slight improvement for direct signaling due to the varying distance between the mobile nodes and d (cp. Figure 6.15).

These measurement results for a practical cooperative WLAN clearly show that the gains expected from theory can be reached in real wireless scenarios.

6.6 Summary of contributions and future work

Contributions

Prototyping a cooperative WLAN transceiver, we made the following contributions.

Simplified combining scheme Theoretical results, simulation, and measurement have shown that complex combining schemes are not required in cooperative WLANs. With low to medium mobility, MRC (and all heuristics based on this scheme) provide only insignificant gains compared to Packet Selection (PS). PS simply selects the first correctly decoded packet, is almost trivial to implement, does not depend on accurate channel knowledge, and does not restrict the choices of rate adaptation.

Cooperative signaling for WLANs From our theoretical results in Section 3.4 and from the measurement results in this chapter we can conclude that cooperative MAC protocols fail to provide diversity gains when control frames are transmitted directly (so-called *direct signaling*). To overcome this *direct signaling problem*, we design the *Cooperative Signaling (CSIG)* protocol for the IEEE 802.11 MAC which protects control frames by cooperation diversity. The high performance of CSIG is demonstrated by measurements in an indoor and vehicular scenario. Unlike cooperation with direct signaling, CSIG maintains a high data rate even at low transmission power and improves the PER by more than one order of magnitude.

Cooperative IEEE 802.11a/g transceiver We describe a transceiver design to integrate PS and CSIG into IEEE 802.11a/g. Our design is lightweight, clearly separates the extensions from IEEE 802.11a/g functions and, thus, includes standard operation as a legacy mode.

Based on this design we implement a prototype that performs Combining-based Selection Relaying (CSR) at the high data rates of IEEE 802.11a/g. This prototype and our extensive field measurements clearly demonstrate that *cooperative* WLAN transceivers (1) are feasible even with today's technology and (2) reach the high gains promised by theory even in real scenarios.

Future work

Rate/relay adaptation Cooperation under the orthogonality constraint reduces the data rate if the wireless channel is in a "good" state. This multiplexing loss can be avoided by dynamically choosing between direct transmission and cooperative relaying according to the channel state. More generally, the transmitter jointly adapts its rate and the number of employed relays (including direct transmission as special case) to the channel. In IEEE 802.11 and many other systems, rate adaptation is already performed to which such joint *rate/relay adaptation* can be integrated by adding one dimension to the rate adaptation matrix. Based on theoretical work [LEG06, LVvM$^+$09], such adaptation schemes have to be designed from a practical point of view, implemented, and studied in field measurements.

Further studies Naturally, the scope of our above transceiver design and measurements is limited. Further studies should widen this scope to more scenarios and systems. In terms of scenarios, we limited our scope to a single indoor and to a single vehicular situation. While the indoor scenario is typical for an office or computer lab situation, the results of a vehicular scenario can be only considered as a guideline for studying other mobile environments. At system level, we focused on IEEE 802.11a/g with the OFDM

PHY. Although this system is relevant and a technical foundation of upcoming IEEE 802.11 and IEEE 802.16 systems [Per08, PH09], different transceiver designs are required for communication at higher mobility and at lower data rate. For such systems (e.g., in wireless sensor or cellular networks) practical designs have to be proposed and studied in theory and by measurements.

Chapter 7

Conclusions and future research

In this thesis, we bridged substantial gaps between theoretical and practical research on cooperative relaying. We studied how realistic assumptions degrade the theoretical performance of selection relaying protocols, proposed practical schemes to deal with these constraints, applied cooperation to improve resource allocation, and, finally, demonstrated a prototype for cooperative Wireless Local Area Networks (WLANs). Based on our analysis, simulation, and field measurements, we draw the following conclusions.

Conclusions

Practical constraints and schemes Cooperative relaying's performance that was so far promised by theory, substantially degrades with limited Channel State Information (CSI), erroneous control frames, limited network connectivity, and autocorrelated fading channels. Each of these practical constraints has strong consequences on the design of cooperative relaying protocols.

With *limited CSI*, Path allocation-based Selection Relaying (PSR) protocols strongly suffer from feedback errors and overhead. Since this fact is often ignored in the literature, it was necessary to revalidate these protocols. We found that PSR protocols perform poorly at low SNR and when high robustness is required. In this regime, the overall performance is restricted by the feedback channel's capacity and Combining-based Selection Relaying (CSR) protocols (not relying on feedback) prevail. At high SNR or low required robustness, this situation reverses and PSR protocols should be selected. By reaching their best performance in different SNR and reliability regions, both protocol classes complement one another.

Like errors during CSI feedback, *erroneous control frames* limit the performance of a cooperation protocol. Many previous cooperation protocol designs ignore this fact and – as our measurements show – perform poorly in realistic scenarios. Our *Cooperative Signaling (CSIG)* protocol protects its control frames by cooperation, seamlessly integrates into the IEEE 802.11 MAC, and maintains high performance where other protocols fail.

Limited network connectivity is another practical constraint that was not consistently studied so far. Especially in urban scenarios, links are frequently blocked and the performance of a cooperative relaying protocol drops. We know now that this loss is the higher the more a protocol relies on a specific network configuration. Thus, protocols have to be designed such that a high performance is reached with many different configurations. This is not the case in many current designs.

Also the effect of *autocorrelated fading* on selection relaying was not studied in previous work. Instead, the research community focused on the block fading model which implies that the forwarding decision is always optimal in time. By generalizing this model to autocorrelated fading we showed that selection relaying substantially loses performance if a relay does not decide frequently "enough". Hence, for general time-selective fading channels an optimization in the value *and* time domain is required. Our practical *Partial Forwarding (PF)* system demonstrates that such frequent forwarding decisions can be efficiently realized with soft output decoding. Even with autocorrelated fading, a performance close to the theoretically ideal case can be reached.

Cooperation and resource allocation   Our analysis points out that cooperative relaying and resource allocation interact beneficially. With resource allocation, packets are prioritized and, by relaying only the most important packets, high gains can be expected at small multiplexing loss.

We exploit this interaction in two new approaches. First, *Traffic-Aware Cooperation Diversity (TACD)* allocates more cooperation diversity branches to the more important parts of a video stream. This improves video quality and can be integrated into selection relaying protocols without overhead. Second, *Cooperative Feedback (CFB)* strengthens the CSI feedback channels, avoids scheduling errors, and improves the sum capacity of Multiuser Diversity (MUD) systems. This new approach is promising for future WLANs, WMANs, and cellular networks that will heavily rely on accurate CSI feedback [LHL+08].

Prototyping and field measurements   From prototyping a *cooperative* IEEE 802.11g WLAN transceiver we conclude that cooperative relaying is not only promising but already practical with today's technology. We have described how to simplify cooperative relaying protocols and combining schemes such that only a slight modification of current MAC and PHY designs is required but still high performance is reached. Our field measurements demonstrate these high gains in real scenarios and are, thus, a strong motivation to include cooperative relaying into future standards and systems.

Future research

Based on our above findings, we suggest the following fields of future research.

Join combining and path allocation   So far, our analysis and the literature separates three extreme transmission schemes: Direct transmission (use $n = 0$ relays), Path allocation-based Selection Relaying (PSR) (use $n = 1$ relay per hop), and Combining-based Selection Relaying (CSR) (use all $n = N$ available relays per hop). Future cooperative relaying protocols may join these cases by adapting $n \in [0, N]$ according to the current channel situation. As a theoretical concept to perform the diversity/multiplexing tradeoff [ZT03] over multiple hops, such n-adaptive protocols may provide further insight in the capacity of cooperative multi-hop networks.

Join cooperation and temporal diversity With our Partial Forwarding (PF) approach, selection relaying can provide spatial diversity gains in fading scenarios where also temporal diversity can be exploited. In this intermediate region between slow and fast fading, it can be beneficial to join PF with temporal diversity schemes (e.g., interleaving, HARQ, or rateless codes). Since cooperation and temporal diversity perform best with different channel statistics and impose different constraints on feedback and delay, joining both approaches may lead to interesting tradeoffs but also to practical schemes which cope well with varying mobility.

Diversity-aware resource allocation By allocating cooperation diversity branches we substantially improved the video quality of a cooperative transmission. This is only one example of a fundamental new resource allocation approach that uses diversity order as a new criterion for resource allocation. By considering the diversity order for each allocated resource portion the scheduler can improve the performance and the complexity of its decision. This certainly demands further studies.

Feedback errors To isolate the effect of feedback errors and cooperation we studied Cooperative Feedback (CFB) only for a basic resource allocation scheme. Many practical schedulers (e.g., in OFDMA downlinks) operate under multiple resource/delay/fairness constraints and, thereby, may react differently to CSI feedback errors (and to methods avoiding them). The interaction between scheduler and CSI feedback scheme is not treated in current literature and seems promising for future research.

More prototypes and measurements Prototyping and measuring cooperative systems is only at its beginning. Although our cooperative WLAN transceiver overcomes the performance and flexibility limitations of current prototypes, it is restricted to IEEE 802.11g operation and was only studied in two example scenarios. Further transceiver designs, prototypes, and measurement campaigns have to provide representative results for LTE and IEEE 802.16 systems. Here, cooperative relaying promises high gains and should be strongly considered for standardization.

Appendix A

BER of partial forwarding

The end-to-end Bit Error Rate (BER_{e2e}) of partial forwarding is derived for a single relay in the CTR network (Figure 3.1(b)), and i.i.d. Rayleigh fading channels. As all cooperating nodes use BPSK, the modulation-dependent parameters in (4.3) are $\alpha_M = 1/2, \beta_M = 1$ [Pro00, (5.2-11)]. FEC coding is ignored and the source employs Maximum Ratio Combining (MRC) with ideal coherent detection.

A.1 BER of uncoded BPSK

For the above assumptions, the closed-form expressions for the BER of the direct link and combined signal are known [Pro00, (14.4-15)]. The BER for an arbitrary direct link (i, j) with i.i.d. Rayleigh fading, BPSK modulation, and no FEC coding is

$$\text{BER}_{i,j} = \frac{1 - \mu_{i,j}}{2} \qquad (A.1)$$

where we define

$$\mu_{i,j} := \sqrt{\frac{\bar{\gamma}_{i,j}}{1 + \bar{\gamma}_{i,j}}}. \qquad (A.2)$$

This expression also provides the closed-form solution for the SER $P^s_{\text{Ray}}(\bar{\gamma}_{i,j})$ in (4.4).

In the CTR, d combines two signals. The BER after this operation is also given in closed-form by [Pro00, (14.4-15)] as

$$\text{BER}_{\text{mrc}} = \begin{cases} \frac{1}{2}(1 - \mu_{r,d})^2 \left(1 + \frac{\mu_{r,d}}{2}\right) & ; \ \bar{\gamma}_{r,d} = \bar{\gamma}_{s,d} \\ \frac{1}{2}\left[1 - \frac{1}{\bar{\gamma}_{s,d} - \bar{\gamma}_{r,d}}\left(\bar{\gamma}_{s,d}\mu_{s,d} - \bar{\gamma}_{r,d}\mu_{r,d}\right)\right] & ; \ \text{otherwise} \end{cases} \qquad (A.3)$$

obtaining $\mu_{r,d}$ and $\mu_{s,d}$ as in (A.2).

A.2 Fraction of symbols not forwarded

Since, with uncoded BPSK, BER and SER are equally expressed by (A.1), we can use this expression to derive the number of symbols not forwarded by the relay F_{drop}. Inserting (A.1) for link (s, r) into (4.6) and (4.8) provides

$$F_{\text{drop,c1}} = P_{\text{Ray}}^s(\tilde{\gamma}_{s,r}) = \frac{1-\mu_{s,r}}{2} \tag{A.4}$$

for Case 1 when the relay decides at least once per fading block. Again, $\mu_{s,r}$ is defined as in (A.2). Inserting (A.1) for link (s,r) into (4.8) results in

$$F_{\text{drop,c2}} = 1 - (1 - P_{\text{Ray}}^s(\tilde{\gamma}_{s,r}))^{1/D_b} = 1 - \left(\frac{1+\mu_{s,r}}{2}\right)^{1/D_b} \tag{A.5}$$

for Case 2 when the relay decides less than once per fading block.

A.3 End-to-end BER of partial forwarding

For the CTR network we assume symmetrical mean SNR, i.e., $\tilde{\gamma}_{s,d} = \tilde{\gamma}_{s,r} = \tilde{\gamma}_{r,d}$ and use the corresponding case in (A.3). Inserting $F_{\text{drop,c1}}$ (A.4) and the BER terms (A.1) and (A.3) into (4.9) provides the end-to-end BER for Case 1

$$\begin{aligned}\text{BER}_{\text{e2e,c1}} &= P_{\text{Ray}}^s(\tilde{\gamma}_{s,r})\text{BER}_{s,d} + (1 - P_{\text{Ray}}^s(\tilde{\gamma}_{s,r}))\text{BER}_{\text{mrc}} \\ &= \frac{1}{4}\left[(1-\mu_{s,r})(1-\mu_{s,d}) + (1+\mu_{s,r})(1-\mu_{r,d})^2\left(1+\frac{\mu_{r,d}}{2}\right)\right].\end{aligned} \tag{A.6}$$

Inserting $F_{\text{drop,c2}}$ (A.5) and the BER terms (A.1) and (A.3) into (4.9) results in

$$\begin{aligned}\text{BER}_{\text{e2e,c2}} &= \left[1 - (1 - P_{\text{Ray}}^s(\tilde{\gamma}_{s,r}))^{1/D_b}\right]\text{BER}_{s,d} + (1 - P_{\text{Ray}}^s(\tilde{\gamma}_{s,r}))^{1/D_b}\text{BER}_{\text{mrc}} \\ &= \left[1 - \left(\frac{1+\mu_{s,r}}{2}\right)^{1/D_b}\right]\frac{1-\mu_{s,d}}{2} \\ &+ \frac{1}{2}\left[\left(\frac{1+\mu_{s,r}}{2}\right)^{1/D_b}(1-\mu_{r,d})^2\left(1+\frac{\mu_{r,d}}{2}\right)\right]\end{aligned} \tag{A.7}$$

as the end-to-end BER for Case 2.

Note that at $D_b = 1$ the end-to-end BER of both cases is equal, since (A.7) reduces to (A.6).

Appendix B

Details on the measurement platform and scenarios

To detail the scenario description in Section 6.5, this appendix describes specifics of the SORBAS devices and important scenario factors. First, we provide an insight into the hardware and software of the SORBAS prototyping platform. Second, we explain the outliers in Figure 6.13 by characterizing a mismatch between the selected and the actual transmission power at the SORBAS antenna port. Finally, we take a closer look at the link budget for the indoor and for the vehicular scenario. To this end, we measure the mean noise plus interference power and characterize the mean path loss in both scenarios. For the indoor scenario, actual path loss measurements allow to estimate the path loss exponent and offset. For the vehicular scenario, these values are predicted by the familiar free space model. Based on these estimations, the average power and the mean SINR at the receivers is predicted.

B.1 SORBAS prototyping platform

The cooperative IEEE 802.11a/g transceiver described in Chapter 6 is implemented on the SORBAS 101 prototyping platform. A brief description of the components that are most relevant to this work is provided here. A more detailed discussion of the platform design, features, and performance can be found in [SDH+04, UU07, LVE+07].

SORBAS is a Software Defined Radio (SDR) [Mit95] that runs a complete IEEE 802.11a/g PHY and DLC in software and in real time. All functions of the DLC and the physical baseband run on off-the-shelf DSPs and Field Programmable Gate Arrays (FPGAs) and can, thus, be modified using standard programming tools.

B.1.1 Hardware overview

Figure B.1 shows a photo of the SORBAS 101 hardware platform. At the front (left) one antenna port for the 5.2 GHz and one port for the 2.4 GHz band is shown. The rear view (right) shows the IEEE 1149.1

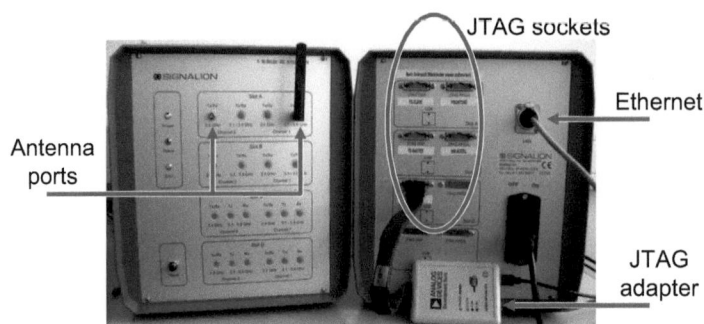

Figure B.1: Front and rear view of a SORBAS 101 device.

Joint Test Action Group (JTAG) sockets at the SORBAS device. A JTAG adapter is used to connect the SORBAS device to a host computer for debugging, memory inspection, and re-programming the internal memory. During the experiments, Ethernet and UDP/IP is used to exchange data and control commands between host PC and SORBAS device.

SORBAS is a modular system that consists of the following main components:

SRFC board: Contains one Infineon PMB8680 RF chip set with D/A and A/D converters, RF amplifier, Received Signal Strength Indication (RSSI) generation, and Clear Channel Assessment (CCA),

Two SDCxC boards: Each with one Xilinx FPGA and one Analog Devices TigerSHARC floating point DSP for PHY processing, and

SMAC board: One Analog Devices Blackfin fixed-point DSP for MAC processing and interfacing to the host computer.

Due to the tremendous processing power required at the PHY, *two* SDCxC boards are necessary per SORBAS device. Each processor has its own memory and operates in a chain with the other processors and FPGAs. The processing units are interconnected at high speed via the so-called *link port* bus.

B.1.2 Software overview

Figure B.2 shows the connection of the processors and FPGAs and how particular PHY and MAC functions are mapped to these hardware components [UU07].

Physical layer The PHY is divided into a *master* part on the SDCxC 2 board and a *slave* part on the SDCxC 1 board. The master performs scrambling/de-scrambling, convolutional encoding/Viterbi decoding, and interleaving/de-interleaving. While the Viterbi decoding is performed on the FPGA, all other components are written in C and run on the DSP. SDCxC 1 contains the slave part which focuses on

B.1. SORBAS prototyping platform

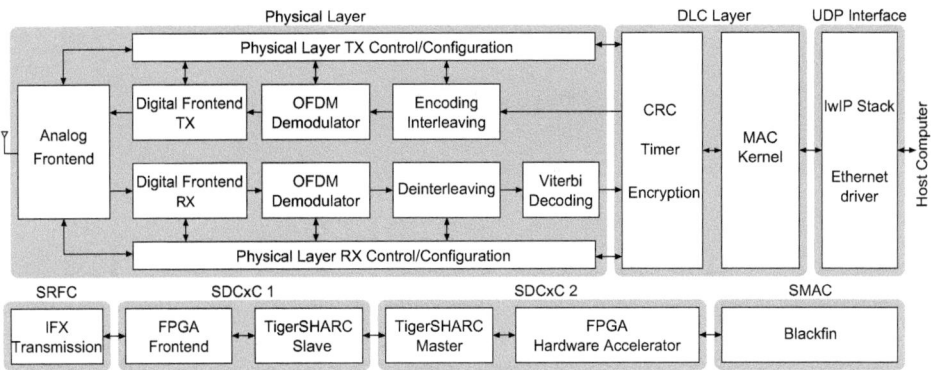

Figure B.2: Overview of the SORBAS 101 hardware and mapping of PHY and DLC functions to hardware components.

mapping/de-mapping and the Fast Fourier Transform (FFT) and its inverse. Since the FFT is performance-critical, it is written entirely in assembler.

The separated design of the PHY exploits parallelization through pipelining. When the master DSP receives a MAC frame as a bitstream from the upper layer, it performs scrambling, convolutional encoding, interleaving, and puncturing on the bitstream and divides it into chunks. These chunks contain as many bits as are to be mapped to OFDM symbols. Then, Direct Memory Access (DMA) is used to transfer one or more chunks via link port to the slave DSP for mapping and inverse FFT. As a consequence, the master DSP can continue with processing the next sequence of bits while the slave simultaneously performs the mapping and computes the inverse FFT.

Data link control layer The MAC protocol is mainly implemented on the Blackfin DSP. Time-critical functions, in particular CRC and timers, are performed at the attached FPGA. The MAC protocol is implemented as an automaton in the Specification and Description Language (SDL) [ITU02]. However, significant parts of the SDL code were replaced by hand-optimized C code to meet real-time requirements. The MAC comprises the complete IEEE 802.11 standard except for security components (that are not used in this thesis). The SORBAS MAC and PHY service primitives are controlled from a host computer using the UDP interface.

Programming aspects Its pipeline-based architecture makes SORBAS 101 a hardware-efficient but also difficult platform for PHY programming. In particular, the physical layer pipeline relies on carefully adjusted I/O rates among the PHY functions. Each function has to keep a processing time (1) short enough such that the overall latency is not increased above the frame time but (2) long enough such that the input buffer of the subsequent function does not overflow. Keeping this balance among the runtimes of the PHY functions makes implementing PHY extensions on the SORBAS devices an error-prone and time-intense task.

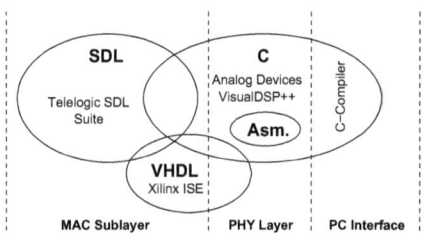

Figure B.3: Programming languages and tools that are used to implement IEEE 802.11a/g functions on the SORBAS platform.

PHY programming is done in C, assembler, and VHDL. The MAC protocol automaton is specified in SDL, translated into C code, and finally compiled for the Blackfin DSP. Figure B.3 summarizes the specification and programming languages that are used to prototype a wireless communication system on SORBAS.

B.1.3 Measurement and control software

The SORBAS devices are integrated into a toolchain for automatically controlling and monitoring a large number of experiments. This control software was developed in the context of this thesis and consists of the following main components.

Linux driver A Linux kernel driver allows to use the SORBAS 101 devices like a standard WLAN adapter. Furthermore, a /proc interface is provided to access parameters on the SORBAS devices via a Unix file handle. This simplifies monitoring and controlling since now any user space program can access the SORBAS device. The complete documentation of the Linux driver is given in [BEF$^+$06].

Measurement framework Based on the Linux driver, a complete measurement framework was developed. This framework configures the SORBAS devices according to the parameter tuple of the current experiment, conducts and monitors the experiments, and captures error events. In case of an error or timeout, the affected SORBAS device is automatically rebooted and the experiment is restarted. In combination with remote control, this framework simplifies running a large number of experiments for several days (the longest continuous measurement in the context of this thesis lasted 8 days). The measurement framework is detailed in [BBF$^+$07] and [BFK$^+$08].

B.2 Transmit power mismatch

For several protocols, Figure 6.13 shows an unexpectedly low data rate if a transmission power of -13 or -12 dBm is selected. We will now show that these outliers result from a transmit power mismatch in the

B.2. Transmit power mismatch

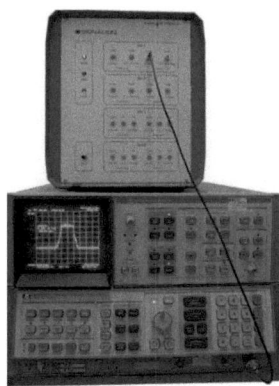

Figure B.4: Setup to measure transmit power mismatch: The antenna port of the transmitting SORBAS is directly connected to the spectrum analyzer.

SORBAS 101 RF frontend. Due to this mismatch, in some cases the power at the antenna port is lower than selected leading to an unexpected low data rate.

B.2.1 Experimental setup

The experimental setup is simple. Using an RG-174 cable, we directly connect the 2.4 GHz antenna port of the transmitting SORBAS 101 device to the inlet of an HP8566B spectrum analyzer. As during all experiments in Section 6.5, we chose the carrier frequency of $f_c = 2.472$ GHz. At this frequency, cable and connectors add a loss of $L_c = -5$ dB to the transmission power at the antenna port.

B.2.2 Measurement results

We vary the selected transmission power in $P_{tx} \in [-20, -3]$ dBm and measure the signal power at the spectrum analyzer P_{rx}. Each mean P_{rx} value is measured for 3000 transmitted PLCP frames; each frame lasts 2 ms. From the measured P_{rx} we obtain the transmission power at the antenna port $P_{tx,o}$ by substracting the cable/connector loss, more formally, $P_{tx,o} = P_{rx} - L_c$. The resulting P_{tx} to $P_{tx,o}$ mapping is shown in Figure B.5.

While at most levels $P_{tx,o}$ matches well with the selected power, this is clearly not the case at $P_{tx} \in [-13, -12]$ dBm. At $P_{tx} = -13$ dBm, $P_{tx,o}$ is 1 dB less than configured and at $P_{tx} = -12$ dBm only $P_{tx,o} = -12.9$ dBm are returned. In our experiments in Section 6.5, this mismatch leads to less power on air than configured and, consequently, to a lower data rate than expected.

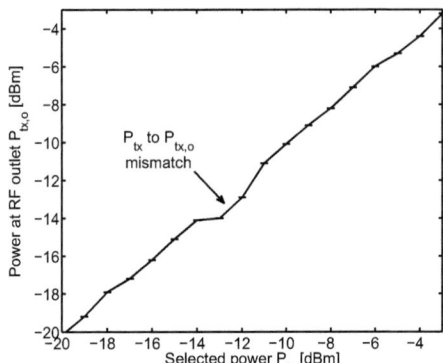

Figure B.5: Mismatch between selected transmission power P_{tx} and actual transmission power at the antenna port of the SORBAS 101 device $P_{tx,o}$.

B.3 Path loss and link budget

Before setting up an experiment, we can estimate the received power and Signal-to-Interference plus Noise Ratio (SINR) by a link budget analysis [Pro00, Section 5.5.2]. Although this approximation is rather rough, it allows to choose the interesting transmit power region and serves as a sanity check for the received values. An important factor in link budget analysis is path loss, which we discuss first.

B.3.1 Indoor scenario

The propagation environment of the indoor scenario is equivalent to the NLOS situation in Figure 6.10. With ferroconcrete walls, closed metal window shutters, computer cases, and monitors there is a large number of reflectors in the propagation environment. The LOS path is covered by the shielding material of the rotating disc (rotation is switched off during path loss measurements) and by the metal cases of the SORBAS devices (cp. Figure 6.10).

In this scenario, we measure mean noise plus interference power and mean path loss. Fitting the results of the common power law path loss model to our measurements allows to estimate the path loss exponent.

Experimental setup

The setup differs from the indoor scenario in Section 6.5.2 only as follows. The relay device is switched off and the destination device is replaced by an Rx antenna bracket. This maintains the antenna position of the destination but allows to measure P_{rx} with an HP8566B spectrum analyzer. To this end, an additional Rx cable connects the Rx antenna in the bracket to the spectrum analyzer. This cable and the connectors

B.3. Path loss and link budget

Table B.1: Link budget: Constant power losses and gains at $f_c = 2.472\,\text{GHz}$.

Component	Type	Adds to P_{tx}
Tx antenna	$\lambda/2$ omni	$G_{tx} = 5\,\text{dBi}$
Tx feeder		$L_{tx,f} = -3\,\text{dB}$
Rx antenna	$\lambda/2$ omni	$G_{rx} = 5\,\text{dBi}$
Rx feeder		$L_{rx,f} = -3\,\text{dB}$
Rx cable	RG-58	$L_{rx,c} = -7\,\text{dB}$

introduce additional power losses. Table B.1 summarizes all components which add a constant power loss or gain to the link budget. The feeder losses result from the antenna connectors at the SORBAS devices.

Per measured P_{rx} value, the source transmits 3000 PLCP frames. Each frame lasts 2 ms and is transmitted at a constant power of $P_{tx} = -4\,\text{dBm}$.

Path loss

To obtain path loss, we measure P_{rx} for a varying distance between the antenna of the source and of the destination. This separation distance $D_{s,d}$ is varied between 2.7 m and 4.5 m. Note that $D_{s,d} = 2.7\,\text{m}$ is the source-to-destination distance in Section 6.5.2 which is, here, used as the reference distance D_0.

From the measured P_{rx} we obtain the mean path loss PL by substracting all other gains and losses (Table B.1), i.e.,

$$\text{PL}(D_{s,d}) = P_{rx} - P_{tx} - L_{tx,f} - G_{tx} - G_{rx} - L_{rx,c} \;\;[\text{dB}]. \tag{B.1}$$

Two specifics of (B.1) have to be noted. First, $L_{rx,c}$ has to be included instead of $L_{rx,f}$ as now no SORBAS device but an additional cable is used to connect the spectrum analyzer. Second, this standard method [Pro00, (5.5-13)] does not separately account for shadowing. Thus, shadowing losses are included in PL. The result of (B.1) is shown by the measured values in Figure B.6. At the reference distance this leads to a mean path loss of $\text{PL}(D_0) = -56.2\,\text{dB}$.

Based on these measurement results we can approximate the path loss exponent α by using the power law model [Rap02, (4.68)]

$$\text{PL}(D_{s,d}) = \text{PL}(D_0) - \alpha \cdot 10\log_{10}\left(\frac{D_{s,d}}{D_0}\right) \;\;[\text{dB}]. \tag{B.2}$$

Choosing $\alpha = 2$ leads to the reference curve in Figure B.6 which corresponds to free space adjusted by the reference path loss $\text{PL}(D_0)$. At $\alpha = 2.75$, the Mean Squared Error (MSE) between the results of model (B.2) and our measurements is minimized to $2.14 \cdot 10^{-6}$. The resulting fitted curve is shown in Figure B.6. Consequently, with the parameters $\alpha = 2.75$ and $\text{PL}(D_0) = -56.2\,\text{dB}$ the path loss model (B.2) suitably reflects our indoor measurements.

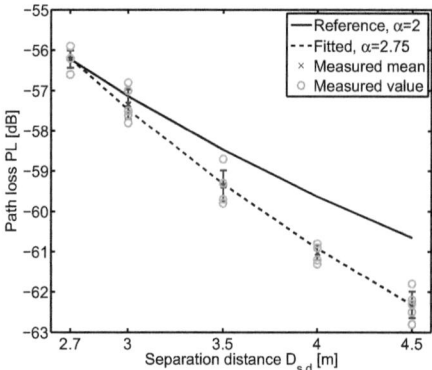

Figure B.6: Path loss of the indoor scenario vs. source-destination separation distance $D_{s,d}$.

Link budget

With the path loss and the constants from Table B.1, the received power in the indoor scenario can be readily approximated by

$$P_{rx} = P_{tx} + L_{tx,f} + G_{tx} + \text{PL}(D_{s,d}) + G_{rx} + L_{rx,f} \text{ [dBm]}. \tag{B.3}$$

To account for the indoor scenario, $L_{rx,c}$ is ignored but $L_{rx,f}$ is included. As in Figure 6.13, we assume that the transmission power is varied between $P_{tx} \in [-18, -6]$ dBm and that $D_{s,d} = 2.7$ m. With these parameters, we can expect a received power within $P_{rx} \in [-70.2, -58.2]$ dBm.

Mean noise plus interference power

The mean noise plus interference power N_{0I} is measured directly at the spectrum analyzer using an $\lambda/2$ omnidirectional antenna. To limit interference from external devices, all controllable radios in the neighborhood are switched off. Nevertheless, the indoor setup is close to a large campus WLAN. Monitoring showed that during measurements approximately 20 to 30 neighboring IEEE 802.11g/b legacy nodes transmitted in the 2.4 GHz band.

In a two days measurement campaign, $N_{0I} = -75.5$ dBm was obtained within 40 MHz bandwidth around the used carrier frequency of $f_c = 2.472$ GHz. During this time, a maximum noise plus interference power of $\hat{N}_{0I} \approx -63$ dBm was measured.

Signal-to-Interference plus Noise Ratio (SINR) and discussion

With the link budget and the measured mean noise plus interference power N_{0I}, we can conclude that a mean SINR between 5.3 dB and 17.3 dB can be expected in the indoor scenario.

This SINR matches to the full operation region of typical IEEE 802.11g receivers, e.g., [Ath07]. Nevertheless, our measurements indicate that neighboring interferers can significantly reduce the mean SINR. We cope with this issue by (1) measuring during the weekends (when less interferers are present), (2) scrambling the experimental matrix (which distributes all measurements for a single factor over the measurement period), and (3) by measuring continuously until the confidence intervals reach the desired size.

B.3.2 Vehicular scenario

The propagation environment of the vehicular scenario is illustrated in Figure 6.5.1. This scenario corresponds to a LOS situation in a rural propagation environment. There are no buildings or trees in the area around the transmitters $\{s,r\}$ (both placed on the RailCab vehicle) and destination d (placed in the center of the elliptic track). The ground is covered with high grass. During the *data rate* measurement campaign, the weather conditions where clear. With a mean relative humidity of 37 % the air was considerably dry.

Path loss

Due to dry air we can ignore atmospheric attenuation on the LOS path. Assuming high absorption from the grassy ground allows to ignore ground reflection. This allows to assume single-ray free space propagation and to predict path loss by Friis well-known equation [Rap02, (4.1)]

$$\text{PL}(D_{\{s,r\},d}) = 20\log_{10}\left(\frac{\lambda}{4\pi d}\right) \; [\text{dB}] \tag{B.4}$$

implying a path loss exponent of $\alpha = 2$. The separation distance $D_{\{s,r\},d} := D_{s,d} = D_{r,d}$ between the transmitters $\{s,r\}$ and destination d varies between 44 m and 90 m. Depending on this distance, the path loss varies between $\text{PL}(D_{\{s,r\},d}) \in [-79.4, -73.2]$ dB.

In literature, only a few outdoor measurements in the 2.4 GHz band are described [HXB99, BBCS02, LRD07]. These papers focus on scenarios in urban or suburban environments with a large number of reflectors and scatterers compared to the vehicular scenario in Figure 6.5.1. This work is, therefore, not included in further discussion.

Link budget

We can estimate the mean received power P_{rx} by inserting $\text{PL}(D_{\{s,r\},d})$ in (B.3). As the RF cabling in indoor and vehicular scenario was identical, the values from Table B.1 can be used as above. In addition to the varying separation distance, we assume that the transmission power is selected between $P_{tx} \in [-7,-1]$ dBm. Depending on the chosen P_{tx} the mean received power is $P_{rx} \in [-82.4, -76.4]$ dBm at the maximum separation distance of 90 m and increases to $P_{rx} \in [-76.2, -70.2]$ dBm at the minimum distance of 44 m. With these intervals, we expect that the total studied P_{rx} region is $P_{rx} \in [-82.4, -70.2]$ dBm.

Mean noise plus interference power

During the one day measurement campaign a mean noise plus interference power of $N_{0I} = -97$ dBm was obtained.

Signal-to-Interference plus Noise Ratio (SINR) and discussion

With the link budget and the measured mean noise plus interference power N_{0I}, we can predict the SINR in the vehicular scenario. At maximum separation distance, an SINR between 14.6 dB and 20.6 dB can be expected according to the selected transmission power. At minimum distance, SINR between 20.8 dB and 26.8 dB can be configured. Thus, we expect that the studied mean SINR is between 14.6 dB and 26.8 dB.

Note that these SINR values are above the SINR required by typical IEEE 802.11g transceivers to operate at 18 Mbits/s transmission rate, e.g., SINR $\geq$ 11 dB in [Ath07]. Thus, the chosen P_{tx} range includes a safety margin if the above path loss prediction (B.4) is too optimistic or if fading and shadowing further reduce the received power.

B.4 Summary of experimental setup and parameters

This section summarizes the parameters and components employed during our experiments.

Table B.2 lists the non-conventional hardware and software used in both scenarios. The table lists the SORBAS firmware that was provided by the vendors and then modified to incorporate cooperative relaying (Section 6.4).

Table B.3 summarizes the relevant parameters and factors for the indoor scenario. Most MAC and PHY parameters match to the IEEE 802.11 and IEEE 802.11g standards [IEE03, IEE99] and are, thus, not mentioned here.

Table B.4 lists the relevant parameters and factors for the vehicular scenario. Note that only those parameters are listed that have changed with respect to the indoor scenario. Due to unknown but significant atmospheric attenuation, P_{rx} and SINR are not listed for the PER measurement campaign. Nonetheless, from the results in Figure 6.16, we expect that the increased P_{tx} compensated for this atmospheric loss such that the P_{rx} and SINR during PER measurements is similar to the values of the data rate measurement campaign.

B.4. Summary of experimental setup and parameters

Table B.2: Hardware and software used in the indoor and vehicular scenario.

Component (vendor)	Type/Version	Description
Antennas	WL-IW151S	$\lambda/2$ omnidirectional whip, 5 dBi gain
SORBAS devices (Signalion)	101	SDR platform (Section B.1)
SORBAS firmware		
FPGA (Signalion)	1.6	Baseband filter and Viterbi decoding [UU07]
PHY (Signalion)	060929_UPB	IEEE 802.11a/g OFDM PHY [UU07]
MAC (Signalion)	060929_UPB	IEEE 802.11 MAC [Ung05]
MAC automata (IHP)	04-Jan-2006	IEEE 802.11, SDL specification [THL05]
Development software		
SDT (Telelogic)	4.6	SDL specification/test suite
VisualDSP++ (Analog Devices)	4.0	ASM, C development and compiler suite

Table B.3: Parameters and factors for the indoor scenario.

Parameter/Factor	Values
Carrier frequency f_c	2.472 GHz
Signal bandwidth W	20 MHz
Assumed propagation environment	NLOS
Tangential velocity	1 m/s
UDP/IP packet length	1052 Bytes
PHY transmission rate, signaling (BPSK, $R_c = 1/2$)	6 Mbits/s
PHY transmission rate, data (QPSK, $R_c = 3/4$)	18 Mbits/s
Distance $D_{s,r}$	1.44 m
Distances $D_{s,d} = D_{r,d}$	2.7 m
Reference path loss at $D_{s,d}$	-56.2 dB
Path loss exponent α	2.75
Mean noise plus interference power N_{0I}	-75.5 dBm
Transmission power P_{tx}	$[-18, -6]$ dBm
Estimated received power P_{rx}	$[-70.2, -58.2]$ dBm
Estimated mean SINR	$[5.3, 22.3]$ dB

Table B.4: Parameters and factors for the vehicular scenario.

Parameter/Factor	Values
Assumed propagation environment	LOS, free space
Linear velocity	5 m/s
Distance $D_{s,r}$	1.61 m
Distances $D_{s,d} = D_{r,d}$	$[44, 90]$ m
Path loss exponent α	2
Mean noise plus interference power N_{0I}	-97 dBm
Transmission power P_{tx} (PER)	$[2, 7]$ dBm
Transmission power P_{tx} (data rate)	$[-7, -1]$ dBm
Estimated received power P_{rx} (data rate)	$[-82.4, -70.2]$ dBm
Estimated mean SINR (data rate)	$[14.6, 20.6]$ dB

Bibliography

[3GP01] 3GPP, "Physical layer aspects of UTRA high speed downlink packet access," 3GPP, TSG-RAN technical report 25.848, v. 4.0.0, 2001.

[ADF+09] D. Astely, E. Dahlman, A. Furuskär, Y. Jading, M. Lindström, and S. Parkvall, "LTE: the evolution of mobile broadband," *IEEE Commun. Mag.*, vol. 47, no. 4, pp. 44–51, Apr. 2009.

[AFYP08] A. Adinoyi, Y. Fan, H. Yanikomeroglu, and H. V. Poor, "On the performance of selection relaying," in *Proc. Vehicular Technology Conf. (VTC-Fall)*, Sep. 2008, pp. 1–5.

[Ala98] S. M. Alamouti, "A simple transmit diversity technique for wireless communications," *IEEE J. Sel. Areas Commun.*, vol. 16, no. 8, pp. 1451–1458, Oct. 1998.

[AMI07] G. Acosta-Marum and M. A. Ingram, "Six time and frequency selective empirical channel models for vehicular wireless LANs," *IEEE Veh. Technol. Mag.*, vol. 2, no. 4, pp. 4–11, Dec. 2007.

[ASH+08] J. Andrews, S. Shakkottai, R. Heath, N. Jindal, M. Haenggi, R. Berry, D. Guo, M. Neely, S. Weber, S. Jafar, and A. Yener, "Rethinking information theory for mobile ad hoc networks," *IEEE Commun. Mag.*, vol. 46, no. 12, pp. 94–101, Dec. 2008.

[AT07] A. Avestimehr and D. Tse, "Outage capacity of the fading relay channel in the low-SNR regime," *IEEE Trans. Inf. Theory*, vol. 53, no. 4, pp. 1401–1415, Apr. 2007.

[Ath07] *AR5414 Technical specifications*, Atheros, 2007, 6th Generation.

[BA07] E. Beres and R. Adve, "Outage probability of selection cooperation in the low to medium SNR regime," *IEEE Commun. Lett.*, vol. 11, no. 7, pp. 589–597, July 2007.

[BA08] ——, "Selection cooperation in multi-source cooperative networks," *IEEE Trans. Wireless Commun.*, vol. 7, no. 1, pp. 118–127, Jan. 2008.

[BBCS02] P. Baldassaro, C. Bostian, L. Carstensen, and D. Sweeney, "Path loss predictions and measurements over urban and rural terrain at frequencies between 900 MHz and 28 GHz," in *Proc. IEEE Int. Symp. of the Antennas and Propagation Society (APS)*, vol. 2, 2002, pp. 302–305.

[BBF+07] D. Bergen, T. Biermann, R. Funke, M. Jürgens, C. Kunzmann, S. Lutters, D. Platz, D. Protte, S. Valentin (ed.), and H. Karl (ed.), "Implementing and evaluating IEEE 802.11-based cooperative MAC protocols using the SORBAS software-defined radio," University of Paderborn, Student research project, final documentation, Oct. 2007.

[BBKT96] P. Bhagwat, P. Bhattacharya, A. Krishna, and S. K. Tripathi, "Enhancing throughput over wireless LANs using channel state dependent packet scheduling," in *Proc. Ann. Joint Conf. of the IEEE Computer Societies (INFOCOM)*, vol. 3, 1996, pp. 1133–1140.

[BCJR74] L. Bahl, J. Cocke, F. Jelinek, and J. Raviv, "Optimal decoding of linear codes for minimizing symbol error rate," *IEEE Trans. Inf. Theory*, vol. 20, no. 2, pp. 284–287, Mar. 1974.

[BEF+06] W. Badis, F. Eitzen, T. Freitag, Q. Hasi, H. S. Lichte, W. Reisch, M. Röhs, B. Schmidt, K. Song, B. Stelte, Z. Yuan, S. Valentin (ed.), and H. Karl (ed.), "Implementing 802.11a cross-layer optimization on a software-defined radio," University of Paderborn, Student research project, final documentation, Sep. 2006.

[BFK+08] L. Banach, L. Fernhomberg, A. Klass, P. Krümmelbein, A. Malki, R. Petrlic, T. Rheker, S. Valentin (ed.), H. S. Lichte (ed.), and H. Karl (ed.), "Implementation and performance study of cooperative MAC protocols," University of Paderborn, Student research project, final documentation, Sep. 2008.

[BFY04] J. Boyer, D. Falconer, and H. Yanikomeroglu, "Multihop diversity in wireless relaying channels," *IEEE Trans. Commun.*, vol. 52, no. 10, pp. 1820–1830, Oct. 2004.

[BFY07] J. Boyer, D. D. Falconer, and H. Yanikomeroglu, "Diversity order bounds for wireless relay networks," in *Proc. IEEE Wireless Commun. and Netw. Conf. (WCNC)*, Mar. 2007.

[BKRL06] A. Bletsas, A. Khisti, D. Reed, and A. Lippman, "A simple cooperative diversity method based on network path selection," *IEEE J. Sel. Areas Commun.*, vol. 24, no. 3, pp. 659–672, Mar. 2006.

[BL06a] X. Bao and J. Li, "Progressive network coding for message-forwarding in ad-hoc wireless networks," in *Proc. Ann. Conf. on Sensor, Mesh and Ad Hoc Commun. and Networks (SECON)*, vol. 1, Sep. 2006, pp. 207–215.

[BL06b] A. Bletsas and A. Lippman, "Implementing cooperative diversity antenna arrays with commodity hardware," *IEEE Commun. Mag.*, vol. 44, pp. 33–40, Dec. 2006.

[BL07] X. Bao and J. Li, "Efficient message relaying for wireless user cooperation: Decode-amplify-forward (DAF) and hybrid DAF and coded-cooperation," *IEEE Trans. Wireless Commun.*, vol. 6, no. 11, pp. 3975–3984, Nov. 2007.

[BM05] S. Biswas and R. Morris, "Opportunistic routing in multi-hop wireless networks," in *Proc. Ann. Conf. of the Special Interest Group on Data Commun. (SIGCOMM)*, 2005.

[Bre03] D. Brennan, "Linear diversity combining techniques," *Proc. IEEE*, vol. 91, no. 2, pp. 331–356, Feb. 2003.

[BS04] I. N. Bronstein and K. A. Semendjajew, *Handbook of Mathematics*, 4th ed. Springer, Apr. 2004.

[BSE04] A. R. S. Bahai, B. R. Saltzberg, and M. Ergen, *Multi-Carrier Digital Communications Theory and Applications of OFDM*, 2nd ed. Springer, Inc., 2004.

[BSW07] A. Bletsas, H. Shin, and M. Z. Win, "Cooperative communications with outage-optimal opportunistic relaying," *IEEE Trans. Wireless Commun.*, vol. 6, no. 9, pp. 3450–3460, Sep. 2007.

[Cav00] J. Cavers, *Mobile Channel Characteristics*. Kluwer Academic, 2000.

[CBD02] T. Champ, J. Boleng, and V. Davies, "A survey of mobility models for ad hoc network research," *Wireless Communication & Mobile Computing (WCMC)*, vol. 2, no. 5, pp. 483–502, 2002.

[CBH08] J. Chen, R. Berry, and M. Honig, "Limited feedback schemes for downlink OFDMA based on sub-channel groups," *IEEE J. Sel. Areas Commun.*, vol. 26, no. 8, pp. 1451–1461, Oct. 2008.

[CC84] R. Comroe and J. Costello, D., "ARQ schemes for data transmission in mobile radio systems," *IEEE J. Sel. Areas Commun.*, vol. 2, no. 4, pp. 472–481, Jul. 1984.

[CG79] T. M. Cover and A. A. E. Gamal, "Capacity theorems for the relay channel," *IEEE Trans. Inf. Theory*, vol. 25, no. 5, pp. 572–584, Sep 1979.

[Cha66] R. W. Chang, "Synthesis of band-limited orthogonal signals for multichannel data transmission," *Bell Systems Technical Journal*, vol. 45, Dec. 1966.

[Cha85] D. Chase, "Code combining – a maximum-likelihood decoding approach for combining an arbitrary number of noisy packets," *IEEE Trans. Commun.*, vol. 33, no. 5, pp. 385–393, May 1985.

[CK02] C.-N. Chuah and R. H. Katz, "Characterizing packet audio streams from Internet multimedia applications," in *Proc. IEEE Int. Conf. on Commun. (ICC)*, vol. 2, 2002, pp. 1199–1203.

[CKL06] Y. Chen, S. Kishore, and J. Li, "Wireless diversity through network coding," in *Proc. IEEE Wireless Commun. and Netw. Conf. (WCNC)*, vol. 3, 3-6 April 2006, pp. 1681–1686.

[CLL+07] P. Chan, E. Lo, V. Lau, R. Cheng, K. Letaief, R. Murch, and W. H. Mow, "Performance comparison of downlink multiuser MIMO-OFDMA and MIMO-MC-CDMA with transmit side information – multi-cell analysis," *IEEE Trans. Wireless Commun.*, vol. 6, no. 6, pp. 2193–2203, Jun. 2007.

[CLRS01] T. H. Cormen, C. E. Leiserson, R. L. Rivest, and C. Stein, *Introduction to Algorithms*, 2nd ed. The MIT press, 2001.

[CRWC07] I. Chatzigeorgiou, M. Rodrigues, I. Wassell, and R. Carrasco, "Comparison of convolutional and turbo coding for broadband FWA systems," *IEEE Trans. Broadcast.*, vol. 53, no. 2, pp. 494–503, Jun. 2007.

[CT91] T. M. Cover and J. A. Thomas, *Elements of Information Theory*. Wiley, 1991.

[DM09] G. Y. Dai and W. Mow, "Realizing wireless cooperative communications with the one-bit soft forwarding technique," in *Proc. IEEE Wireless Commun. and Netw. Conf. (WCNC)*, Apr. 2009, pp. 1–6.

[GE04] D. Gunduz and E. Erkip, "Joint source-channel cooperation: Diversity versus spectral efficiency," in *Proc. IEEE Int. Symp. on Inf. Theory (ISIT)*, Jun. 2004, pp. 392–392.

[GGKW06] J. Gross, H.-F. Geerdes, H. Karl, and A. Wolisz, "Performance analysis of dynamic OFDMA systems with inband signaling," *IEEE J. Sel. Areas Commun.*, vol. 24, no. 3, pp. 427–436, Mar. 2006.

[GK00] P. Gupta and P. R. Kumar, "The capacity of wireless networks," *IEEE Trans. Inf. Theory*, vol. 46, no. 2, pp. 388–404, Mar. 2000.

[GK08] S. Gollakota and D. Katabi, "ZigZag decoding: Combating hidden terminals in wireless networks," in *Proc. Ann. Conf. of the Special Interest Group on Data Commun. (SIGCOMM)*, Aug. 2008.

[GKKW04] J. Gross, J. Klaue, H. Karl, and A. Wolisz, "Cross-layer optimization of OFDM transmission systems for MPEG-4 video streaming," *Computer Communications*, vol. 27, pp. 1044–1055, 2004.

[GNU09] GNU Radio, "The GNU software radio, project homepage," http://gnuradio.org/, 2009, link verified on Jul. 12th, 2010.

[GRTK08] D. Gesbert, C. V. Rensburg, F. Tosato, and F. Kaltenberger, *UMTS Long Term Evolution (LTE): From theory to practice*. Wiley, 2008, ch. 7: Multiple antenna techniques.

[GVKW05] J. Gross, S. Valentin, H. Karl, and A. Wolisz, "A study on the impact of inband signaling and realistic channel knowledge for an example dynamic OFDM-FDMA system," *Euro. Trans. Telecomms.*, vol. 16, no. 1, pp. 37–49, Jan. 2005.

[GWAC05] A. Ghosh, D. Wolter, J. Andrews, and R. Chen, "Broadband wireless access with WiMAX/802.16: Current performance benchmarks and future potential," *IEEE Commun. Mag.*, vol. 43, no. 2, pp. 129–136, Feb. 2005.

[Hag88] J. Hagenauer, "Rate-compatible punctured convolutional codes (RCPC codes) and their applications," *IEEE Trans. Commun.*, vol. 36, no. 4, pp. 389–400, Apr. 1988.

[Her05] P. Herhold, "Cooperative relaying – protocols and performance," Dissertation, TU Dresden, Mar. 2005.

[HH89] J. Hagenauer and P. Hoeher, "A Viterbi algorithm with soft-decision outputs and its applications," in *Proc. IEEE Global Telecommun. Conf. (GLOBECOM)*, Nov. 1989, pp. 1680–1686.

[HKA08] K.-S. Hwang, Y.-C. Ko, and M.-S. Alouini, "Performance analysis of incremental relaying with relay selection and adaptive modulation over non-identically distributed cooperative paths," in *Proc. IEEE Int. Symp. on Inf. Theory (ISIT)*, Jul. 2008, pp. 2678–2682.

[HKK+07] L. Hentilä, P. Kyösti, M. Käske, M. Narandzic, and M. Alatossava, "MATLAB implementation of the WINNER Phase II Channel Model ver1.1," http://www.ist-winner.org/phase_2_model.html, Dec. 2007, link verified on Jul. 12th, 2010.

[HM02] A. Høst-Madsen, "On the capacity of wireless relaying," in *Proc. Vehicular Technology Conf. (VTC-Fall)*, vol. 3, Sep. 2002, pp. 1333–1337.

[HMZ05] A. Høst-Madsen and J. Zhang, "Capacity bounds and power allocation for wireless relay channels," *IEEE Trans. Inf. Theory*, vol. 51, no. 6, pp. 2020–2040, Jun. 2005.

[HN02] T. E. Hunter and A. Nosratinia, "Cooperation diversity through coding," in *Proc. IEEE Int. Symp. on Inf. Theory (ISIT)*, Jul. 2002, p. 220.

[Hos09] HostAP, "Open-source driver for Intersil Prism 2/2.5/3 chip-sets," http://hostap.epitest.fi/, 2009, link verified on Jul. 12th, 2010.

[HSLK10] S. V. H. S. Lichte and H. Karl, "Expected interference in wireless networks with geometric path loss – a closed-form approximation," *IEEE Commun. Lett.*, vol. 14, pp. 130–132, Feb. 2010.

[HSN06] T. E. Hunter, S. Sanayei, and A. Nosratinia, "Outage analysis of coded cooperation," *IEEE Trans. Inf. Theory*, vol. 52, no. 2, pp. 375–391, Feb. 2006.

[HTL+06] I. Haratcherev, J. Taal, K. Langendoen, R. Lagendijk, and H. Slips, "Optimized video streaming over 802.11 by cross-layer signaling," *IEEE Commun. Mag.*, vol. 44, no. 1, pp. 115–121, Jan. 2006.

[HW04] J. Hamalainen and R. Wichman, "Performance of multiuser diversity in the presence of feedback errors," in *Proc. IEEE Ann. Int. Symp. on Personal, Indoor and Mobile Radio Commun. (PIMRC)*, vol. 1, Sep. 2004, pp. 599–603.

[HWR07] L. Hanzo, J. Woodard, and P. Robertson, "Turbo decoding and detection for wireless applications," *Proc. IEEE*, vol. 95, no. 6, pp. 1178–1200, Jun. 2007.

[HXB99] D. Har, H. Xia, and H. Bertoni, "Path-loss prediction model for microcells," *IEEE Trans. Veh. Technol.*, vol. 48, no. 5, pp. 1453–1462, Sep. 1999.

[HZF04] P. Herhold, E. Zimmermann, and G. Fettweis, "A simple cooperative extension to wireless relaying," in *Proc. Int. Zurich Sem. on Commun.*, 2004, pp. 36–39.

[ID08] R. Irmer and F. Diehm, "On coverage and capacity of relaying in LTE-advanced in example deployments," in *Proc. IEEE Ann. Int. Symp. on Personal, Indoor and Mobile Radio Commun. (PIMRC)*, Sep. 2008.

[IEE99] IEEE, "Standard for information technology – telecommunications and information exchange between systems – LAN/MAN specific requirements – part 11: Wireless LAN MAC and PHY layer specifications," *ANSI/IEEE Std 802.11-1999*, 1999.

[IEE03] ——, "Standard for information technology – telecommunications and information exchange between systems – LAN/MAN specific requirements – part 11: Wireless LAN MAC and PHY layer specifications – amendment 4: Further higher-speed physical layer extension in the 2.4 GHz band," *IEEE Std 802.11g-2003*, Jun. 2003.

[IEE05] ——, "Standard for local and metropolitan area networks – part 16: Air interface for fixed and mobile broadband wireless access systems – amendment 2: Physical and medium access control layers for combined fixed and mobile operation in licensed bands," *IEEE Std 802.16e-2005*, Nov. 2005.

[IEE09a] ——, "Standard for local and metropolitan area networks – part 16: Air interface for fixed and mobile broadband wireless access systems – amendment 1: Multiple relay specification," *IEEE Std 802.16j-2009*, Jun. 2009.

[IEE09b] IEEE-SA Standards Board, "IEEE 802.16 Task Group m," Website: http://wirelessman.org/tgm/, 2009, link verified on Jul. 12th, 2010.

[IH07] R. Islam and W. Hamouda, "An efficient MAC protocol for cooperative diversity in mobile ad hoc networks," *Wireless Commun. and Mobile Computing*, Apr. 2007.

[Int01a] *ISL37300P – PRISM 2.5 11 Mbps Wireless Local Area Network PC Card*, Intersil Americas Inc., Dec. 2001.

[Int01b] *ISL3873 – Wireless LAN Integrated Medium Access Controller with Baseband Processor*, Intersil Americas Inc., Feb. 2001.

[ISO00] ISO, "Overview of the MPEG-4 standard," ISO/IEC JTC1/SC29/WG11, Document N3536, July 2000.

[ITU93] ITU-T, "Video codec for audiovisual services at $p \times 64$ kbits," ITU-T Recom. H.261, Mar. 1993.

[ITU96] ——, "Subjective video quality assessment methods for multimedia applications," ITU-T Recom. P.910, Aug. 1996.

[ITU02] ——, "Specification and description language (SDL)," ITU-T Recom. Z.100, Aug. 2002.

[Jak62] W. C. Jakes, *Microwave Mobile Communications*. Wiley, 1962.

[JHHN04] M. Janani, A. Hedayat, T. E. Hunter, and A. Nosratinia, "Coded cooperation in wireless communications: Space-time transmission and iterative decoding," *IEEE Trans. Signal Process.*, vol. 52, no. 2, pp. 362–371, Feb. 2004.

[KGG05] G. Kramer, M. Gastpar, and P. Gupta, "Cooperative strategies and capacity theorems for relay networks," *IEEE Trans. Inf. Theory*, vol. 51, no. 9, pp. 3037–3063, Sep. 2005.

[KHL05] A. Kwasinski, Z. Han, and K. Liu, "Cooperative multimedia communications: Joint source coding and collaboration," in *Proc. IEEE Global Telecommun. Conf. (GLOBECOM)*, vol. 1, Nov. 2005, p. 5.

[KK08] A. Kühne and A. Klein, "Throughput analysis of multi-user OFDMA-systems using imperfect CQI feedback and diversity techniques," *IEEE J. Sel. Areas Commun.*, vol. 26, no. 8, pp. 1440–1450, Oct. 2008.

[KKEP09] T. Korakis, M. Knox, E. Erkip, and S. Panwar, "Cooperative network implementation using open-source platforms," *IEEE Commun. Mag.*, vol. 47, no. 2, pp. 134–141, Feb. 2009.

[KMY06] G. Kramer, I. Marić, and R. D. Yates, "Cooperative communications," *Foundations and Trends in Netw.*, vol. 1, no. 3, pp. 271–425, 2006.

[KNBP06] T. Korakis, S. Narayanan, A. Bagri, and S. Panwar, "Implementing a cooperative MAC protocol for wireless LANs," in *Proc. IEEE Int. Conf. on Commun. (ICC)*, vol. 10, June 2006, pp. 4805–4810.

[Kra06] G. Kramer, "The relay channel," Handout 4 – Tutorial on Cooperative Communications, Sep. 2006.

[KSW+08] A. Köpke, M. Swigulski, K. Wessel, D. Willkomm, P. T. K. Haneveld, T. Parker, O. Visser, H. S. Lichte, and S. Valentin, "Simulating wireless and mobile networks in OMNeT++: The MiXiM vision," in *Proc. Int. Workshop on OMNeT++ collocated with SIMUTools*, Mar. 2008.

[LAW+08] L. Loyola, I. Aad, J. Widmer, H. S. Lichte, and S. Valentin, "Increasing the capacity of IEEE 802.11 wireless LAN through cooperative coded retransmissions," in *Proc. Vehicular Technology Conf. (VTC-Spring)*, May 2008.

[LCSK07] Y.-B. Lin, T.-H. Chiu, Y. Su, and M. Kao, "An iterative resource allocation algorithm for cooperative multimedia communications," in *Proc. Vehicular Technology Conf. (VTC-Fall)*, Sep. 2007, pp. 1767–1771.

[LEG06] Z. Lin, E. Erkip, and M. Ghosh, "Rate adaptation for cooperative systems," in *Proc. IEEE Global Telecommun. Conf. (GLOBECOM)*, Dec. 2006.

[LES06] Z. Lin, E. Erkip, and A. Stefanov, "Cooperative regions and partner choice in coded cooperative systems," *IEEE Trans. Commun.*, vol. 54, no. 7, pp. 1323–1334, Jul. 2006.

[LG01] L. Li and A. Goldsmith, "Capacity and optimal resource allocation for fading broadcast channels – Part I. ergodic capacity," *IEEE Trans. Inf. Theory*, vol. 47, no. 3, pp. 1083–1102, Mar. 2001.

[LHL+08] D. Love, R. Heath, V. Lau, D. Gesbert, B. Rao, and M. Andrews, "An overview of limited feedback in wireless communication systems," *IEEE J. Sel. Areas Commun.*, vol. 26, no. 8, pp. 1341–1365, Oct. 2008.

[LHV07] C. Lo, W. Heath, and S. Vishwanath, "Opportunistic relay selection with limited feedback," in *Proc. Vehicular Technology Conf. (VTC-Spring)*, Apr. 2007, pp. 135–139.

[LK08] A. Lie and J. Klaue, "Evalvid-RA: Trace driven simulation of rate adaptive MPEG-4 VBR video," *Multimedia Systems*, vol. 14, no. 1, pp. 33–50, Jun. 2008.

[LL06] G. Li and H. Liu, "Resource allocation for OFDMA relay networks with fairness constraints," *IEEE J. Sel. Areas Commun.*, vol. 24, no. 11, pp. 2061–2069, Nov. 2006.

[LLM+09] A. Larmo, M. Lindström, M. Meyer, G. Pelletier, J. Torsner, and H. Wiemann, "The LTE link-layer design," *IEEE Commun. Mag.*, vol. 47, no. 4, pp. 52–59, Apr. 2009.

[LNDX04] T. Le-Ngoc, N. Damji, and Y. Xu, "Dynamic resource allocation for multimedia services over OFDM downlink in cellular systems," in *Proc. Vehicular Technology Conf. (VTC-Spring)*, vol. 4, May 2004, pp. 1864–1868.

[LRD07] L. Liechty, E. Reifsnider, and G. Durgin, "Developing the best 2.4 GHz propagation model from active network measurements," in *Proc. Vehicular Technology Conf. (VTC-Fall)*, Oct. 2007, pp. 894–896.

[LSC07]   M.-H. Lu, P. Steenkiste, and T. Chen, "Time-aware opportunistic relay for video streaming over WLANs," in *Proc. IEEE Int. Conf. on Multimedia & Expos (ICME)*, Jul. 2007, pp. 1782–1785.

[LSSK09]   K. J. R. Liu, A. K. Sadek, W. Su, and A. Kwasinski, *Cooperative Communications and Networking*. Cambridge University Press, 2009.

[LTL+06]   P. Liu, Z. Tao, Z. Lin, E. Erkip, and S. Panwar, "Cooperative wireless communications: A cross-layer approach," *IEEE Wireless Communications*, vol. 13, pp. 84–92, Aug. 2006.

[LTN+07]   P. Liu, Z. Tao, S. Narayanan, T. Korakis, and S. S. Panwar, "CoopMAC: a cooperative MAC for wireless LANs," *IEEE J. Sel. Areas Commun.*, vol. 25, no. 2, pp. 340–354, 2007.

[LTP05]   P. Liu, Z. Tao, and S. Panwar, "A cooperative MAC protocol for wireless local area networks," in *Proc. IEEE Int. Conf. on Commun. (ICC)*, vol. 5, May 2005, pp. 2962–2968.

[Lub02]   M. Luby, "LT codes," in *Proc. Ann. IEEE Symp. on Foundations of Computer Science (FOCS)*, 2002, pp. 271–280.

[LV08]   H. S. Lichte and S. Valentin, "Implementing MAC protocols for cooperative relaying: A compiler-assisted approach," in *Proc. Int. Conf. on Simulation Tools and Techniques for Commun., Networks and Systems (SIMUTools)*, Mar. 2008, best paper award.

[LVE+07]   H. S. Lichte, S. Valentin, F. Eitzen, M. Stege, C. Unger, and H. Karl, "Integrating multiuser dynamic OFDMA into IEEE 802.11a and prototyping it on a real-time software-defined radio testbed," in *Proc. Int. Conf. on Testbeds and Research Infrastructures for the Development of Netw. and Communities (TridentCom)*, May 2007.

[LVK+08]   H. S. Lichte, S. Valentin, H. Karl, I. Aad, L. Loyola, and J. Widmer, "Design and evaluation of a routing-informed cooperative MAC protocol for ad hoc networks," in *Proc. Ann. Joint Conf. of the IEEE Computer Societies (INFOCOM)*, Apr. 2008.

[LVK09a]   H. S. Lichte, S. Valentin, and H. Karl, "Automated development of cooperative MAC protocols: A compiler-assisted approach," *Mobile Networks and Applications*, Sep. 2009.

[LVK+09b]   H. S. Lichte, S. Valentin, H. Karl, I. Aad, and J. Widmer, "Analyzing space/capacity tradeoffs of cooperative wireless networks using a probabilistic model of interference," in *Proc. ACM Int. Conf. on Modeling, Analysis and Simulation of Wireless and Mobile Systems (MSWiM)*, Oct. 2009, to appear.

[LVvM+09]   H. S. Lichte, S. Valentin, H. von Malm, H. Karl, A. B. Sediq, and I. Aad, "Rate-per-link adaptation in cooperative wireless networks with multi-rate combining," in *Proc. IEEE Int. Conf. on Commun. (ICC)*, Jun. 2009.

[LVWD06]   Y. Li, B. Vucetic, T. Wong, and M. Dohler, "Distributed turbo coding with soft information relaying in multihop relay networks," *IEEE J. Sel. Areas Commun.*, vol. 24, no. 11, pp. 2040–2050, Nov. 2006.

[LWT01]   J. N. Laneman, G. W. Wornell, and D. N. C. Tse, "An efficient protocol for realizing cooperative diversity in wireless networks," in *Proc. IEEE Int. Symp. on Inf. Theory (ISIT)*, Jun. 2001, p. 294.

[LWT04] ——, "Cooperative diversity in wireless networks: Efficient protocols and outage behavior," *IEEE Trans. Inf. Theory*, vol. 50, no. 12, pp. 3062–3080, Dec. 2004.

[Mad09] MadWifi, "Open-source driver, project homepage," http://madwifi-project.org/, 2009, link verified on Jul. 12th, 2010.

[Mit95] J. Mitola, "The software radio architecture," *IEEE Commun. Mag.*, vol. 33, no. 5, May 1995.

[MKP07] M. Morelli, C.-C. Kuo, and M.-O. Pun, "Synchronization techniques for orthogonal frequency division multiple access (OFDMA): A tutorial review," *Proc. IEEE*, vol. 95, no. 7, pp. 1394–1427, Jul. 2007.

[Moo05] T. K. Moon, *Error Correction Coding: Mathematical Methods and Algorithms*. Wiley, Jul. 2005.

[NBKL04] H. Nguyen, J. Brouet, V. Kumar, and T. Lestable, "Compression of associated signaling for adaptive multi-carrier systems," in *Proc. Vehicular Technology Conf. (VTC-Spring)*, vol. 4, May 2004, pp. 1916–1919.

[NH07] A. Nosratinia and T. E. Hunter, "Grouping and partner selection in cooperative wireless networks," *IEEE Journal on Selected Areas in Communications*, vol. 25, no. 2, pp. 369–378, Feb. 2007.

[NHH04] A. Nosratinia, T. E. Hunter, and A. Hedayat, "Cooperative communication in wireless networks," *IEEE Commun. Mag.*, vol. 42, no. 10, pp. 74–80, Oct. 2004.

[OAF$^+$07] F. A. Onat, A. Adinoyi, Y. Fan, H. Yanikomeroglu, and J. S. Thompson, "Optimum threshold for SNR-based selective digital relaying schemes in cooperative wireless networks," in *Proc. IEEE Wireless Commun. and Netw. Conf. (WCNC)*, Mar. 2007.

[OAF$^+$08] F. A. Onat, A. Adinoyi, Y. Fan, H. Yanikomeroglu, J. S. Thompson, and I. D. Marsland, "Threshold selection for SNR-based selective digital relaying in cooperative wireless networks," *IEEE Trans. Wireless Commun.*, vol. 7, no. 11, pp. 4226–4237, Nov. 2008.

[OFYT08] F. A. Onat, Y. Fan, H. Yanikomeroglu, and J. Thompson, "Asymptotic BER analysis of threshold digital relaying schemes in cooperative wireless systems," *IEEE Trans. Wireless Commun.*, vol. 7, no. 12, pp. 4938–4947, Dec. 2008.

[OP99] B. O'Hara and A. Petrick, *IEEE 802.11 Handbook: A designers companion*. IEEE Press, 1999.

[Per08] E. Perahia, "IEEE 802.11n development: History, process, and technology," *IEEE Commun. Mag.*, vol. 46, no. 7, pp. 48–55, Jul. 2008.

[PH09] S. W. Peters and R. W. Heath, "The future of WiMAX: Multihop relaying with IEEE 802.16j," *IEEE Commun. Mag.*, vol. 47, no. 1, pp. 104–111, Jan. 2009.

[PM07] D. Piazza and L. Milstein, "Analysis of multiuser diversity in time-varying channels," *IEEE Trans. Wireless Commun.*, vol. 6, no. 12, pp. 4412–4419, Dec. 2007.

[PNG03] A. Paulraj, R. Nabar, and D. Gore, *Introduction to Space-Time Wireless Communications*. Cambridge University Press, May 2003.

[Pro00] J. G. Proakis, *Digital Communications*, 4th ed. McGraw-Hill, 2000.

[PWS+04] R. Pabst, B. Walke, D. Schultz, P. Herhold, H. Yanikomeroglu, S. Mukherjee, H. Viswanathan, M. Lott, W. Zirwas, M. Dohler, H. Aghvami, D. Falconer, and G. Fettweis, "Relay-based deployment concepts for wireless and mobile broadband radio," *IEEE Commun. Mag.*, vol. 42, no. 9, pp. 80–89, Sep. 2004.

[Rai02] Rail Technology Consortium, "New rail technology of Paderborn," Booklet available at project web page http://www.railcab.de/, 2002, link verified on Jul. 12th, 2010.

[Rai07] ——, "New rail technology of Paderborn – demonstration videos," http://nbp-www.upb.de/index.php?id=57, 2007, link verified on Jul. 12th, 2010.

[Rap02] T. S. Rappaport, *Wireless Communications Principles And Practice*, 2nd ed. Prentice Hall, Inc., 2002.

[RC00] W. Rhee and J. M. Cioffi, "Increase in capacity of multiuser OFDM system using dynamic subchannel allocation," in *Proc. Vehicular Technology Conf. (VTC-Spring)*, vol. 2, May 2000, pp. 1085–1089.

[RF09] P. Rost and G. Fettweis, "Analysis of a mixed strategy for multiple relay networks," *IEEE Trans. Inf. Theory*, vol. 55, no. 1, pp. 174–189, Jan. 2009.

[RJ08] N. Ravindran and N. Jindal, "Multi-user diversity vs. accurate channel feedback for mimo broadcast channels," in *Proc. IEEE Int. Conf. on Commun. (ICC)*, May 2008, pp. 3684–3688.

[Ros96] S. M. Ross, *Stochastic Processes*, 2nd ed. Wiley, 1996.

[RVH95] P. Robertson, E. Villebrun, and P. Hoeher, "A comparison of optimal and sub-optimal MAP decoding algorithms operating in the log domain," in *Proc. IEEE Int. Conf. on Commun. (ICC)*, vol. 2, Jun. 1995, pp. 1009–1013.

[SA04] M. K. Simon and M.-S. Alouini, *Digital Communications over Fading Channels*, 2nd ed. Wiley, 2004.

[SCTG05] N. S. Shankar, C. Chun-Ting, and M. Ghosh, "Cooperative communication MAC (CMAC) – a new MAC protocol for next generation wireless LANs," in *Proc. Int. Conf. on Wireless Networks, Commun. and Mobile Computing*, Jun. 2005.

[SDH+04] M. Stege, T. Dräger, M. Henker, T. Hentschel, M. Hossmann, M. Löhning, C. Unger, A. Zoch, and G. Fettweis, "Hardware in a loop – a wireless communication system prototyping platform for IEEE 802.11n," in *Proc. Int. OFDM-Workshop*, Sep. 2004.

[SE03] A. Stefanov and E. Erkip, "On the performance analysis of cooperative space-time coded systems," in *Proc. IEEE Wireless Commun. and Netw. Conf. (WCNC)*, vol. 2, Mar. 2003, pp. 729–734.

[SE04] ——, "Cooperative coding for wireless networks," *IEEE Trans. Commun.*, vol. 52, no. 9, pp. 1470–1476, Sep. 2004.

[SEA98] A. Sendonaris, E. Erkip, and B. Aazhang, "Increasing uplink capacity via user cooperation diversity," in *Proc. IEEE Int. Symp. on Inf. Theory (ISIT)*, Aug. 1998, p. 156.

[SEA03a] ——, "User cooperation diversity. Part I. system description," *IEEE Trans. Commun.*, vol. 51, no. 11, pp. 1927–1938, Nov. 2003.

[SEA03b] ——, "User cooperation diversity. Part II. implementation aspects and performance analysis," *IEEE Trans. Commun.*, vol. 51, no. 11, pp. 1939–1948, Nov. 2003.

[Sha49] C. E. Shannon, "Communication in the presence of noise," *Proc. of the IRE*, vol. 37, no. 1, pp. 10–21, Jan. 1949.

[Sho06] A. Shokrollahi, "Raptor codes," *IEEE Trans. Inf. Theory*, vol. 52, no. 6, pp. 2551–2567, Jun. 2006.

[SL05a] G. Song and Y. Li, "Cross-layer optimization for OFDM wireless networks – Part I: theoretical framework," *IEEE Trans. Wireless Commun.*, vol. 4, no. 2, pp. 614–624, Mar. 2005.

[SL05b] ——, "Cross-layer optimization for OFDM wireless networks – Part II: algorithm development," *IEEE Trans. Wireless Commun.*, vol. 4, no. 2, pp. 625–634, Mar. 2005.

[SPG+03] S. Simoens, P. Pellati, J. Gosteau, K. Gosse, and C. Ware, "The evolution of 5 GHz WLAN toward higher throughputs," *IEEE Wireless Commun.*, vol. 10, no. 6, pp. 1536–1284, Dec. 2003.

[SSL07] A. K. Sadek, W. Su, and K. J. R. Liu, "Multinode cooperative communications in wireless networks," *IEEE Trans. Signal Processing*, vol. 55, no. 1, pp. 341–355, Jan. 2007.

[SV05] H. H. Sneessens and L. Vandendorpe, "Soft decode and forward improves cooperative communications," in *IEE Int. Conf. on 3G and Beyond*, Nov. 2005, pp. 1–4.

[SW73] D. Slepian and J. Wolf, "Noiseless coding of correlated information sources," *IEEE Trans. Inf. Theory*, vol. 19, no. 4, pp. 471–480, Jul. 1973.

[SY08] A. B. Sediq and H. Yanikomeroglu, "Diversity combining of signals with different modulation levels in cooperative relay networks," in *Proc. of the Wireless World Research Forum Meeting (WWRF)*, Apr. 2008.

[SZW09] H. Shan, W. Zhuang, and Z. Wang, "Distributed cooperative MAC for multihop wireless networks," *IEEE Commun. Mag.*, vol. 47, no. 2, pp. 126–133, Feb. 2009.

[TH98] D. Tse and S. Hanly, "Multiaccess fading channels. i. polymatroid structure, optimal resource allocation and throughput capacities," *IEEE Trans. Inf. Theory*, vol. 44, no. 7, pp. 2796–2815, Nov. 1998.

[The03] The Internet Society, Network Working Group, "RTP: a transport protocol for real-time applications," RFC 3550, Standards Track, Jul. 2003.

[THL05] K. Tittelbach-Helmrich and J. Lehmann, *User Manual of the Implementation of the IEEE 802.11a MAC Protocol on a BlackFin Processor System for Signalion, Dresden*, IHP, Frankfurt (Oder), Germany, Aug. 2005.

[THN08] B. Timus, J. Hultell, and M. Nilson, "Techno-cconomical viability of deployment strategies for cellular-relaying networks," in *Proc. Vehicular Technology Conf. (VTC-Spring)*, May 2008, pp. 2259–2263.

[TV05] D. Tse and P. Viswanath, *Fundamentals of Wireless Communication*. Cambridge University Press, May 2005.

[TWT08] D. Tung, C. Wong, and C. K. Tham, "Burst mode cooperative MAC protocol in ad hoc wireless networks," in *Proc. IEEE Int. Conf. on Commun. Systems (ICCS)*, Nov. 2008, pp. 1275–1279.

[Ung05] C. Unger, *SORBAS 101 PHY Implementation – MAC-PHY Interface for 802.11a Implementation, Version 1.1*, Signalion GmbH, Jul. 2005.

[UU07] C. Unger and M. Unger, *SORBAS 101 PHY Implementation, Version 0.9*, Signalion GmbH, May 2007.

[Val09] S. Valentin, "TACD video quality study: Visual examples," Available at http://www.cs.upb.de/en/research-group/research-group-computer-networks/projects/docomo, Mar. 2009, link verified on Jul. 12th, 2010.

[vdM71] E. C. van der Meulen, "Three-terminal communication channels," in *Advances in Applied Probability*, vol. 3, 1971, pp. 120–154.

[VFK08] S. Valentin, T. Freitag, and H. Karl, "Integrating multiuser dynamic OFDMA into IEEE 802.11 WLANs – LLC/MAC extensions and system performance," in *Proc. IEEE Int. Conf. on Commun. (ICC)*, May 2008.

[VGKW05] S. Valentin, J. Gross, H. Karl, and A. Wolisz, "Adaptive scheduling for heterogeneous traffic flows in cellular wireless OFDM-FDMA systems," in *Proc. Int. Conf. on Personal Wireless Commun. (PWC)*, Aug. 2005.

[VHW+08] V. Venkatkumar, T. Haustein, H. Wu, E. Schulz, T. Wirth, A. Forck, S. Wahls, and V. Jungnickel, "Field trial results on multi-user MIMO downlink OFDMA in typical outdoor scenario using proportional fair scheduling," in *Proc. Int. ITG/IEEE Workshop on Smart Antennas (WSA)*, Feb. 2008.

[Vid04] Video Quality Experts Group (VQEG), "Video test sequences," http://www.its.bldrdoc.gov/vqeg/downloads/downloads.php, 2004, link verfied on Mar. 16th, 2010.

[Vit67] A. J. Viterbi, "Error bounds for convolutional codes and an asymptotically optimum decoding algorithm," *IEEE Trans. Inf. Theory*, vol. 13, no. 2, pp. 260–269, Apr. 1967.

[VK07a] S. Valentin and H. Karl, "Analyzing the effect of asymmetric mobility and channel configurations on the outage performance of coded cooperative systems," in *Proc. European Wireless (EW)*, Apr. 2007.

[VK07b] ——, "Effect of user mobility in coded cooperative systems with joint partner and cooperation level selection," in *Proc. IEEE Wireless Commun. and Netw. Conf. (WCNC)*, Mar. 2007.

[VK09] ——, "Cooperative feedback to improve capacity and error rate in multiuser diversity systems – An OFDM case study," in *Proc. European Wireless (EW)*, May 2009.

[VKA07] S. Valentin, H. Karl, and I. Aad, "Transceiver apparatus for cooperative wireless networks," Patents EP1962456, JP2008228289 filed by NTT DoCoMo Inc., Feb. 2007.

[VLK+06] S. Valentin, H. S. Lichte, H. Karl, G. Vivier, S. Simoens, J. Vidal, A. Agustin, and I. Aad, "Cooperative wireless networking beyond store-and-forward: Perspectives for PHY and MAC design," in *Proc. of the Wireless World Research Forum Meeting (WWRF)*, Nov. 2006.

[VLK+07] S. Valentin, H. S. Lichte, H. Karl, S. Simoens, G. Vivier, J. Vidal, and A. Agustin, *Cognitive Wireless Networks: Concepts, Methodologies and Visions*. Springer, Sep. 2007, ch. Implementing cooperative wireless networks – Towards feasibility and deployment.

[VLK+08] S. Valentin, H. S. Lichte, H. Karl, I. Aad, L. Loyola, and J. Widmer, "Opportunistic relaying vs. selective cooperation: Analyzing the occurrence-conditioned outage capacity," in *Proc. ACM Int. Conf. on Modeling, Analysis and Simulation of Wireless and Mobile Systems (MSWiM)*, Oct. 2008.

[VLK+09] S. Valentin, H. S. Lichte, H. Karl, G. Vivier, S. Simoens, J. Vidal, and A. Agustin, "Cooperative wireless networking beyond store-and-forward: Perspectives in PHY and MAC design," *Wireless Personal Commun.*, vol. 48, no. 1, pp. 49–68, Jan. 2009.

[VLW+08] S. Valentin, H. S. Lichte, D. Warneke, T. Biermann, R. Funke, and H. Karl, "Mobile cooperative WLANs – MAC and transceiver design, prototyping, and field measurements," in *Proc. Vehicular Technology Conf. (VTC-Fall)*, Sep. 2008.

[VTL02] P. Viswanath, D. Tse, and R. Laroia, "Opportunistic beamforming using dumb antennas," *IEEE Trans. Inf. Theory*, vol. 48, no. 6, pp. 1277–1294, Jun. 2002.

[VVA+08a] S. Valentin, T. Volkhausen, F. Atay Onat, H. Yanikomeroglu, and H. Karl, "Decoding-based channel estimation for selective cooperation diversity protocols," in *Proc. IEEE Ann. Int. Symp. on Personal, Indoor and Mobile Radio Commun. (PIMRC)*, Sep. 2008.

[VVA+08b] ——, "Enabling partial forwarding by decoding-based one and two-stage selective cooperation," in *Proc. IEEE Int. Conf. on Commun. Workshops (ICC WS)*, May 2008.

[VvK07] S. Valentin, H. v. Malm, and H. Karl, "Traffic-aware asymmetric cooperation diversity for media streaming in wireless networks," in *Proc. IEEE Ann. Int. Symp. on Personal, Indoor and Mobile Radio Commun. (PIMRC)*, Sep. 2007.

[VVK08] S. Valentin, T. Volkhausen, and H. Karl, "Verfahren und Vorrichtung zur Schätzung von Kanalparametern," German patent application DE 10 2008 007 113.7, filed by UPB, Jan. 2008.

[VVK+09] S. Valentin, T. Volkhausen, H. Karl, F. Atay Onat, and H. Yanikomeroglu, "Decoding-based channel state estimation for channel-adaptive communication," International patent application PCT/DE 2009/000126, filed by UPB, Jan. 2009.

[VvMK06] S. Valentin, H. von Malm, and H. Karl, "Evaluating the GNU Software Radio platform for wireless testbeds," University of Paderborn, Tech. Rep. TR-RI-06-273, Feb. 2006.

[VWVK09] S. Valentin, D. H. Woldegebreal, T. Volkhausen, and H. Karl, "Combining for cooperative WLANs – a reality check based on prototype measurements," in *Proc. IEEE Int. Conf. on Commun. Workshops (ICC WS)*, Jun. 2009.

[WAR09] WARP Project, "Wireless open-access research platform," http://warp.rice.edu/, 2009, link verified on Jul. 12th, 2010.

[WCLM99] C. Y. Wong, R. S. Cheng, K. B. Letaief, and R. D. Murch, "Multiuser OFDM with adaptive subcarrier, bit, and power allocation," *IEEE J. Sel. Areas Commun.*, vol. 17, no. 10, pp. 1747–1758, Oct. 1999.

[Wil04] A. Willig, "Intermediate checksums for improving goodput over error-prone links," in *Proc. Vehicular Technology Conf. (VTC-Fall)*, Sep. 2004.

[WP09] S. Wolf and M. Pinson, "Fast Low Bandwidth Video Quality Model (VQM) Description and Reference Code," ITU-T Contribution COM9-C5-E, Feb. 2009.

[WSBL03] T. Wiegand, G. Sullivan, G. Bjontegaard, and A. Luthra, "Overview of the H.264/AVC video coding standard," *IEEE Trans. Circuits Syst. Video Technol.*, vol. 13, no. 7, pp. 560–576, Jul. 2003.

[Wu01] P.-Y. Wu, "On the complexity of turbo decoding algorithms," in *Proc. Vehicular Technology Conf. (VTC-Spring)*, vol. 2, May 2001, pp. 1439–1443.

[WVK07] D. Woldegebreal, S. Valentin, and H. Karl, "Outage probability analysis of cooperative transmission protocols without and with network coding: Inter-user channels based comparison," in *Proc. ACM Int. Conf. on Modeling, Analysis and Simulation of Wireless and Mobile Systems (MSWiM)*, Oct. 2007.

[WVK08] D. H. Woldegebreal, S. Valentin, and H. Karl, "Incremental network coding in cooperative transmission wireless networks," in *Proc. Vehicular Technology Conf. (VTC-Fall)*, Sep. 2008.

[XGEW05] X. Xu, D. Gunduz, Erkip, and Y. Wang, "Layered cooperative source and channel coding," in *Proc. IEEE Int. Conf. on Commun. (ICC)*, vol. 2, May 2005, pp. 1200–1204.

[YC06] D. Yu and J. Cioffi, "Iterative water-filling for optimal resource allocation in OFDM multiple-access and broadcast channels," in *Proc. IEEE Global Telecommun. Conf. (GLOBECOM)*, Dec. 2006, pp. 1–5.

[YK08] Z. Yi and I.-M. Kim, "Diversity order analysis of the decode-and-forward cooperative networks with relay selection," *IEEE Trans. Wireless Commun.*, vol. 7, no. 5, pp. 1792–1799, May 2008.

[ZJZ09] Q. Zhang, J. Jia, and J. Zhang, "Cooperative relay to improve diversity in cognitive radio networks," *IEEE Commun. Mag.*, vol. 47, no. 2, pp. 111–117, Feb. 2009.

[ZLE[+]05] F. Zhai, C. E. Luna, Y. Eisenberg, T. N. Pappas, R. Berry, and A. K. Katsaggelos, "Joint source coding and packet classification for real-time video transmission over differentiated services networks," *IEEE Trans. Multimedia*, vol. 7, no. 4, pp. 716–726, Aug. 2005.

[ZT03] L. Zheng and D. Tse, "Diversity and multiplexing: A fundamental tradeoff in multiple-antenna channels," *IEEE Trans. Inf. Theory*, vol. 49, no. 5, pp. 1073–1096, May 2003.

[ZV03] B. Zhao and M. Valenti, "Distributed turbo coded diversity for the relay channel," *IEEE Electron. Lett.*, vol. 39, no. 10, pp. 786–787, May 2003.

[ZV05] ——, "Practical relay networks: A generalization of hybrid-ARQ," *IEEE J. Sel. Areas Commun.*, vol. 23, no. 1, pp. 7–18, Jan. 2005.

Die VDM Verlagsservicegesellschaft sucht für wissenschaftliche Verlage abgeschlossene und herausragende

Dissertationen, Habilitationen, Diplomarbeiten, Master Theses, Magisterarbeiten usw.

für die kostenlose Publikation als Fachbuch.

Sie verfügen über eine Arbeit, die hohen inhaltlichen und formalen Ansprüchen genügt, und haben Interesse an einer honorarvergüteten Publikation?

Dann senden Sie bitte erste Informationen über sich und Ihre Arbeit per Email an *info@vdm-vsg.de*.

Sie erhalten kurzfristig unser Feedback!

VDM Verlagsservicegesellschaft mbH
Dudweiler Landstr. 99   Telefon +49 681 3720 174
D - 66123 Saarbrücken   Fax   +49 681 3720 1749
www.vdm-vsg.de

Die VDM Verlagsservicegesellschaft mbH vertritt

Printed by Books on Demand GmbH, Norderstedt / Germany